THE ESSENTIAL

TORAH
TEMIMAH

תורת ה' תמימה משיבת נפש

The Torah of Hashem is complete — it restores the soul.

PSALMS 19:8 תהילים יט:ח

THE ESSENTIAL
TORAH
TEMIMAH

by Harav Boruch Halevi Epstein

Translated and elucidated by
SHRAGA SILVERSTEIN

BERESHITH

FELDHEIM PUBLISHERS
Jerusalem / New York

First published 1989 • ISBN 0-87306-504-2

Philipp Feldheim Inc.   Feldheim Publishers Ltd.
200 Airport Executive Park POB 6525
Spring Valley, NY 10977   Jerusalem, Israel

Printed in Israel

מוקדש לזכר נשמת

חותני

ר׳ צבי ב״ר דוב לוינברון ז״ל

נפטר ט״ז אלול תשכ״ה

וחותנתי

אסתר בת ר׳ משה מאיר ז״ל

נפטרה י״ט תמוז תשר״ז

Acknowledgments

My special thanks and gratitude to: Melach Lehman, for his typical *chesed*. To Rabbi Chaim Kramer, for his friendship. To Rebbetzin Zippora Bromberg, for her devoted work and expert workmanship. Above all, to my wife, Tova, for her faith and loyalty.

It is a source of personal pleasure and gratification to have *The Essential Torah Temimah* produced by Yaakov Feldheim in Yerushalayim in this semicentennial year of Feldheim Publications. It was Mr. Philipp Feldheim who, with great patience and kindness, started me out on my own Torah library in a little bookshop on the Lower East Side many years ago. I am delighted to salute him and his remarkable achievement on this golden anniversary and to wish him and Feldheim Publications many more years of *haromas keren haTorah*.

Shraga Silverstein
Yerushalayim, 5749

Translator's Introduction

The Work

The *Torah Temimah*, by Harav Boruch Halevi Epstein (son of Harav Yechiel Michel Halevi Epstein, author of the monumental *Aruch Hashulchan*) — a telescoped synthesis of the Written and Oral Law — has become one of the most popular classics of our Torah literature, going through many editions in a relatively short space of time. The scope of the work can best be understood by some brief excerpts from the author's extensive introduction:

> "It has been our aim to show that this Torah, the Written Law, is a twin sister, as it were, to the Oral Law. They are inseparable — as body and soul, as flame and wick — the one, intimately enmeshed with the other. And so long as the Written Law is not conjoined with the explanations and addenda of the Oral Law, it is not a complete Torah. Its message is not complete and its mitzvah is not complete."

> [It is the aim of the *Torah Temimah*] "to conjoin and amalgamate the two Laws as one — one beside the other — *so that eye and sense can assimilate both as one.*"

> "I have called this work *Torah Temimah* ["the complete Torah"], as the name implies. For this Torah, the Written Law, the five books of Moses, when completely unified with the Oral Law — the entire Talmudic literature — becomes whole and complete, lacking nothing that properly appertains to the mitzvoth and the laws, the statutes and the judgments, as the Creator Himself joined them in the very beginning, in their original transmission at Sinai. And, having done so, the tent of Torah shall be one."

The Translation

Given the immense importance and popularity of the *Torah Temimah*, it is more than remarkable that no translation of it has yet appeared. It is to fill this glaring void that the present translation was undertaken.

The Essential Torah Temimah features:

- A new translation of the Biblical verses *in accordance with the Talmudic derivations*

- A translation of all the Talmudic sources, designed to reveal the derivations as *implicit in the verse*

- Incorporation within the translation [in brackets] of whatever commentary [predominantly the author's] is necessary to elucidate the source with maximum clarity and concision

- Language that is fluent, literate, articulate — the optimal medium for conveying the meaning

The Essential Torah Temimah — How It Works

Below is one example of *The Essential Torah Temimah* in operation:

The Essential Torah Temimah rendering of the verse (*Bamidbar* 30:7):

> And if be, she shall be, to a man, and her vows be upon her, or the utterance of her lips wherewith she bound her soul,

The conventional translation is: "And if she be married to a husband, when she vowed, or uttered aught out of her lips, with which she bound herself." This tells us nothing about the Talmudic derivation [see example which follows]. The new translation is especially designed to show *where* that derivation is coming from (or, in essence, to demonstrate how the Oral Law is implicit in the Written Law).

The Essential Torah Temimah rendering of the Talmudic commentary:

And if be she shall be to a man, etc. — If her husband [i.e., the one to whom she is betrothed] dies, the option of annulling her vows is [again] exclusively her father's, it being written: "And if *be*, she shall *be*, to a man, and her vows be upon her" — the pre-second "being" [i.e., her status before her possible second betrothal] is likened to her pre-first "being" [i.e., her status before her first betrothal]. Just as in her pre-first "being" her father annulled by himself, so in her pre-second "being" her father annuls by himself (Nedarim 70a).[56]

- A bracketed comment supplying a qualification without which the Talmudic citation is incomprehensible

- A *felicitious, concise, meaningful* rendering of the Talmudic phrase (which, rendered literally, would be: "permission is emptied out to her father")

- Illuminating italicizing to highlight the *source* of the derivation

- Approximation to the language of the Talmudic phrase with sufficient explanatory information to make its meaning readily apparent

- Superscript numbers matching those in the Hebrew *Torah Temimah* for easy cross-reference

- A *totality*, eliminating confusing, distracting footnoting, showing as concisely as possible, in one visual locale, how Written and Oral Law create a unified whole — a *Torah Temimah*

Note on Translation of Aggadic Material

Special care has been taken with Aggadic material to provide a translation which is not only faithful to the text, but which flows and "reads" well [a feature sadly lacking in conventional translations], and which brings out the point of the passage. One illustration will suffice:

Soncino Talmud, Chagigah 12b, Page 68

'And the earth was unformed and void'. Consider: [Scripture] began at first with heaven, why then does it proceed to relate [first] the work of the earth? — The School of R. Ishmael taught: It is like a human king who said to his servants: Come early to my door. He rose early and found women and men. Whom does he praise? The ones who are not accustomed to rise early but yet did rise early.

The Essential Torah Temimah, Bereshith, Page 2

1:2 And the earth was, etc.: If the heavens came first, why is the status of the earth described first? It was taught in the forum of R. Yishmael: "This is analogous to a king's commanding his subjects to arrive early at his door and finding the women there as well as the men. Whom will he single out for commendation? Those who are not in the habit of rising early, but have done so, nevertheless, in deference to his command." [The earth is the habitual late riser in the analogy (weighted down, as it were, with the sluggishness of matter).]

Author's Introduction

This book, the Torah of Hashem, its mitzvoth, statutes, and judgments, which was given to us at Sinai, was given to us only as principles, fundamentals, and foundations. That is, only the principles, fundamentals, and foundations of each mitzvah, and each statute and judgment. And these, Moses our teacher wrote down for us from the mouth of the Holy One Blessed be He, a Divine charter for all of Israel. But its specifics and ramifications, its elucidation and interpretation, because of the multiplicity of detail and sub-detail, entailing deep probing, subtle analysis, uncommon understanding, and broad knowledge — these were orally transmitted by the Holy One to Moses our teacher, so that he would teach them to those who were fit to be taught, and cause them to be understood by those capable of understanding. And it is thus that we have received the interpretation of the Blessed One's dictum (*Shemoth* 24:12): "And I will give you the tablets of stone and the Torah and the mitzvah": "Torah" — this is the Written Law; "and the mitzvah" — this is its interpretation. And it is this interpretation which is called the Oral Law, as opposed to the generic framework of Torah, which, being given at the outset, as has been said, in written form, is referred to as the Written Law.

And Moses our teacher taught this Oral Law that he had received to the seventy elders, and, at the end of his days, to Joshua. He, in turn, taught it to the elders of his generation, who afterwards taught it and passed it down orally to the sages of each generation, the elder to the younger, generation after generation, until the generation of Rabbeinu Hakadosh, R. Yehudah Hanasi. He, witnessing the exile of the Jews, their dispersal among the nations, and their dislocations and wanderings, and fearing that the Oral Law might thereby be forgotten, arose in company with the sages of his generation and compiled the book of the *Mishnah*, which contains the fundamentals and foundations of the Oral Law, so that every Jew would be conversant with them. He was the first since the days of Moses to write a work for all Jews for the study of the Oral Law.

However, since the *Mishnah*, likewise, is composed of only the principles and fundamentals of the Oral Law — concise, epitomized *halachoth* — and does not furnish us with an overall conception of the interrelationship between the Oral and Written Laws as transmitted to Moses our teacher through the thirteen hermeneutical rules, the parallels, the juxtapositions, and the intimations of Scripture and of its ancillary signs — this work, too, did not suffice to banish the fear of forgetting the Oral Law in its entirety and in its distinctive character.

Therefore, the sages after Rabbeinu Hakadosh arose and composed to this end various works such as the *Sifra, Sifrei, Tosefta,* and *Mechilta* — the end of which is to elucidate the principles and themes of the *Mishnah* — and the two Talmuds, redacted in Eretz Yisrael and Babylonia, as a gloss upon the *Mishnah* and the derivational and interrelational procedures subserving the Oral and Written Laws and the formulation of the *halachoth* received and transmitted by the sages of each generation. So that with the completion of the two Talmuds, the repositories of the Oral Law, the Written Law had been definitively analyzed, fully elucidated, and adequately interpreted. The Talmuds and the *baraithoth* could be compared to a many-branched tree, its roots reaching out and fixing themselves in a pure, holy, central core — the bequest of the Blessed One to Moses our teacher.

We have expatiated somewhat upon the progress of the Oral Law from its original source, though these things, essentially, have been long and well known. (See at length Maimonides' introduction to his *Yad Hachazakah.*) It has been our aim, however, to show that this Torah, the Written Law, is a twin sister, as it were, to the Oral Law. They are inseparable — as body and soul, as flame and wick — the one, intimately enmeshed with the other. And so long as the Written Law is not conjoined with the explanations and addenda of the Oral Law, it is not a complete Torah. Its message is not complete and its mitzvah is not complete.

In spite of all this, however, our eyes are witness to a strange and saddening phenomenon. As obvious as the absolute interdependence of the two Laws — their being, to all intents and purposes, two that are one — so, the enormity of the rift between them. The Written Law is relegated to one corner, and its sister, the Oral Law, to another. The Torah has become two Torahs. We know instinctively that the Written Law is correctly illumined only in conjunction with the Oral Law. But when we are confronted with a section of the Written Law we find it impossible to bring to the fore all of the Oral Law generated by it. And why so? Because of the profuseness of its dispersion in the literature of the Talmud, a literature vaster and broader than the sea. So that, for example, one section of Written Law may be commented upon in every single tractate of the Talmud and in a variety of scattered, non-related *baraithoth.* Similarly, in practically every tractate we find allusions to matters scattered throughout all five books of the Written Law — one here, the other there. So that it becomes impossible even for great Torah scholars in the exigency of study to assemble the requisite complement of Oral Law for even one section of Written Law.

And we know not what to say of this — that from the time of the closing of the Talmuds not one of the sages has arisen to rectify this glaring omission in the fabric and foundation of our Torah, to conjoin and amalgamate the two Laws as one — one beside the other — so that eye and sense can assimilate both as one, and so that we might know the mitzvah of the Torah in depth and essence, as the Creator forged it at the outset. Wonder of wonders!

And if this omission in the literature of the Written Law was matter for concern in the earlier generations, in those glorious days, days of eternity and majesty for the wisdom of Torah, when Torah study, individual and collective, was universal, when the yeshivoth were overflowing with sages and scholars in the thousands and ten thousands, when the mind of every Torah sage was broad in wisdom, when Torah was his solitary occupation, when each scholar had the Oral Law, to a greater or lesser extent, "in his hip pocket" as it were, and when, with greater or lesser application, the relevant teachings of the Oral Law were brought to the fore in the study of the Written Law itself — how much more so in our time, when we are confronted with manifold tribulations, the struggle for survival, the yoke of earning a livelihood, the proliferation of secular studies, the comings and goings from one country to another, the study of the Oral Law flickering out, so that both sage and disciple are constrained to find a short, paved path for their studies — how much more are we compelled, for the survival of the Oral Law, to conjoin it, clearly and concisely, with the Written Law, so that when one studies the Written Law he will find at his side, readily accessible to him, all that has been superadded in the Oral Law in respect to the particular section he is studying — sparing him weariness of flesh and spirit, omitting all the convolutions of deliberation, adducing only the pith and essence of the oral commentary and the definitive *halachah* emerging therefrom through the medium of the hermeneutical rules for the exegesis of the Written Law. In this way, he will come to perceive the two Laws as one, the Oral Law as inexorably generated by the Written Law, a branch growing together with the tree; and the Torah of Israel will not appear to him as two Torahs. Only thus can we rest confident in the survival of the Oral Law, when it is thus conjoined and engrafted with the Written Law, the enduring possession of all Israel.

Therefore, I have betaken myself, "the youngest of the house of Levi," and, with the help of the Lord, who "elected" the Torah, have girded my loins in a spirit of strength and determination, and have put forth this compendium to the end of all that has been stated herein. I have gathered and assembled, with great attention and care, every statement and every theme, every commentary and every decision, in *halachah* and *aggadah*, in *mussar* and *derech eretz* (except for those of unusual length or not relevant to the subject at hand) — all that is spread and scattered throughout the entire range of Talmudic literature, *Bavli* and *Yerushalmi, Sifra* and *Sifrei, Tosefta* and *Mechilta, Avoth d'R. Nathan*, and minor tractates, and others. I have arranged and ordered every statement and subject alongside its referent in the Written Law, one next to the other, clearly, concisely, lucidly, in the language of the sages, indicating the source of each citation in the Oral Law, and furnishing as much commentary as is necessary to elucidate the manner of derivation of the teachings and *halachoth* that the sages have deduced from the language and content of the verses...

I have called this work *Torah Temimah* ["the complete Torah"], as the name implies. For this Torah, the Written Law, the five books of Moses, when completely unified with the Oral Law — the entire Talmudic literature — becomes whole and complete, lacking nothing that properly appertains to the mitzvoth and the laws, the statutes and the judgments, as the Creator Himself joined them in the very beginning, in their original transmission at Sinai. And, having done so, the tent of Torah shall be one.

Bereshith

1:1   In the beginning, G-d created the heavens and the earth.

In the beginning - The world was created with ten pronouncements. Which are they? All of the "And He saids" in the chapter *Bereshith*. [And although there are] only nine, "In the beginning," too, is considered a pronouncement, as it is written (*Psalms* 33:6): "By the word of the L-rd, the heavens were made" (*Rosh Hashanah* 32a).[1-3]

In the beginning - It was taught: "Why was the world created with a *bet* [the second letter of the alphabet "*B*ereshith"] and not with an *aleph* [the first letter]? Because *bet* intimates "*b*erachah" [blessing], whereas *aleph* intimates "*a*rirah" [cursing]. The Holy One Blessed be He said: "I shall not create it with an *aleph*, so that it not be said: 'How can a world created within the context of cursing endure?' but I shall create it with a *bet*, within the context of blessing — and would that it endured ! " (*Yerushalmi, Chagigah* 2:1).[4]

In the beginning, G-d created - Once, King Ptolemy assembled seventy-two elders in seventy-two separate houses and said to each of them: "Transcribe for me [into Greek] the Torah of Moses your teacher." The Holy One Blessed be He placed goodly counsel in the heart of each of them, and they all wrote as one: "G—d created in the beginning" [so that Ptolemy could not structure the words as: "In the beginning, god *was* created"] (*Megillah* 9a).[5]

In the beginning, G-d created [bara Elokim] - The heretics asked R. Simlai: "How many gods created the world?" He answered: "Go and ask Adam, as it is written (*Deuteronomy* 4:32): 'For ask now of the days that are past ... from the day that G-d created [*bara Elokim*] man upon the earth.' It is not written "*baru*" [plural], but "*bara*" [singular]." At this, they asked: "But is it not written: 'In the beginning, *Elokim* [seemingly "gods"] created'?" To this he answered: "Is it written '*baru*' ['*they* created']? It is written '*bara*' ['*He* created']!" (*Yerushalmi, Berachoth* 9:1).[6-8]

the heavens [shamayim] - Why is the sky called "*shamayim*"? R. Yossi
b. R. Chanina said: "*Sham mayim*" ["There is water there"]. In a
Baraitha it was taught: "*Shamayim*" — "*Esh umayim*" ["fire and
water"]: this teaches us that the Holy One Blessed be He brought them
together, intermixed them, and made the firmament from them"
(*Chagigah* 12a).[9]

the heavens and the earth - From here we derive that the heavens and
the earth were created on the first day (*Ibid.*).[10]

the heavens and the earth [et hashamayim ve'et ha'aretz] - Why are
"*et*" and "*ve'et*" needed? Nachum Ish Gamzu expounded: "If
'*shamayim vaaretz*' alone were stated, I might have said that '*shamayim
vaaretz*' were the names of the Holy One Blessed be He, but '*et*
hashamayim *ve'et* haaretz' indicates that each is a created entity in itself.
Still, why must I have *ve'et* haaretz [for the above requirement would be
satisfied without it]? To indicate that the heavens were created before
the earth [and not together with it]" .(*Ibid.*).[11,12]

the heavens and the earth - But another verse states (2:4): "On the day
that the L-rd G-d created earth and heaven" [first earth, then heaven!]
Resh Lakish answered: "In creation, heaven preceded earth, but in
extension, earth preceded heaven" (*Ibid.*).[13]

the heavens and the earth - Alexander of Macedonia asked the elders of
the Negev: "What was created first — heaven or earth?" They
answered: "Heaven was created first, as it is written: 'the heavens and
the earth.' " He questioned further: "What was created first — light or
darkness?" To this, they said: "This cannot be answered." But why
could they not have told him that darkness was created first, as it is
written: "And there was darkness on the face of the deep," and, later:
"And there was light"? They feared that if they did so he might come to
ask what was "above" and what "below" [i.e., mysteries to which man
is barred access] (*Tamid* 32a).[14,15]

1:2   And the earth was formless and void, and there was
       darkness on the face of the deep, and a wind of G-d swept
       along the surface of the waters.

And the earth was, etc. - If the heavens came first, why is the status of the earth described first? It was taught in the forum of R. Yishmael: "This is analogous to a king's commanding his subjects to arrive early at his door and finding the women there as well as the men. Whom will he single out for commendation? Those who are not in the habit of rising early, but have done so, nevertheless, in deference to his command." [The earth is the habitual late riser in the analogy (weighted down, as it is, with the sluggishness of matter)] (*Chagigah* 12b).[16]

formless [tohu] and void [vohu] - It was taught: "*Tohu* is a green line which encircles the entire world and from which darkness issues forth, as it is written (*Psalms* 18:11): 'He has made darkness His secret place, round about Him.' "*Bohu* — these are sponge-like stones embedded in the deep, from which water issues forth, as it is written (*Isaiah* 34:11): 'And He shall stretch out upon it the line of *tohu* and the stones of *bohu*'" (*Ibid.*).[17,18]

formless and void [tohu vavohu] - "Formless and void, and darkness on the face of the deep, and a wind from G-d swept along the surface of the waters": From here it is derived that *tohu, vohu*, darkness, wind, and water were all created on the first day (*Ibid.*a).[19]

swept along, etc. - R. Yehudah b. Pazzi expounded: "In the beginning the world consisted of water conjoined with water, as it is written: 'And a wind from G-d swept along the surface of the waters.' The water was then transformed to snow, which, in turn, was transformed to earth, as it is written (*Job* 37:6): 'For He says to the snow: "Be earth!"'" (*Yerushalmi Chagigah* 2:1).[20]

1:3   And G-d said: "Let there be light," and there was light.

Let there be light - This teaches us that the light was created on the first day. And though it is written (17): "And G-d set them [the luminaries] in the firmament of heaven ... and it was evening and it was morning the *fourth* day," the understanding is that they were *suspended* on the fourth day (*Chagigah* 18a).[21]

1:4   And G-d saw the light that it was good, and G-d divided the light from the darkness.

that it was good - R. Elazar said: "Even one righteous man would justify the creation of a world, as it is written: 'And G-d saw the light that it was good,' and "good" is nothing other than a righteous man, as it is written (*Isaiah* 3:10): 'Say of the righteous one that he is good' " (*Yoma* 38b).[22]

that it was good - R. Elazar said: "With the light that the Holy One Blessed be He created on the first day man could look from one end of the world to the other. But when the Holy One Blessed be He envisioned the perverse deeds of the generation of the flood and of the generation of the Tower of Babel, He arose and secreted it for the righteous in time to come, as it is written: 'And G-d saw the light, that it was good,' and "good" is nothing other than a righteous man, as it is written (*Isaiah* 3:10): 'Say of the righteous one that he is good' " (*Chagigah* 12).[23]

that it was good - R. Yehoshua b. Levi said: "If one sees the letter *tet* in a dream, he may take it as a propitious sign, for the letter *tet* does not appear from 'In the beginning' until 'that it was good' [*"ki Tov"*] (*Bava Kamma* 58a).[24]

and G-d divided - R. Zeira expounded in the name of R. Avahu: [Whence is it derived that the Sabbath eve blessing on the candle (*Havdalah*) is not made until benefit can be derived from its light?] "From the verse: 'And He divided' [*vayavdel*]" (*Yerushalmi, Berachoth* 8:6).[25]

1:5   And G-d called to the light, day, and to the darkness He called night.

to the light, day - Not that the light is day, but rather that G-d called to the light and commanded it to preside in the day; and He called to the darkness and commanded it to preside at night (*Pesachim* 2a).[26]

to the light, day - This is analogous to a king's having two princes, one saying: "I will preside by day," and the other saying: "I will preside by day" — at which the king calls to the first and says: "The day will be your domain," and to the second, and says: "The night will be your domain." This is the intent of the verse: "And G-d called to the light, day," viz.: to the light He said: "The day will be your domain," and to the darkness: "The night will be your domain" (*Yerushalmi Berachoth* 8:6).[27]

and it was evening, etc. - From what time is the *Shema* recited in the evening? From the time that the Cohanim go in to eat their *terumah*. And from what time is the *Shema* recited in the morning? From the time that one can tell the difference between blue and white. Why is "evening" discussed first? The order of creation is being followed, as it is written: "And it was evening and it was morning" (*Berachoth* 2a).[28,29]

and it was evening, etc. - This teaches us that the attribute of day and the attribute of night were created on the first day (*Chagigah* 12a).[30]

and it was evening - R. Shila said in the name of Rebbe [R. Judah Hanasi]: "It is written (*Psalms* 104:19): 'He appointed the moon for festivals: the sun knows its setting' — the festivals are reckoned from the time that the sun "knows" its setting [i.e., from the evening of the day (the lunar cycle) and not from the middle of the day (the solar cycle.)"] R. Yochanan said [that the inclusion of the evening in the determination of the festival is intimated in the verse]: "And it was evening, and it was morning, one day" (*Yerusahlmi, Rosh Hashanah* 2:8).[31]

one day - If one erred and did not recite the evening prayer, he prays twice in the morning; for evening and morning are considered one day, as it is written: "And it was evening and it was morning, one day" (*Berachoth* 26a).[32]

one day - R. Yochanan said: "The day of the ingathering of the exile is comparable in greatness to the day of creation of heaven and earth, as it is written (*Hosea* 2:2): 'Then the children of Judah will be gathered in ... and they will make *one* chief for themselves,' and: 'And it was evening and it was morning, *one* day' " (*Pesachim* 88a).[33]

one day - In the "one day" of the creation, the day follows the night, as it is written: "And it was evening and it was morning, one day" (*Chullin* 83a).[34]

1:6   And G-d said: "Let there be a firmament in the midst of the waters, and let it separate water from water."

Let there be a firmament [rakia] - Rav said: " 'Let there be a firmament' — let the firmament be strengthened; let the firmament congeal; let the firmament become solid; let the firmament become taut." R. Yehudah b. Pazzi said: "Let there be a kind of plating for the firmament, as it is written (*Exodus* 39:3): 'And they beat [*vayeraku* (similar to "*rakia*")] the gold into thin plates' " (*Yerushalmi, Berachoth* 1:1).[35],[36]

Let there be a firmament, etc. - It was taught: "The men of the watch [in the Temple] would fast every day. On the second day they would fast for those embarking upon sea voyages [it being written of that day]: 'And G-d said: "Let there be a firmament in the midst of the *waters*" ' " (*Yerushalmi, Ta'anith* 4:3).[37]

in the midst of the waters - R. Bun said: " 'Let there be a firmament in the midst of the waters' — let there be a firmament in the very middle" (*Yerushalmi, Berachoth* 1:1).[38]

and let it separate - How much? R. Acha b. Yaakov said: "A hairsbreadth" (*Chagigah* 15a).[39]

1:8   And G-d called the firmament heaven, and it was evening and it was morning, the second day.

the second day - R. Banaah the son of R. Ulla said: "Why is it not said 'that it was good' on the second day? Because the fire of Gehinnom was created upon it" (*Pesachim* 54a).[40]

the second day - The second day of creation, but not the second day of the week, for we do not find the Torah reckoning events by the days of the week (*Yerushalmi, Rosh Hashanah* 1:1).[41]

1:9   And G-d said: "Let the waters be gathered together, which are under the heavens, and let the dry land be seen," and it was so.

Let the waters be gathered together - It was taught: "The men of the watch [in the Temple] would fast every day. On the third day they would fast for those undertaking land journeys [it being written of that day]: 'Let the waters be gathered together ... and let the dry *land* be seen' " (*Yerushalmi, Taanith* 4:3).[42]

1:10   And the ingathering of the waters He called oceans, and G—d saw that it was good.

And the ingathering, etc. - R. Yossi said; "All oceans are unfit for ritual purification vis à vis a *zav* [one afflicted with a genital discharge], a leper, and the preparation of the "sprinkling waters." Why so? Because the Torah refers to the oceans as "ingathering of waters," as it is written: 'And the ingathering of the waters He called "oceans."'" [Ritual purification for the above requires *mayim chayim* ("living waters," i.e., pools, deriving their "life" from a different source)] (*Parah* 8:3).[43]

1:11   And G-d said: "Let the earth bring forth grass, herb yielding seed, and fruit tree producing fruit after its kind, whose seed is in it upon the earth," and it was so.

Let the earth bring forth, etc. - It was taught: "R. Eliezer said: 'How do we know that the world was created in Tishrei? For it is written: "Let the earth bring forth grass, herb yielding seed, and fruit tree." Which is the month when the earth is full of grass and the trees full of fruit? Tishrei. And though it is written (12): "And trees *producing* fruit" [and fruit are not produced until Nissan], this refers to their future cycle [and not to their actual state at the time of creation]'" (*Rosh Hashanah* 11a).[44]

producing fruit after its kind - R. Chanina b. Pappa expounded: "When the Holy One Blessed be He said 'after its kind' in respect to trees, the grass reasoned a fortiori in respect to itself: 'Now if trees, which, by their very nature, cannot grow in close proximity to each other, are exhorted by the Holy One Blessed be He: "after its kind," how much more so should we do so! — whereupon each variety sprung up according to its kind. At this, the regent of the world proclaimed (*Psalms* 104:31): 'May the glory of the L-rd endure forever; let the L-rd rejoice in His works' " (*Chullin* 60a).[45]

1:12   And the earth brought forth grass, herb yielding seed after
         its kind, trees producing fruit, whose seed was in it, after
         its kind, and G-d saw that it was good. And it was evening
         and it was morning, the third day.

And the earth brought forth grass - R. Assi asked: "In respect to the
third day it is written: 'And the earth brought forth grass,' and yet, in
respect to the sixth day it is written (2:5): 'And no plant of the field was
yet in the earth!' This teaches us that the grass rose up to the surface of
the earth, where it remained until Adam came and implored mercy
upon it, so that it rained, and it sprouted — this, to teach us that the
Holy OneBlessed be He longs for the prayers of the righteous" (*Ibid.*
b).[46]

and trees, producing fruit - Even normally non-fruit producing trees
produced fruit (*Yerushalmi, Kilayim* 1:7).[47]

1:14   And G-d said: "Let there be luminaries in the firmament
         to divide the day from the night, and they shall be for
         signs and for festivals, and for days and for years."

Let there be luminaries - It was taught: "The men of the watch [in the
Temple] would fast every day. On the fourth day they would fast that
diphtheria not enter the mouths of infants [it being written of that day]:
'And G-d said: "Let there be luminaries [*meorot*]' " — but it is written
defective [*meairot* — "blight"] (*Yerushalmi, Ta'anith* 4:3).[48]

for signs and for festivals - R. Shila said in the name of Rebbe [R.
Judah Hanasi]: "It is written (*Psalms* 104:19): 'He appointed the moon
for festivals; the sun knows its setting' — the festivals are reckoned from
the time the sun "knows" its setting." [See 1:5] R. Simon said: " 'And
they shall be for signs and festivals' — on the basis of both, the sun and
the moon" (*Yerusahlmi, Rosh Hashanah* 2:8).[49]

and for years - Here is intimated the blessing over the sun in its twenty-
eight year cycle [in which it returns to its position at creation]
(*Yerushalmi, Berachoth* 9:2).[50]

1:16   And G-d made the two great luminaries, the great
         luminary to rule the day and the small luminary to rule the
         night, and the stars.

the two great luminaries - R. Shimon b. Pazzi asked: "It is written: 'the
two great luminaries,' and: 'the great luminary' and 'the small
luminary'! The moon said before the Holy One Blessed be He: 'Is it
possible for two kings to share one crown?' At this, He said to it: 'Go
and diminish yourself!' " (*Chullin* 60b).[51]

1:17   And G-d set them in the firmament of heaven to give light
         upon the earth.

in the firmament of heaven - From here we derive that sun, moon,
stars, and constellations are embedded in the firmament (*Chagigah*
12b).[52]

1:20   And G-d said: "Let the waters swarm with moving
         creatures that have life, and let birds fly above the earth
         upon the firmament of heaven."

Let the waters swarm - One verse states: "Let the *waters* swarm
abundantly with moving creatures that have life, and let birds fly," and
another verse states (2:19): "And the L-rd formed out of the *ground* ...
and every bird of the air." We see, then, that they were created from the
earth! How can this be? They were created from alluvial mud (*Chullin*
27b).[53]

moving creatures that have life - It was taught: "The men of the watch
[in the Temple] would fast every day. On the fifth day they would fast
that pregnant women not miscarry and that nursing infants not die [it
being written of that day]: 'And G-d said: "Let the waters swarm
abundantly with all moving creatures that have *life*"'" (*Yerushalmi,
Ta'anith* 4:3).[54]

1:21   And G-d created the great sea-serpents, and every living
         creature that moves, which the waters brought forth

abundantly, after their kind, and every winged bird after
its kind. And G-d saw that it was good.

the great sea-serpents - Translate it: "the mammoth beasts of the sea."
R. Yochanan said: "It is the bolt-like serpentine leviathan [the male],
and the convoluted serpentine leviathan [the female] (*Bava Bathra*
74b).[55,56]

1:22   And G-d blessed them, saying: "Be fruitful and multiply,
and fill the waters in the seas, and let birds multiply in the
earth."

And G-d blessed them - Bar Kappara taught: "A virgin is wed on the
fourth day, and lived with on the fifth, for on that day the fish were
blessed, as it is written: 'And G-d blessed them, saying: "Be fruitful and
multiply" ' " (*Kethuvoth* 5a).[57]

1:26   And G-d said: "Let us make a man in our image, after our
likeness, and let them have dominion over the fish of the
sea and over the birds of the air, and over the cattle, and
over all the earth, and over every creeping thing that
creeps on the earth."

Let us make a man - Once King Ptolemy assembled seventy-two elders
in seventy-two separate houses, and told each one: "Transcribe [into
Greek] the Torah of Moses your teacher." The Holy One Blessed be He
placed goodly counsel into the heart of each of them, and they all wrote
as one: "*I* will make a man in image and form." [So that he would not
be able to argue for a plurality of gods] (*Megillah* 9a).[58]

Let us make a man - R. Yochanan said: "Wherever the Sadducees
found room for their heresies their answer is at their side. They argue
heretically from the verse: 'Let *us* make a man in our image, according
to our form.' What follows immediately thereafter? 'And G-d created
man in *His* image' " (*Sanhedrin* 38b).[59]

1:27   And G-d created man in His image. In the image of G-d
He created him. Male and female He created them.

in His image - This teaches us that Adam was born circumcised (*Avoth d'R. Nathan* 2).[60]

He created him - R. Yehudah asked: "It is first written: 'In the image of G-d, He created *him*,' and then: 'Male and female, He created *them*!' How can this be? He projected two in thought, and created one in deed [from which He later formed two]" (*Kethuvoth* 8a).[61]

male - R. Yitzchak said in the name of R. Ammi: "When a male comes to the world, peace comes to the world. '*Zachar*' [male] — [acronymically] '*zeh kar*' ["This is a lamb" — of peace], as it is written (*Isaiah* 16:1): 'Send the lamb [as an offering of peace] to the ruler of the land' " (*Niddah* 31b).[62]

male and female - R. Yitzchak said in the name of R. Ammi: "When a male comes to the world, his "loaf" comes with him. '*Zachar*' — '*zeh kar*' ["This is a loaf"], as it is written (II *Kings* 6:23): 'And he prepared a great feast [*kairah*] for them.' '*Nekevah*' [female] — '*nekiah baah*' ["A clean one (i.e., void of possessions) comes."] Unless she asks for food, she has none, as it is written (30:28): 'State what you request ["*nakvah*" (similar to "*nekevah*")] as wages, and I shall give it' " (*Ibid.*).[63]

1:28   And G-d blessed them, and G-d said to them: "Be fruitful and multiply, and fill the earth and subdue it. And have dominion over the fish of the sea, and over the birds of the air, and over every living thing that moves on the earth."

And G-d blessed them - Bar Kappara taught: "A widow is married on the fifth day and lived with on the sixth, for on that day man was blessed, [as it is written: 'And G-d blessed them, and G-d said to them: ["Be fruitful and multiply" ' "] (*Kethuvoth* 5a).[64]

and subdue it - The *mitzvah* of begetting children devolves upon the man and not upon the woman, for it is written: "And subdue it" [*vekivshuhah*]. It is written defective [without the *vav* after the *shin*, implying that only *one* is being addressed.] Who is a "subduer"? Man and not woman (*Yevamoth* 65b).[65]

1:29 And G-d said: "Behold, I have given you every herb bearing seed which is upon the face of all the earth, and every tree, on which is the fruit yielding seed. It will be for you to eat."

It will be for you to eat - R. Yehudah said in the name of Rav: "Animal flesh was not permitted to Adam, as it is written: 'It [vegetation] will be for you to eat and for all the animals of the earth' — but the animals of the earth will not be food for you. And though it is written (28): 'And have dominion over the fish of the sea, and over the birds of the air, and over every living thing that moves on the earth,' the "dominion" in question is in respect to work" (*Sanhedrin* 59b).[66]

1:31 And G-d saw all that He did, and it was very good. And it was evening and it was morning the sixth day.

all that He did - R. Elazar said: "Though 'that it was good' is not stated in respect to the second day, it was, nevertheless, included in the blessing of the sixth day, as it is written: 'And G-d saw *all* that He did, and it was very good' " (*Pesachim* 54a).[67]

the sixth day - Why the superfluous *heh* ["*ha*shishi"]? Resh Lakish said: "This teaches us that the Holy One Blessed be He made a condition with the creation, telling it: 'If Israel accepts the Torah ["*The* sixth" alludes to the sixth of Sivan when the Torah was given], you shall endure, and if not, I shall return you to formlessness and void' " (*Shabbath* 88a).[68]

2:1 And the heavens and the earth were finished, and all of their hosts.

And they were finished [Vayechulu] - R. Hamnuna said: "All who pray on the eve of the Sabbath and say '*Vayechulu*' are accounted by Scripture as partners to the Holy One Blessed be He in the act of creation, as it is written: '*Vayechulu* the heavens and the earth.' Read it not '*Vayechulu*' [plene — 'and they (heaven and earth) were finished'], but '*Vayechalu*' [defective — 'and they (the Creator and those who acknowledge Him as such) completed']" (*Shabbath* 119b).[1]

and all of their hosts - R. Yehoshua b. Levi said: "The entire creation was created in full stature, in full cognition, in full distinctiveness, as it is written: 'And the heavens and the earth were finished, and all of their hosts.' Read it not 'their hosts' [*tzeva'am*], but 'their distinctiveness' [*tzivyonam*]" (*Rosh Hashanah* 11a).[2,3]

2:2   And G-d finished on the seventh day the work which He had done, and He rested on the seventh day from all His work which He had done.

on the seventh day - Once King Ptolemy assembled seventy-two elders in seventy-two separate houses, and told each one: "Transcribe for me [into Greek] the Torah of Moses your teacher." The Holy One Blessed be He placed goodly counsel into the hearts of each of them, and they all wrote as one: "And G-d finished on the sixth day, and He rested on the seventh day" [so that Ptolemy could not argue from the verse that G-d worked on the seventh day] (*Megillah* 9a).[4]

2:3   And G-d blessed the seventh day and He sanctified it; for on it He rested from all of His work which G-d had created to do.

And G-d blessed ... and He sanctified - With what did He bless and sanctify? With the *manna*. [It did not fall on the Sabbath; a double share fell on Friday] (*Mechilta, Yithro*).[5]

2:4   These are the generations of heaven and earth when they were created, on the day that the L-rd G-d made earth and heaven.

These are the generations - Immediately preceding this it is written: "And G-d completed all of His work." What is the connection? A day comes, a day goes; a week comes, a week goes; a month comes, a month goes; a year comes, a year goes — and still: 'These are the generations of heaven and earth on the day [i.e., as on the same day] that G-d made earth and heaven.' All is in its pristine freshness" (*Yerushalmi Berachoth* 1:1).[6]

the generations of heaven and earth - It was taught: "R. Eliezer Hagadol said: 'These are the generations of heaven and earth' — what is "heavenly" in nature was created from the heavens, and what is "earthly" in nature, from the earth" (*Yoma* 54b).[7]

when they were created - R. Yehudah b. R. Ilai expounded: "G-d created two worlds; one with a *heh* and one with a *yod*. I would not know which with a *heh* and which with a *yod*, if not for the fact that it is written: 'These are the generations of heaven and earth *behibaram*'; do not read it "*behibaram*" ["when they were created"], but "*beheh baram*" ["He created them with a *heh*"] — from which we derive that this world was created with a *heh* [(and the world to come, with a *yod*)] (*Menachoth* 29b).[8,9]

earth and heaven - Scripture always places heaven before earth, but here it places earth before heaven, to teach us that they are equal (*Yerushalmi, Chagigah* 2:1).[10]

2:6   And a mist went up from the earth and watered the whole face of the ground.

And a mist went up - It was taught: "R. Eliezer said: 'And a mist went up from the earth and watered the whole face of the ground' — this teaches us that it was the time of fructification, and rain came down and caused the soil to sprout — from which we derive that the world was created on Tishrei" (*Rosh Hashanah* 11a).[11,12]

And a mist went up - "It was taught: "R. Eliezer said: 'The entire world derives rain by way of Oceanus [and not from a heavenly source], as it is written: "And a mist went up from the *earth* and watered." ' R. Yeshoshua countered: 'But are the waters of Oceanus not salty?' To this, R. Eliezer responded: 'They are sweetened in the clouds' " (*Ta'anith* 9b).[13,14]

And a mist went up - Immediately afterwards it is written: "And the L—rd G-d formed man of the dust of the ground" — as a woman who kneads her dough in water and then separates *challah*. This teaches us that Adam was called the "*challah*" of the world — and Eve brought about his death. She was, therefore, given the *mitzvah* of *challah* to observe (*Yerushalmi, Shabbath* 2:6).[15]

And a mist went up - It was taught: "Adam was the 'blood' of the world, as it is written: 'And a mist [analogous to blood] went up ... and the L-rd created Adam' — and Eve brought about his death. Woman was, therefore, given the *mitzvah* of *niddah*" (*Ibid.*).[16,17]

And a mist ["ed"] went up - Resh Lakish expounded: "It is written: 'And an *ed* went up from the earth.' As soon as "breaking" ["*ed*" — as used here, the breaking of one's heart in prayer] goes up from below, rain comes down from above" (Yerushalmi, Ta'anith 2:1).[18]

And a mist ["ed"] went up - It was taught: "Why is a cloud called '*ed*'? Because it 'breaks' those who inflate prices." [When there is ample rain, there is ample food, and prices are lower] (*Yerushalmi, Ta'anith* 3:3).[19]

From the earth - This teaches us that clouds "grow" from the ground [See 13, 14 above] (*Succah* 11b).[20]

2:7   And the L-rd G-d formed man, dust from the earth, and breathed into his nostrils the breath of life, and man became a living soul.

And the L-rd G-d formed [Vayitzer] - Why is "*Vayitzer*" written with two *yods*? As R. Shimon b. Pazzi says: "Woe is me by virtue of my Creator ["*Yotzri*" - if I violate His will]; woe is me by virtue of my evil inclination ["*yitzri*" - which it is painful to suppress.]" Or, as R. Yirmiah b. Elazar says: "The Holy One Blessed be He created Adam with two visages, as it is written (*Psalms* 139:4): 'You formed me behind and before' " (*Berachoth* 61a).[21,22]

And He formed [Vayitzer] - Why is "*Vayitzer*" written with two *yods*? R. Zeira said in the name of R. Huna [It alludes to two different terms of creation (gestation)]: "A seven-month creation, and a nine-month creation" (*Yerushalmi, Yevamoth* 4:2).[23]

dust from the earth - R. Yuden b. Pazzi said: "The Holy One Blessed be He took a spoonful of dust from the site of the altar and created man with it, as it is written: 'And the L-rd G-d created man dust from the *earth*' and (*Exodus* 20:21): 'Make an altar of *earth* for me.' Just as 'earth' there refers to the earth of the altar, so 'earth' here refers to the earth of the altar. The Holy One Blessed be He said: 'Would that, being created from the site of the altar, he could yet endure!' " (*Yerushalmi, Nazir* 7:2).[24,25]

a living soul - R. Yossi said: "An individual is not permitted to mortify himself with fasting, lest he be cast upon the mercies of others, and they not have mercy upon him. R. Yehudah said in the name of Rav: "Whence does R. Yossi derive this? From the verse: 'And man became a living soul' — the soul that I gave you, keep it in life" (*Ta'anith* 22b).[26]

2:8   And the L-rd G-d planted a garden in Eden, eastward ["*mikedem*"], and He put there the man that He had formed.

a garden in Eden "mikedem" - This teaches us that the Garden of Eden was created before ["*kodem*"] the world was created (*Pesachim* 54a).[27]

and he put there - "there" — in the *garden* [and not in Eden.] And lest you say that the garden and Eden are one and the same, it is explicitly stated (10): "And a river went out of Eden to water the garden" — which clearly indicates that the garden and Eden are distinct entities (*Berachoth* 34b).[28]

2:10   And a river went out of Eden to water the garden, and from there it separated, and branched into four streams.

And a river went out of Eden - R. Yehoshua b. Levi said: "The entire world derives rain from the essence of the Garden of Eden, as it is written: 'And a river went out of Eden to water the garden' [and we derive our rain from the essence of that water]" (*Ta'anith* 10a).[29]

2:12   And the gold of that land is good. There, is bdellium and shoham stone.

And the gold, etc. - "And the gold of that land is good." R. Chisda said: "This teaches us that 'gold' and 'good gold' are two distinct varieties" (*Yoma* 44b).[30]

and the gold, etc. - "and the gold of that land is good." R. Yitzchak said: "Good at home [i.e., easily secured]: good on the road [i.e., easily redeemable]" (*Yerushalmi, Yoma* 4:4).[31]

2:14   And the name of the third river is Chidekel. That is the one which goes east of Ashur. And the fourth river is Perat.

Chidekel - What is signified by "Chidekel"? R. Chisda said: "Its waters are 'crisp' [*chaddin*] and light [*kallin*]" (*Berachoth* 59b).[32]

east of Ashur - R. Yosef taught: "Ashur is Seleucia." — But did Seleucia exist at that time! — The verse speaks in terms of the future (*Kethuvoth* 10b).[33]

It is Perat - R. Yehudah said in the name of Rav: "All rivers emanate from these three rivers, and these three rivers emanate from Perat." But is it not written: 'And the *fourth* river is Perat'? R. Nachman b. Yitzchak answered: "It is the same as the first-mentioned "river" (10) [in which verse it is clear that Perat is the source of the other three]" (*Berachoth* 55b).[34,35]

It is Perat - It was taught: "R. Meir said: 'Its real name is Yuval, as it is written (*Jeremiah* 17:8): "And he shall be like a tree planted by the waters, that spreads its roots out by Yuval." Why, then, is it called Perat? Because its waters are fruitful and multiply [*parim* (similar to "*Perat*"), *veravim* (without rain)] (*Ibid.*).[36]

2:15   And the L-rd G-d took the man, and He placed him in the Garden of Eden to work it and to keep it.

to work it and to keep it - It was taught: "R. Shimon b. Elazar said: 'Great is labor, for even Adam tasted nothing until he had worked, as it is written: "And He placed him in the Garden of Eden to work it and to keep it," and only afterwards: "From all the trees of the garden, you may eat" ' " (*Avoth d'R. Nathan* 11).[37]

2:16   And the L-rd G-d commanded man, saying: "Of every tree of the garden, eat, you may eat."

And the L-rd commanded, etc. - The Rabbis taught: "Seven *mitzvoth* were prescribed for the Noachides: to establish courts, not to bless [euphemism for "curse"] the name of the L-rd, and to keep from: idol worship, adultery, bloodshed, robbery, and from eating flesh torn from a living animal [*ever min hachai*]. As Scripture states: 'And the L-rd G-d commanded man, saying: "Of every tree of the garden, eat, you may eat"': "And He *commanded*" — this alludes to the establishment of courts, as it is written (18:19): 'For I have known him because he will *command* his children ... to do justice and judgment'; "The *L-rd*" — this alludes to "blessing" of the Name, as it is written (*Leviticus* 24:16): 'And he who blasphemes the name of the *L-rd* shall surely be put to death'; "*G-d*" — this alludes to idol worship, as it is written (*Exodus* 19:3): 'You shall have no other gods beside me'; "*man*" — this alludes to bloodshed, as it is written (9:6): 'He who spills the blood of a *man*, etc.'; "*saying*" — this alludes to adultery, as it is written (*Jeremiah* 3:1): '*Saying* if a man send away his wife, and she go from him and become another man's, etc.'; "of every tree of the garden" — and not from what is stolen; "eat, you may eat" — [i.e., you may eat what is already fit to be eaten] and not flesh torn from a living animal" (*Sanhedrin* 56b).[38,39]

2:18   And the L-rd G-d said: "It is not good for man to be alone. I shall make him a help against him."

It is not good, etc. - R. Nachman said in the name of Shmuel: "Though a man has several children, he is forbidden to remain without a wife, as it is written: 'It is not good for man to be alone' "(*Yevamoth* 61b).[40]

It is not good - R. Chanilai said: "Whoever does not have a wife abides without good, as it is written: 'It is not good for man to be alone' " (*Ibid.* 62b).[41]

I shall make him a help - R. Yossi found Elijah and asked him: "It is written: 'I shall make him a help.' How does a woman help a man?" He answered: "A man brings wheat from the field. Can he chew wheat? He brings flax. Can he wear flax? The result is that [by woman's processing what man brings] she brightens his eyes and puts him on his feet" (*Ibid.* 63a).[42]

a help against him - R. Elazar said: " 'I shall make him a help against him' — if he is meritorious, she helps him; if not, she is against him." Others say: "R. Elazar asks: 'It is written "*kenegdo*" ["against him"], but it can be read "*kenigdo*" ["as flogging him"]! — if he is meritorious, she is "against" him [i.e., at his side]: if not, she "flogs" him" (*Ibid.*).[43]

2:22   And the L-rd G-d built the side that he had taken from man into a woman, and He brought her to the man.

And He built - Rav and Shmuel differ on this. One says that Eve was a form in herself, connected to Adam; the other, that she was constructed from Adam's caudal appendage. Now, according to the latter view, how are we to understand: "And He closed up the flesh beneath it"? — The reference is to the site of the incision (*Berachoth* 61a).[44]

And He built - R. Shimon b. Menassia expounded: " 'And the L-rd built the side' — this teaches us that the Holy One Blessed be He plaited Eve's hair and brought her to Adam; for in the cities of the sea, plaiting is called 'building' " (*Ibid.*).[45,46]

And He built - R. Chisda said (some say it was taught in a *baraitha*) ["And the L-rd G-d built the side"]: "This teaches us that the Holy One Blessed be He built Eve as a receptacle. Just as a storage-bin is narrow on top and wide on the bottom for the receiving of fruit, so a woman is narrow on top and wide on the bottom for the receiving of the child" (*Ibid.*).[47]

And He built [Vayiven] - R. Chisda said: " 'And the L-rd G-d built' — He placed greater intuition [*binah* - same root as *Vayiven*] in woman than in man" (*Niddah* 45b).[48]

And He brought her to the man - R. Yirmiah b. Elazar said: "This teaches us that the Holy One Blessed be He became a groomsman to Adam. The Torah hereby taught us proper conduct — that one of higher station should act as groomsman to one of lower station, and not be uneasy about it" (*Berachoth* 61a).[49]

2:23 And the man said: "This time, bone of my bone, and flesh of my flesh. This one shall be called 'woman' because this one was taken from man."

This time - "'This time, bone of my bone, and flesh of my flesh'" — this teaches us that Adam was intimate with every beast and animal, but was not fulfilled until he was intimate with Eve (*Yevamoth* 63a).[50]

2:24 For this, a man shall leave his father and his mother and he shall cleave to his wife, and they shall be one flesh.

his father, etc. - R. Akiva said: "His father" — this intimates the prohibition of sexual relationships with his father's wife; "his mother" — this intimates the prohibition of sexual relationships with his mother (*Sanhedrin* 58a).[51]

and he shall cleave to his wife - "And he shall cleave" — not with a male; "to *his* wife" — not his neighbor's (*Ibid.*).[52]

and he shall cleave to his wife - Rava said: "A Noachite who has pederastic intercourse with his neighbor's wife is not liable, for it is written: 'And he shall cleave to his wife' — '*his* wife,' not his neighbor's wife; 'and he shall *cleave*' — not pederastically" (*Ibid.* 58b).[53]

and he shall cleave to his wife - It was taught: "A Noachite who performs even the surface stage [*hearah*] of a forbidden sexual act is liable, as it is written: 'And he shall cleave to *his* wife' — and not to his neighbor's wife; 'and he shall cleave' — even peripheral cleaving. And the same ["even peripheral cleaving"] holds true for sexual relationships with other males or with animals (*Yerushalmi, Kiddushin* 1:1).[54,55]

and they shall be one flesh - An adulterous Noachitess also receives the death penalty; for although it is written: "Therefore, a *man* should cleave ... " — a man and not a woman — it is written afterwards: "And they shall be one flesh" — Scripture re-combines them (*Sanhedrin* 57b).[56]

and they shall be one flesh - Such relationships are permitted as result in one flesh [a child, in whom the flesh of father and mother become one] — to exclude relationships with beasts or animals, that do not result in one flesh (*Ibid.* 58a).[57]

3:1   And the serpent was subtler than all the beasts of the field which the L-rd G-d had made. And he said to the woman: "Did G-d really say that you should not eat of all the trees of the garden?"

And the serpent was subtler - [What was his subtlety?] He said: "I know that the Holy One Blessed be He said: 'For the day that you eat from it you shall die.' I shall go and deceive man and his wife; they will eat and be punished, and I shall inherit the land for myself" (*Yerushalmi, Kiddushin* 4:1).[1]

3:3   But from the fruit of the tree which is in the midst of the garden, G-d said: "Do not eat of it and do not touch it, lest you die."

and do not touch it - Chizkiah said: "How do we know that all who add [to a command] detract [from its effectiveness]? For it is written: 'G-d said: "Do not eat from it, and do not touch it." ' " [G-d had not said: "Do not touch it." The serpent pushed Eve against the tree and proved to her that touching does not produce death — why, then, should eating?] (*Sanhedrin* 29a).[2]

3:7   And the eyes of both of them were opened, and they knew that they were naked, and they sewed fig leaves together, and they made belts for themselves.

and they sewed fig leaves together - It was taught: "R. Nechemiah said: 'The tree from which Adam ate was a fig tree; for by means of the

very object through which they had gone astray, they were corrected —
as it is written: 'And they sewed together leaves of a fig tree' " (*Ibid.*
70b).[3]

3:9   And the L-rd G-d called to Adam and He said to him:
           "Where are you?"

And the L-rd G-d called - It was taught: "One should never enter his
neighbor's house unexpectedly, but should follow the example of the
Holy One Blessed be He, who stood at the entrance to the garden and
called to Adam, as it is written: 'And the L-rd G-d called to Adam' "
(*Derech Eretz* 5).[4]

And He said to him: "Where are you?" - R. Yehudah said in the name
of Rav: "Adam was a Sadducee, as it is written: 'And He said to him:
"Where are you?"' — Where has your heart strayed?" (*Sanhedrin*
38b).[5]

3:11   And He said to him: "Who told you that you were naked?
           Did you eat of the tree of which I commanded you not to
           eat?"

of the tree - Some Epiphanians asked R. Mathnah: "Where is Haman
alluded to in the Torah? He answered: " '*Hamin* [similar in appearance
to "Haman"] *haetz* ... ['Did you eat of the tree of which I commanded
you not to eat?']" (*Chullin* 139b).[6]

3:12   And Adam answered: "The woman that You gave with
           me — she gave me from the tree and I ate."

The woman that You gave - The Rabbis taught: "Adam was an ingrate,
as it is written: 'The woman that You gave with me — she gave me from
the tree and I ate'!" (*Avodah Zarah* 5b).[7]

3:14   And L-rd G-d said to the serpent: "Because you have
           done this, you are more accursed than any beast and any

animal of the field. On your belly shall you walk, and dust shall you eat all the days of your life."

And the L-rd G-d said to the serpent - It was taught: "Rebbi [R. Judah Hanasi] said: 'In cursing, the order is from inferior to superior; for the serpent was cursed first, then Eve, then Adam, as it is written: 'And the L—rd G-d said to the serpent' — then to Eve and to Adam" (*Berachoth* 61a).[8]

And the L-rd G-d said to the serpent - From here it is to be derived that one does not furnish a defense for an instigator [in this case, the serpent]. Which defense could have been furnished? "The words of the Master [G—d], and the words of the disciple [the serpent] — whose words should be heeded? Naturally, the Master's!" (*Sanhedrin* 29a).[9]

And the L-rd G-d said to the serpent - It was taught: "Why do serpents mate face to face? Because the *Shechinah* [the Divine Presence] addressed the serpent, as it is written: 'And the L-rd G-d said to the serpent' " (*Bechoroth* 8a).[10,11]

you are more accursed, etc. - The Rabbis taught: "All who set their eyes upon what is not theirs, what they desire is not given them, and what they possess is taken from them. For so we find with the primal serpent, who set his eyes upon what was not his. What he desired was not given him, and what he possessed was taken from him. The Holy One Blessed be He said: 'I said: "Be king over every beast and animal " — and now: you are more accursed than any beast and any animal of the field. I said: "Walk upright" — and now: walk upon your belly. I said that he should eat the food of men — and now: let him eat dust. He said: 'I shall kill Adam and Eve' — and now: I shall place hatred between you and the woman" (*Sotah* 9b).[12,13]

than any beast and any animal of the field - If he is more accursed than any beast, does it not stand to reason that he is more accursed than any animal of the field? — The meaning is that to the same extent that the beast is more accursed than the animal, conceiving only one time to the latter's seven, to that extent is the serpent more accursed than the beast.

What are "the beast" and "the animal" in question? The ass [which
conceives once a year], and the cat [which conceives every fifty-two
days]. The serpent is accursed in like degree above the beast [ass] in
that it conceives only once in seven years (*Bechoroth* 8a).[14,15]

3:16   To the woman He said: "I shall increase your sorrow and
       your child-bearing. In sorrow shall you bring forth
       children, and to your husband is your desire, and he shall
       rule over you."

To the woman He said - through an intermediary (*Yerushalmi, Sotah*
7:1).[16]

I shall increase [lit., "make more and more"] - "More and more" —
these are the two drippings of blood: that of *niddah* and that of the
hymen (*Eruvin* 100b).[17]

your sorrow and your child-bearing - "Your sorrow" — this is the
ordeal of child-rearing; "your child-bearing" — this is the ordeal of
pregnancy (*Ibid.*).[18,19]

and to your husband is your desire - This teaches us that a woman has a
desire for her husband when he is about to set out on a journey. This is
the basis for the Rabbis' ruling: "One must 'remember' his wife before
he sets out on a journey" (*Yevamoth* 62).[20,21]

and he shall rule over you - This teaches us that a woman "solicits" in
her heart, and a man, verbally. And this is a commendable trait in a
woman (*Eruvin* 100b).[22]

3:17   And to the man he said: "Because you listened to the
       voice of your wife and ate from the tree from which I
       commanded you not to eat, the earth is accursed for you;
       in sorrow shall you eat it all the days of your life."

the earth is accursed for you - It was taught: "Why was the earth
cursed? R. Yuden b. Shalom said: 'Because it violated the decree of the
Holy One Blessed be He [for it was commanded to bring forth only

unique fruit-producing trees, and it brought forth trees that produced fruit even though they were not especially adapted to the purpose.] R. Pinchas said: 'It is as men say: "Cursed be the demon that gave birth to such as these" ' [Cursed be the earth from which man was formed]" (*Yerushalmi, Kelayim* 1:7).[23,24]

in sorrow shall you eat it - R. Yochanan said: "The attainment of one's sustenance is twice as difficult as child-bearing; for in relation to the latter it is written " *be'etzev*" ["in sorrow"], whereas in relation to the former it is written "*beitzavon*" [which connotes "double sorrow"]" (*Pesachim* 118a).[25]

3:18   And thorns and thistles shall it sprout for you, and you shall eat the grass of the field.

And thorns and thistles - R. Yehoshua b. Levi said: "When the Holy One Blessed be He told Adam: 'And thorns and thistles shall it sprout for you,' his eyes started streaming tears. He said: 'L-rd of the universe, shall I and my ass eat from one manger?' When G-d answered: 'With the sweat of your brow shall you eat bread,' his mind was set at rest" (*Ibid.*).[26,27]

3:19   With the sweat of your brow shall you eat bread until you return to the earth, for from it were you taken; for you are dust and you shall return to dust.

With the sweat of your brow shall you eat bread - This intimates that sweat is a propitious sign for one who is ill (*Berachoth* 57b).[28]

and you shall return to dust - When? R. Achai b. Yashiah said: "A moment before the resurrection" (*Shabbath* 152b).[29]

3:20   And Adam called the name of his wife "Chavah," for she was the mother of all living things.

the mother of all living things - It was taught: A woman ascends [rises to a higher station] with her husband and does not descend. Whence is this derived? R. Elazar said: "From the verse: 'For she was the mother of all living things' — she was given motherhood for "life" [betterment] and not for affliction" (*Kethuvoth* 61a).[30]

3:21   And the L-rd G-d made for man and his wife vestments of skin, and He clothed them.

vestments of skin - Rav and Shmuel differ on this, one interpreting it as clothing that comes from skin [i.e., wool], and the other, as clothing from which the skin derives enjoyment (*Sotah* 11a).[31]

vestments of skin - R. Yehoshua b. Chanina expounded: " 'And the L—rd G-d made for man and his wife vestments of skin, and He clothed them' — this teaches us that the Holy One Blessed be He does not clothe a man [a fetus] with skin until he is fully formed" (*Niddah* 25a).[32]

and He clothed them - From here it is to be derived that it is among the attributes of the Holy One Blessed be He to clothe the naked (*Sotah* 14a).[33]

and He clothed them -R. Simlai expounded: "Great is lovingkindness, for the Torah begins with lovingkindness and ends with lovingkindness. The beginning: 'And the L-rd G-d made for man and his wife vestments of skin and He clothed them.' The end (*Deuteronomy* 34:6): 'And He buried him in the valley' " (*Ibid.*).[34]

4:2   And she bore again, his brother, Hevel. And Hevel was a shepherd of the flock, and Cain was a worker of the earth.

his brother, etc. - "his brother, Hevel" ["*et* achiv *et* Hevel" - the "*et*" indicates an addition] — Hevel and his sister, Cain and his sister (*Yevamoth* 62a).[1]

4:4   And Hevel, he also brought, of the firstlings of his flock and of their fats. And the L-rd looked favorably upon Hevel and his offering.

and of their fats - What is connoted by "And of their fats"? — Of the choicest of them (*Zevachim* 116a).[2]

4:7   If you do well, you shall overcome, and if you do not do well, sin lies at the door, and its desire is to you, but you can rule over it.

If you do well, etc. - It was taught: "Issi b. Yehudah said: 'This is one of the ambiguous verses ["If you do well, you will be forgiven" *or* "You will bear your sin if you do not do well"] (*Yoma* 52b).[3]

If you do well, etc. - It was taught: "The Holy One Blessed be He said to Israel: 'I created an evil inclination, and I created an antidote to it. If you occupy yourself with Torah, you will not succumb to it, as it is written: "If you do well, you shall overcome," and if not, you shall succumb to it, as it is written: "Sin lies at the door." What is more, all of its concourse is with you, as it is written: "And its desire is to you." And if you have the will, you can dominate it, as it is written: "But you can rule over it" ' " (*Kiddushin* 30b).[4-6]

and if you do not do well - R. Meir said: "Any condition which is not like that of the children of Gad and the children of Reuven [i.e., a condition and its opposite - see *Numbers* 32:29] is no condition. And this accounts for the structure: 'If you do well ... and if you do not do well' " (*Ibid.* 61b).[7,8]

sin lies at the door - Rav said: "The evil inclination is like a fly that lies between the two doors of the heart, as it is written (*Ecclesiastes* 10:1): 'The flies of death, etc.' " Shmuel says: "It is like a wheat grain, as it is written: 'Sin [*chatath* - similar to *chitah* (wheat grain)] lies at the door' " (*Berachoth* 61a).[9]

sin lies at the door - Elijah said to R. Yehudah: "You ask why the Messiah has not yet come, when today it is Yom Kippur and many virgins have been violated in Nehardaa!" R. Yehudah, thereupon, asked Elijah: "What does the Holy One Blessed be He say to this!" He answered: " 'Sin lies at the door' " (*Yoma* 19b).[10]

sin lies at the door - Rebbe [R. Judah Hanasi] said: "This was taught me by Antoninus: 'The evil inclination reigns in a man from the time he enters the world, as it is written: "Sin lies at the door [of life]' ' " (*Sanhedrin* 91b).[11]

sin lies at the door - R. Simlai expounded: [When a child is yet in his mother's womb] "he is taught all of the Torah, and as soon as he enters the world, an angel comes, strikes him on the mouth, and causes him to forget the entire Torah, as it is written: 'Sin lies at the door' " (*Niddah* 30b).[12]

4:10   And He said: "What have you done? The voice of your
        brother's bloods cries out to Me from the ground."

The voice of your brother's bloods - Not "your brother's *blood*," but "your brother's *bloods*"— his blood and the blood of his children. This teaches us that the laws involving murder are not like the laws involving monetary violations. In the latter instance, one makes financial restitution and he is forgiven, but in the former, he is responsible for the blood of his victim and the blood of his unborn descendants until the end of time (*Sanhedrin* 37a).[13]

The voice of your brother's bloods - Not "your brother's *blood*," but your brother's *bloods*." This teaches us that his blood was bespattered on trees and on stones (*Ibid.*).[14]

The voice of your brother's bloods - R. Yehudah the son of R. Chiyya said [Not "your brother's *blood*," but "your brother's *bloods*]: "This teaches us that Cain inflicted many blows and wounds upon Abel, not knowing whence the soul departed — until he came to his throat" (*Ibid.*).[15]

4:13   And Cain said to the L-rd: "My sin is too great to
        forgive."

My sin is too great to forgive - The Rabbis taught: "Cain remonstrated with the Holy One Blessed be He, as it is written: 'My sin is too great to forgive.' He said to Him: 'L-rd of the universe, is my sin greater than that of the six hundred thousand Jews who are destined to sin, and whom You will yet forgive?' " (*Sanhedrin* 101b).[16]

My sin is too great to forgive - It was taught: "In relation to the shedding of blood it is stated: 'My sin is too *great* to forgive,' and in relation to slander (*Psalms* 12:4): 'The tongue that speaks *great* things' — to teach us that the sin of the slanderer comes close to being as great as that of the murderer" (*Erchin* 15b).[17]

My sin is too great to forgive - This teaches us that bloodshed is one of those sins for which punishment is exacted in this world, with the "core" remaining for the next world, as it is written: "And Cain said: 'My sin is too great to forgive' " (*Yerushalmi, Peah* 1:).[18]

4:14   You have driven me out this day from the face of the earth, and from Your face I shall be hid, and I shall be a fugitive and a vagabond in the earth; and it shall be that whoever finds me will kill me.

whoever finds me will kill me - R. Alexander said: "When a man's end arrives, all rule over him, as it is written: 'And whoever finds me will kill me' " (*Nedarim* 41a).[19]

4:16   And Cain left the presence of the L-rd, and he dwelt in the land, a vagabond, east of Eden.

and he dwelt in the land, a vagabond - R. Yehudah the son of R. Chiyya said: "Exile atones for half of a man's sins. In the beginning it is written: 'And I shall be a fugitive and a vagabond,' and in the end: 'And he dwelt in the land, a vagabond' " (*Sanhedrin* 37b).[20]

4:19   And Lemech took for himself two wives. The name of one was Addah, and the name of the other was Tzilah.

Addah and Tzilah - "Addah" — he would take pleasure [*mitaden*] in her body [and kept her from having children]; "Tzilah" — he sat in the shade [*tzel*] of the children that she bore (*Yerushalmi, Yevamoth* 6:5).[21]

4:23   And Lemech said to his wives, Addah and Tzilah: "Hear

> my voice, wives of Lemech; hearken to my speech. For I
> have killed a man for wounding me, and a young man for
> my hurt."

wives of Lemech - Should we not have: "my wives"? — This is the style
of Scripture. Similarly (19:24): "And the L-rd rained down upon
Sodom and upon Gemorrah brimstone and fire from the L-rd." Should
we not have: "from Him"? But such is the style of Scripture (*Sanhedrin*
38b).[22]

4:25   And Adam knew his wife again, and she bore a son and
        called his name Sheth — for G-d has given ["*shath*"] me
        another seed instead of Hevel, whom Cain killed.

And Adam knew - When the son of R. Yochanan b. Zakkai died, his
disciples came to console him. R. Elazar said to him: "Adam had a son
who died, and he allowed himself to be consoled for him, as it is written:
'And Adam knew Eve, his wife, again.' You, too, allow yourself to be
consoled" (*Avoth d'R. Nathan* 14).[23]

5:1   This is the book of the generations of man. On the day
        that G-d created man, in the image of G-d He made him.

This is the book, etc. - Resh Lakish asked: "Now did Adam have a
book? What is to be understood, rather, is that the Holy One Blessed be
He showed Adam each generation and its exegetes, each generation and
its sages" (*Avodah Zarah* 5a).[1]

This is the book, etc. - It was taught: "R. Akiva said (*Leviticus* 18:18):
'And you shall love your neighbor as yourself' — this is a great principle
in the Torah." Ben Azai said: 'This is the book of the generations of
man' — this is an even greater principle" (*Yerusahlmi, Nedarim* 9:4).[2]

5:2   Male and female He created them, and He blessed them.
        And He called their name "Man" on the day He created
        them.

Male and female He created them - R. Akiva asked: "It is written: 'Male and female He created *them*,' and 'In the image of G-d He made *man*'! How can this be? — He projected the creation of two, and actually created one [from which He later formed two]" (*Berachoth* 61a).[3,4]

Male and female He created them - Once King Ptolemy assembed seventy-two elders in seventy-two separate houses and said to each one: "Transcribe for me [into Greek] the Torah of Moses your teacher." The Holy One Blessed be He placed goodly counsel into the heart of each of them, and they all wrote as one: "Male and female He created *him*" [to ward off the question asked above by R. Akiva] (*Megillah* 9a).[5]

Male and female He created them - It was taught: "Bet Hillel said: 'One has not fulfilled the *mitzvah* of begetting children unless he has a son and a daughter, as it is written: 'Male and female He created them' '" (*Yevamoth* 61b).[6]

And He called their name "Man" - R. Elazar said: "Anyone who does not have a wife is not a man, as it is written: 'Male and female He created them, and He called their name "Man" ' " (*Ibid.* 63a).[7]

5:3   And Adam lived one hundred and thirty years, and he begot a son in his own likeness according to his image, and he called his name Sheth.

and he begot a son in his own likeness according to his image - R. Yirmiah b. Elazar said: "All those years that Adam was an outcast, he begot spirits, shades, and night-demons, as it is written: 'And Adam lived one hundred and thirty years, and he begot a son in his own likeness according to his image,' from which it may be inferred that up to that time he had not begotten according to his image" (*Eruvin* 18b).[8]

and he begot a son in his own likeness according to his image - This teaches us that Sheth was born circumcised. [Adam was born circumcised - see 1:27] (*Avoth d'R. Nathan* 2).[9]

5:29   And he called his name Noah, saying: "This one will comfort us for our work and the toil of our hands because of the ground, which the L-rd cursed."

This one will comfort us - It was taught: "When a righteous one enters the world, good enters the world, as it is written: 'This one will comfort us for our work and the toil of our hands' " (*Sanhedrin* 113b).[10]

5:32   And Noah was five hundred years old, and Noah begot Shem, Cham and Jefet.

Shem, etc. - It was taught: "Shem was the youngest, but they are listed in rank order of wisdom. Know this to be so, for it is written: 'And Noah was five hundred years old, and Noah begot Shem, Cham and Jefet.' [If Shem were the oldest], how much older would Shem be than Cham? [Let us assume] one year. And Cham would be one year older than Jefet. This would make Shem two years older than Jefet. But it is written: (7:6): 'And Noah was six hundred years old when the flood of waters was upon the earth,' and (11:10): 'These are the generations of Shem. Shem was one hundred years old, when he begot Arpachshad, two years after the flood.' Now, would he be one hundred? Would he not be one hundred and two? It is clear, then, that they are listed in rank order of wisdom [and not in order of birth] (*Sanhedrin* 69b).[11]

6:1   And it was, when men began to multiply on the face of the earth, and daughters were born to them.

when men began, etc. - It was taught: "And it was, when men began to multiply [*larov*], etc. and daughters were born to them" — R. Yochanan said: "*Revayah* [multiplication (of children)] came to the world." [More daughters make for more children.] Resh Lakish said: "*Merivah* [quarreling] came to the world [through the increase of women]" (*Bava Bathra* 16b).[1]

6:2   And the sons of G-d saw the daughters of man, that they were goodly, and they took for themselves wives of all that they selected.

And they saw, etc. - It was taught: "R. Yossi said: 'The generation of the flood had the presumption to sin only because of the eye-ball, which is similar to water, as it is written: 'And the sons of G-d *saw* the daughters of man, that they were goodly, and they took for themselves wives of all that they selected.' They were, therefore, judged through water, which is similar to the eye-ball — as it is written (7:11): 'All the fountains of the great deep opened, and the windows of heaven opened'" (*Sanhedrin* 108a).[2]

6:3   And the L-rd said: "My spirit shall not judge forever in man while he is still flesh, and his days will be one hundred and twenty years."

My spirit will not judge - The Rabbis taught: "The generation of the flood have no share in the world to come and do not rise to be judged [at the resurrection], as it is written: 'My spirit shall not judge' — neither judgment [for the resurrection] nor spirit [for the after-life]" (*Sanhedrin* 107b).[3]

forever - Their souls will not return to their receptacles (*Ibid.* 108a).[4]

while he is still flesh [beshegam hu basar] - Some Epiphanians asked R. Massnah: "Where is Moses alluded to in the Torah? He answered: "*Beshegam* hu basar." [The *gematria* (numerical equivalent) of *beshegam* (345) is the same as that of *Moshe*, and the life-span of Moses was one hundred and twenty years, just as the life-span indicated in the verse] (*Chullin* 139b).[5]

one hundred and twenty years - Now, did Adam not live close to one thousand years? How, then, can it be said: "And his days will be one hundred and twenty years?" — The understanding is that one hundred and twenty years [after his death] he becomes a rotted spoonful of dust (*Yerushalmi, Nazir* 7:2).[6]

6:5   And the L-rd saw that great was the evil of man in the earth, and all the impulse of the thoughts of his heart was only evil every day.

that great, etc. - R. Yochanan said: "The generation of the flood went astray with 'great,' as it is written: 'that *great* was the evil of man,' and they were judged with 'great,' as it is written (7:11): 'All the fountains of the *great* deep opened' " (*Sanhedrin* 108a).[7]

only evil - From here it is derived that the (evil) inclination is called "evil" (*Chagigah* 16a).[8]

every day - R. Yitzchak said: "A man's evil inclination intensifies itself every day, as it is written: 'And all the impulse of the thoughts of his heart was only evil every day' " (*Succah* 52a).[9]

6:6   And the L-rd repented that He had made man on the earth, and it grieved Him at His heart.

And the L-rd ... [Vayinachem Hashem] - Rav Dimmi said: "The Holy One Blessed be He said: 'I did well [I am *consoled*] to have prepared graves for them in the land.' How is this meaning implied? It is written here: "*Vayinachem Hashem*," and elsewhere (50:21): "*Vayinacheim otam*" ["and He *consoled* them."] Others say: "He said: 'I did not do well.' [I *repent* (that I created man.)] It is written here: "*Vayinachem Hashem*," and elsewhere (*Exodus* 32:14): "*Vayinachem Hashem al hara'ah*" ["And the L-rd *repented* of the evil"] (*Sanhedrin* 108a).[10]

6:8   And Noah found favor in the eyes of the L-rd.

And Noah found favor - It was taught in the forum of R. Yishmael: "The decree [of the flood] was sealed for Noah, too, but he found favor, as it is written: 'I repent that I have made them — and Noah found favor in the eyes of the L-rd' " (*Ibid.*).[11]

Noah

6:9   These are the generations of Noah. Noah was a righteous
        man. He was perfectly righteous in his generation. With
        G—d did Noah walk.

perfectly righteous - And further it is written (7:1): "And the L-rd said
to Noah: 'I have seen you as righteous [but not "perfectly"] before
Me.'" R. Yirmiah b. Elazar said: "This teaches us that only a portion of
one's praises are recited in his presence, and all of them, when he is not
present" (*Eruvin* 18b).[12]

perfectly righteous - Righteous in his deeds; perfect in his ways (*Avodah
Zarah* 6a).[13]

perfect - This teaches us that Noah was born circumcised (*Avoth d'R.
Nathan* 2).[14]

in his generation - What is signified by "in his generation"? R.
Yochanan said: "In *his* generation, but not in others." Resh Lakish
said: "In *his* generation, and most assuredly in others" (*Sanhedrin*
108a).[15]

6:11   And the land became corrupted before G-d, and the earth
        was filled wih violence.

And the land became corrupted - It was taught in the forum of R.
Yishmael: "Wherever 'corruption' is mentioned, the reference is to
illicit relations and idol worship. Illicit relations — as it is written (12):
'For all flesh has corrupted its way [nature]'; idol worship — as it is
written (*Deuteronomy* 4:16): 'Lest you corrupt yourselves and make an
idol' " (*Ibid.* 47).[16,17]

6:12   And G-d looked upon the earth, and, behold, it was

corrupt; for all flesh had corrupted its way upon the earth.

all flesh - R. Yochanan said: This teaches us that they mated domestic animals with wild ones, and wild animals with domestic ones — and man with all (*Ibid.* 108a).[18]

6:13   And G-d said to Noah: "The end of all flesh is come before Me, for the land is filled with violence before them, and, behold, I will destroy them with the earth."

for the land is filled, etc. - R. Yochanan said: "Come and see how great is the power of violence [pillage]; for the generation of the flood committed all manner of transgressions, and yet their decree was not sealed until they stretched out their hand to steal, as it is written: 'For the land is filled with violence before them; and, behold, I will destroy them with the earth'" (*Ibid.*).[19]

for the land is filled, etc. - It was taught: "What did they steal? If someone walked out carrying a basket full of lupines, they would contrive to steal an amount worth less than a *prutah* so that they would not be liable for court action (*Yerushalmi, Bava Metzia* 4:2).[20]

6:14   Make yourself an ark of gopher wood. Rooms shall you make in the ark, and you shall pitch it within and without with pitch.

gopher wood - What is gopher wood? In the forum of R. Shila it was said to be *mavligah*, and others say that it is *gulmish* [a species of cedar trees] (*Sanhedrin* 108a).[21]

6:16   A window shall you make for the ark, and to a cubit shall you finish it from above; and the door of the ark shall you set in its side; with lower stories, middle stories, and upper stories shall you make it.

a window [tzohar] - R. Yochanan said: "The Holy One Blessed be He said to Noah: 'Set within it precious stones and pearls, so that they shine for you like the afternoon'" [*tzaharayim* - same root as *tzohar*] (*Ibid.* b).[22]

and to a cubit - Why so? For thus it would stand firm (*Ibid.*).[23]

lower stories, etc. - It was taught: "Lower stories for waste, middle stories for the animals, upper stories for the people" (*Ibid.*).[24]

6:17   And I, behold, I will bring a flood of water upon the earth to destroy all flesh in which is the breath of life from under the heaven; all that is on the earth shall die.

And I, etc. - The Rabbis taught: "The generation of the flood became haughty only because of all the good bestowed upon them by the Holy One Blessed be He. They said: 'Is there anything we need Him for except a drop of rain? We have plenty of rivers and wells to supply us.' At this, the Holy One Blessed be He said: 'They are angering me through the good that I have bestowed upon them, and it is through that same element that I will punish them,' as it is written: 'And I, behold, I will bring a flood of *water*' " (*Ibid.* a).[25]

6:18   And I will establish My covenant with you, and you shall come into the ark: you, your sons, and your wife, and your sons' wives with you.

you, your sons, and your wife - But in reference to their leaving the ark it is written (8:16): "You, your wife, and your sons." This teaches us that upon entering the ark, the men and women were forbidden to live with each other (*Ibid.* b).[26]

6:19   And from all of the animals, from all flesh, two of each, bring into the ark to live with you. Male and female shall they be.

And from all of the animals [hachai - lit., "living things"], **etc.** - R. Elazar said: "Whence is it derived that animals deficient in their organs were forbidden to Noachides? From the verse: 'And from all of the

living things, from all flesh, two of each, bring into the ark.' The Torah
is hereby implying: 'Bring only such animals with living [healthy] organ
prominences' " (*Avodah Zarah* 5b).[27,28]

to live with you - *"with you"* — *similar* to you; to exclude a *treifah* [an
animal which has a fatal organic disease and which cannot survive a
year.] But may it not be that Noah himself was a *treifah?* — It is
inconceivable that G-d would tell him: "Take in only sickly ones like
you, and not healthy ones" (*Ibid.* 6a).[29,30]

7:2   Of every clean beast you shall take to you by sevens, man
        and wife. And of beasts that are not clean, by twos, man
        and wife.

man and wife - Can animals be spoken of as "man and wife"! R. Avahu
said [It is written (7:16): "And those who came"]: "Those who came by
themselves [as pairs, who mated only with each other]" (*Sanhedrin*
108b).[1]

7:3   Of birds of the air, also by sevens, male and female, to
        cause seed to live upon the face of all the earth.

to cause seed to live - To exclude a decrepit or emasculated animal
(*Avodah Zarah* 6a).[2]

7:8   From the beasts that are clean, and from the beasts that
        are not clean, and from the birds, and from everything
        that creeps upon the earth.

the beasts that are clean - Were there clean beasts and unclean beasts at
that time? [i.e., How could Noah have known which they were?] R.
Avahu answered (7:16): "And those who came" — those who came by
themselves [and Noah knew that the pairs of seven were clean, and
those of two, unclean] (*Zevachim* 116a).[3]

that are not clean - R. Yehoshua b. Levi said: "Let a man never permit
offensive speech to issue from his mouth, for the Torah resorted to an

eight-letter circumlocution in order to avoid an offensive statement ["unclean beast"], viz.: 'From the beasts that are clean, and from the beasts that are not clean' " (*Pesachim* 3a).[4]

7:10   And it was at the end of the seven days that the waters of the flood were upon the earth.

And it was at the end of the seven days - What was the nature of those "seven days"? Rav said: "These were the days of mourning for Methuselah — to teach us that the mourning period for the righteous holds off the oncoming calamity" (*Sanhedrin* 108b).[5]

And it was at the end of the seven days - What was the nature of those seven days? We are hereby taught that the Holy One Blessed be He reversed the order of creation for them, causing the sun to rise in the west and set in the east (*Ibid.*).[6]

And it was at the end of the seven days - What was the nature of those seven days? The Holy One Blessed be He caused them to taste of what resembled the world to come, so that they would know what good they were depriving themselves of (*Ibid.*).[7]

And it was at the end of the seven days - What was the nature of those seven days? The Holy One Blessed be He kept vigil over His world for seven days [in "mourning" over their impending doom.] From here it may be derived that the mourning period is seven days (*Yerushalmi, Moed Katan* 3:5).[8]

7:11   In the six hundredth year of Noah's life, in the second month, the seventeenth day of the month, on that same day, all the fountains of the great deep were broken open, and the windows of heaven were opened.

in the second month - It was taught: "R. Eliezer said: 'That day was the seventeenth of Marcheshvan. And what is signified by 'in the second month'? The month after the Day of Judgment [in Tishrei]" (*Rosh Hashanah* 11b).[9]

and the windows of heaven - Here we have "windows," and elsewhere [in relation to the manna] (*Psalms* 78:23): "And He commanded the clouds from above and opened the *doors* of heaven" — to teach us that the measure for good is more ample than the measure for evil (*Yoma* 67a).[10]

7:13   In the middle of the day, Noah, and Shem, and Cham, and Yefet, the sons of Noah, and Noah's wife, and the three wives of his sons with them, entered the ark.

Why in the middle of the day? - Because the men of his generation said: "We will not allow him to enter the ark; we will take axes and hatchets and destroy the ark." To this the Holy One Blessed be He said: "I shall bring him into the ark in the middle of the day, and anyone who has the power to stop Me, let him come and do so" (*Sifrei, Ha'azinu*).[11]

7:14   They, and every beast after its kind, and all the cattle after their kind, and every creeping thing that creeps on the earth after its kind, and every bird after its kind, every bird, every winged creature.

every bird, etc. - "Every bird, every winged creature" — "bird" connotes the clean ones, and "winged creature," the unclean (*Chullin* 139b).[12]

every winged creature - R. Elazar expounded: "Every winged creature" — to exclude those whose wing feathers have been torn off, and which Noachides are forbidden to sacrifice (*Yerushalmi, Megillah* 1:11).[13]

7:16   And those who came, male and female, of all flesh, they came, as G-d had commanded him, and the L-rd shut him in.

And those who came - See above, 2 and 8

7:20   Fifteen cubits upwards did the waters prevail, and the mountains were covered.

Fifteen cubits - How is this "fifteen cubits" to be understood? If, fifteen cubits in the valleys and fifteen cubits in the mountains — does water stay at different levels? And, furthermore, how could the ark then rise to the mountain tops? The meaning must be, then, that the subterranean waters rose to the tops of the mountains, and then the rain added fifteen cubits above this (*Yoma* 76a).[14,15]

7:22   All that had the spirit of life in his nostrils, whatever was on the dry land perished.

the spirit of life in his nostrils - This teaches us that the essence of life is in one's nostrils (*Yoma* 85a).[16]

whatever was on the dry land - R. Chisda said: "The decree did not extend to the fishes in the sea, for it is written: 'Whatever was on the dry land perished,' and not the fishes in the sea" (*Zevachim* 113b).[17]

7:23   And He blotted out every living substance that was on the face of the earth, from man until beast and creeping things, and the birds of the heaven, and they were blotted out from the land; and only Noah remained alive, and those who were with him in the ark.

And He blotted out - R. Ami said: "If one eats anything from the soil of Babylonia, it is as if he is eating of the flesh of his ancestors." Some say: "It is as if he is eating unclean creatures and reptiles," for it is written: 'And He blotted out every living substance' " (*Shabbath* 113b).[18,19]

And He blotted out ... and they were blotted out -The Rabbis taught: "The generation of the flood have no portion in the world to come, as it is written: 'And He blotted out every living substance' — this connotes destruction in this world. 'And they were blotted out from the land' — this connotes destruction in respect to the world to come (*Sanhedrin* 108a).[20]

from man until beast - First man, then beast. This teaches us that man is selected first for calamity (*Berachoth* 61a).[21]

from man until beast - If men sinned, how did the animals sin [i.e., Why should they be destroyed?] The Holy One Blessed be He said: "Did I not create beasts and animals for man's sake alone? Now that man has sinned, what need have I of beasts and animals? (*Sanhedrin* 108a).[22]

and only Noah remained - See 14:13

8:1   And G-d remembered Noah and every living thing, and all the cattle that was with him in the ark, and G-d caused a wind to pass over the earth, and the waters subsided.

and the waters subsided [cooled off] - R. Chisda said: "The generation of the flood went astray through heat [boiling] and were punished through heat. They went astray through heat — lustful passion. They were punished through heat [i.e., boiling waters]: it is written here: 'And the waters *subsided*,' and elsewhere (*Esther* 7:10): 'And the king's wrath [boiling] *subsided*'" (*Sanhedrin* 108b).[1]

8:7   And he sent out the raven, and it went back and forth until the waters were dried up from the earth.

And he sent out the raven - Resh Lakish said: "The raven challenged Noah with an irrefutable argument. He said to him: "Your Master hates me, and you hate me. Your Master hates me, because He said: "From the clean ones, seven, and from the unclean, two" [the raven is unclean]; and you hate me, because you refrain from sending out a bird of the species of seven, and send out one of the species of two; and if the power of heat or of cold should strike me, the world would be deprived of one species' " (*Sanhedrin* 108b).[2]

8:8   And he sent out the dove from him to see if the waters were abated from the face of the earth.

the dove from him - R. Yirmiah said: "From here we derive that the abode of the clean birds is with the righteous" (*Ibid.*).[3]

8:11 And the dove came in to him in the evening, and, behold, an olive leaf, torn off, in its mouth, and Noah knew that the waters were abated from the earth.

an olive leaf, etc. - R. Yirmiah said: " 'An olive leaf, torn off, in its mouth' — The dove said to the Holy One Blessed be He: "L-rd of the universe, let my food be as bitter as an olive, and given by Your hand, rather than sweet as honey, and given by the hand of flesh and blood" ' " (*Eruvin* 18b).[4]

8:13 And it was in the six hundred and first year, in the first month, on the first day of the month, that the waters were dried up from off the earth. And Noah removed the covering of the ark, and looked, and, behold, the face of the ground was dry.

in the first month, on the first day of the month - Since it is only the first day of the month, and still called "month," we may infer that one day in a month may be considered a month; and since one day in a month may be considered a month, we may infer that thirty days in a year may be considered a year. [This has certain halachic implications] (*Rosh Hashanah* 10b).[5]

8:16 Go out to the ark; you, and your wife, and your sons, and your sons' wives with you.

you and your wife - But in reference to entering the ark it is written (6:18): "And you shall come into the ark, you and your sons and your wife." This teaches us that upon leaving he was permitted to live with his wife [See 6:18] (*Yerushalmi, Ta'anith* 1:6).[6]

8:19 Every beast, every creeping thing, and every bird, and whatever creeps on the earth, in their families they went out of the ark.

in their families, they went out - In their families they went out, but not they themselves (*Sanhedrin* 108b).[7]

in their families, they went out - Eliezer [Abraham's servant] said to Shem: "My master, it is written: 'In their families, they went out.' Where were you?" [i.e., Why did you not also go out with your wives, but separately?] Shem answered: "We were hard put to it in the ark. Those creatures whose habit it is to eat in the daytime, we fed in the daytime, and those whose habit it is to eat at night, we fed at night [so that we could not make an orderly exit]" (*Ibid.*).[8]

in their families, they went out - R. Chiyya b. Ba said: " 'In their families, they went out from the ark' — Because they preserved their proper familial relationships, they merited being rescued from the ark" (*Yerushalmi, Ta'anith* 1:6).[9]

8:20   And Noah built an altar to the L-rd, and took of all the clean animals and of all the clean birds, and he brought up burnt-offerings upon the altar.

And Noah built an altar - One is not liable for the slaughtering of consecrated animals outside the Temple court until he brings them up to the head of the altar, as it is written: "And Noah built an altar, and he brought up burnt-offerings upon the altar" [It is the "altar" which makes them "offerings"]" (*Zevachim* 108b).[10]

altar [mizbeach] - R. Elazar expounded [acronymically]: "*Mizbeach - maziach* [it *removes* evil decrees from Israel]: *mazin* [it *insures sustenance* for the universe]; *mechavev* [it *endears* Israel to their Father in heaven]: *mechaper* [it *atones* for Israel's sins]" (*Kethuvoth* 10b).[11]

of all the clean animals, etc. - Before the tabernacle had been erected, all were fit to be sacrificed: domesticated animals, undomesticated animals, and birds; male and female, whole and blemished — so long as they were clean animals, and not unclean, as it is written: "And he took of all of the clean animals, and of all of the clean birds" — "Animals" — as implied; undomesticated animals are included in the category of "animals"; ["all"] male and female, whole and blemished (*Zevachim* 115b).[12]

8:21   And the L-rd smelled the sweet savor, and the L-rd said in

His heart:"I will not curse the earth again because of man; for the inclination of man's heart is evil from his youth. And I will not smite again all living things, as I have done."

And the L-rd smelled the sweet savor - R. Chanina said: "One who can be conciliated with a cup of wine emulates the ways of his Creator, as it is written: 'And the L-rd smelled the sweet savor, and the L-rd said in His heart: "I will not curse again" ' " (*Eruvin* 65b).[13]

for the inclination, etc. - There are seven names for the evil inclnation. The Holy One Blessed be He called it "evil," as it is written: "For the inclination of man's heart is evil" (*Succah* 52a).[14]

for the inclination, etc. - The Rabbis taught: "How severe is the evil inclination! Even its Creator called it "evil" as it is written: 'I will not curse again ... for the inclination of man's heart is evil' " (*Kiddushin* 30b).[15]

evil from his youth [mineurav] - R. Yuden said: It is written: *mineurav*, defective [without a *vav*], the connotation being: from the time that he *stirs* [*ninar*] and goes out into the world. This is the basis for the Rabbis' ruling that if a child can eat the size of an olive of grain, one must remove himself four ells from his excrement or his urine in order to recite the *Shema* — for his thoughts are evil (*Yerushalmi, Berachoth* 3:5).[16]

8:22   While the earth remains, seed time and harvest, and cold and heat, and summer and winter, and day and night — they shall not rest.

they shall not rest - Resh Lakish said: "A gentile who rests [from labor an entire day] incurs the death penalty, for it is written: 'They shall not rest' — and the master said: "A gentile who violates an exhortation incurs the death penalty" (*Sanhedrin* 58b).[17]

9:2   And your fear and dread shall be upon all the animals of the field, and upon every bird of the air, upon all that moves upon the earth, and upon all the fishes of the sea; into your hand are they given.

And your fear and dread - It was taught: "R. Shimon b. Elazar said: 'A living one-day-old infant need not be guarded from weasels or mice, but a dead Og, the king of Bashan, must be guarded from weasels and mice, as it is written: "And your fear and dread shall be upon all the animals of the field, etc.' So long as a man is alive his fear is upon all living creatures, but when he dies, this fear departs" (*Shabbath* 151b).[1]

9:3   Every moving thing that lives shall be food for you. As the green herb, I have given you everything.

As the green herb, etc. - R. Yehudah said in the name of Rav: "Animal flesh was not permitted to Adam, but it was permitted to the sons of Noah, as it is written: 'As the green herb, I have given you everything'" (*Sanhedrin* 59b).[2,3]

9:4   Only the flesh with its life, its blood, you shall not eat.

Only the flesh with its life - "flesh with its life" — this refers to *ever min hachai* [flesh torn from a living animal.] We might think that the prohibtion of *ever min hachai* applies to *sheratzim* [unclean reptiles] too, and we are, therefore, told: "Only ... its blood" — only where the blood is distinct from the flesh, to exclude *sheratzim*, whose blood is not distinct from their flesh (*Ibid.*).[4,5]

9:5   And surely your blood for your lives will I require. At the hand of every living thing will I require it, and at the hand of man. At the hand of a man, his brother, will I require the life of man.

And surely your blood, etc. - A Noachide may be killed through one judge, through one witness, without forewarning, only through the testimony of a man and not through that of a woman, and even through the testimony of his kin — as it is written: "And surely your blood for your lives will I require" — even through one judge; "at the hand of every living thing" — even without forewarning; "will I require it, and at the hand of man" — even through one witness; "at the hand of a man" — and not at the hand of a woman; "his brother" — even one's kin (*Ibid.* 57b).[6,7]

for your lives will I require - "And surely your blood for your lives will I require": R. Elazar interpreted: "I shall require your blood from your lives." From here we derive that one is not permitted to cause himself injury (*Bava Kamma* 91b).[8]

and at the hand of man - This teaches us that a Noachide man is killed even by his own testimony [that he has killed] (*Yerushalmi Kiddushin* 1:1).[9]

9:6   One who spills the blood of a man in a man his blood shall be spilled; for in the image of G-d, He made man.

One who spills the blood of a man - a Noachide woman who kills incurs the death penalty as well as a man. And though it is written: "at the hand of a *man*," it is afterwards written: "*One* who spills the blood of a man" — anyone who spills it (*Sanhedrin* 57b).[10]

the blood of a man in a man - It was taught in the name of R. Yishmael: "A Noachide is liable for the killing of a fetus, as it is written: 'One who spills the blood of a man in a man, his blood shall be spilled.' What is 'a man in a man'? A fetus in its mother's womb" (*Ibid.*).[11]

the blood of a man in a man - It was taught: "If one is pursuing his neighbor to kill him, he is to be told: 'Take heed, it is a Jew you are pursuing, a son of the covenant; and the Torah says: "One who spills the blood of a man in a man, his blood shall be spilled" ' — Save the blood of one man [the pursued] through the blood of another [the pursuer]" (*Ibid.* 72b).[12]

his blood shall be spilled - From here we derive that all Noachide executions are carried out by the sword [whereby blood is spilled] (*Sanhedrin* 56a, see Rashi).[13]

for in the image of G-d, etc. - He used to say: "Beloved is man, who was created in the Image. A profusion of love was accorded him by his creation in the Image, it being written: 'For in the image of G-d, He made man'" (*Avoth* 3:18).[14]

9:7   And you, be fruitful and multiply; abound in the earth, and multiply in it.

be fruitful and multiply - It was taught:"Ben Azzai said: 'If one does not fulfill the *mitzvah* of begetting children, it is as if he spills blood and diminishes G-d's image, as it is written: 'One who spills the blood of a man in a man, his blood shall be spilled, for in the image of G-d He made man,' after which it is written: 'And you, be fruitful and multiply'" (*Yevamoth* 63b).[15]

9:15   And I will remember My covenant between Me and you and every living creature of all flesh, and the waters shall no more be a flood to destroy all flesh.

and the waters shall no more be, etc. - R. Elazar said: " 'No' constitutes an oath, as it is written: 'And the waters shall no more be a flood, and (*Isaiah* 54:9): 'For this is the waters of Noah to me, as I have sworn.' " Rava said: "This is on condition that the negation is stated twice, as it is written: 'And *no* more shall all flesh be cut off by the waters of the flood, and the waters shall *no* more be a flood' " (*Shevuoth* 36a).[16]

9:20   And Noah began, a man of the earth, and he planted a vineyard.

And Noah began, etc. - A Galilean passerby expounded: "Thirteen *vav-yods* ["*vai*"-woe] were stated in relation to wine: '*Vay*achel [And he began] ... ' " (*Sanhedrin* 70a).[17]

a man of the earth - What is the intent of "a man of the earth"? The Holy One Blessed be He said to Noah: "Noah, should you not have learned [not to drink wine] from Adam, whose undoing was caused by wine?" [This, according to the view that the tree of knowledge was a grapevine] (*Ibid.*).[18]

9:21   And he drank of the wine, and he became drunk, and he
        uncovered himself in the midst of his tent.

and he became drunk - It was taught: "R. Meir said: 'The tree from
which Adam ate was a grapevine, for there is nothing that brings woe
upon one as wine, as it is written: 'And he drank of the wine and he
became drunk' " (*Berachoth* 40a).[19]

9:23   And Shem and Jefet took the garment, and laid it upon
        both their shoulders, and went backwards, and covered
        the nakedness of their father; and their faces were
        backwards, and they did not see the nakedness of their
        father.

and they did not see the nakedness of their father - R. Yehudah said:
"It is forbidden to recite the *Shema* in the presence of a naked gentile.
One might think, since it is written of them (*Ezekiel* 23:20): 'whose flesh
is the flesh of asses,' that they are like asses in general; we are, therefore,
told that they, too, can be designated as 'naked,' as it is written: 'And
they did not see the nakedness of their father' " (*Berachoth* 25a).[20]

9:24   And Noah awoke from his wine, and he knew what his
        youngest son had done to him.

what his youngest son had done - Rav and Shmuel differ on this, one
saying that Cham emasculated him, and the other that he committed
sodomy with him. According to him who says that Cham emasculated
him — Because he prevented Noah from having a fourth son, Noah
cursed Cham's fourth son [Canaan]. He who says that Cham
committed sodomy with him derives it from: "And he saw - And he
saw," it being written here: "And Cham saw the nakedness of his
father," and elsewhere (34:2): "And Shechem ben Chamor saw her"
[and lived with her] (*Sanhedrin* 70a).[21,22]

9:25   And he said: "Cursed is Canaan, may he be a servant of
        servants to his brother."

a servant of servants - It was taught: "When the Africans came to dispute with Israel, they said: 'The land of Canaan is ours, as it is written (*Numbers* 34:2): "The land of Cannan until its boundaries" — and Canaan is our father.' At this, Geviha ben Pasissa said to them: 'It is written: "Cursed is Canaan, may he be a servant of servants to his brother." If a servant acquires property, to whom does the servant belong, and to whom does his property belong!'" (*Ibid.* 91a).[23]

9:27   G-d will beautify Jefet and cause him to dwell in the tents of Shem, and Canaan will be a servant to him.

God will beautify, etc. - It was taught: "R. Shimon b. Gamliel said: 'The Scriptures were permitted to be written in no tongue [other than the original] except in Greek. Whence is this derived? From the verse: 'G-d will beautify Jefet [the "father" of Greece], and cause him to dwell in the tents of Shem [connotative of "Scripture"]' " (*Megillah* 9b).[24,25]

G-d will beautify - In the second Temple, built by the Persians [who descend from Jefet], the *Shechinah* [the Divine Presence] did not dwell, as it is written: "G-d will beautify Jefet, and dwell in the tents of Shem." Though G-d beautifies Jefet, He dwells only in the tents of Shem (*Yoma* 10a).[26]

10:2   The sons of Jefet: Gomer and Magog and Madai and Yavan and Tuval and Meshech and Tiras.

Gomer, etc. - "Gomer" — this is Germamia; "Magog" — this is Kandia; "Madai" — this is Macedonia; "Yavan" — Greece; "Tuval" — this is Beth Unaiki; "Meshech" — this is Mussia; "Tiras" — R. Simai and the Rabbis differ on this, one saying that it is Beth Tiraiki, and the other, that it is Persia (*Ibid.* 10a)[1-5]

10:7   And the sons of Kush: Shva and Chavilah and Savtah and Raamah and Savtecha; and the sons of Raamah: Sheva and Dedan.

and Savtah, and Raamah, and Savtecha - R..Yosef taught [concerning

Savta and Savtecha]: "One is the inner Sakistan, and the other, the outer; there is a distance of one hundred parasangs between them, and their perimeter is one thousand parasangs (*Ibid.*).[6]

10:10   And the beginning of his kingdom was Babel and Erech and Akad and Calneh in the land of Shinar.

Babel, etc. - "Babel" — Babylonia; "Erech" — this is Orichuth; "Akad" — this is Bashchar; "Calneh" — this is Nopher-Ninphi (*Ibid.*).[7]

In the land of Shinar - It was taught: "Why was Babylonia called Shinar? R. Yochanan said [acronymically]: 'Because all the dead of the flood were shaken out [ninaru] there.' R. Avahu said: 'Because it shakes out [impoverishes] its wealthy ones' " (*Zevachim* 113b).[8,9]

in the land of Shinar - It was taught: "Why was Babylonia called Shinar? [Acronymically:] Because they die in anguish, without light [*ner*] and without baths." Another view: "Because they are shaken out [*menuarim*] of *mitzvoth* without *terumah* and without *maaser*." Another view: "Because it produced a foe and hater [*ar*] of the Holy One Blessed be He, viz., Nebuchadnezzar" (*Yerushalmi, Berachoth* 4:1).[10-12]

10:11   From that land, Ashur went out, and built Ninveh, and Rechovoth Ir, and Kalach

Ashur went out - R. Yosef taught: "Ashur" — this is Seleucia (*Yoma* 10a).[13]

Ninveh, etc. - R. Yosef taught: "Ninveh" — the same; "Rechovoth Ir" — this is Perath of Mishan; "Kalach" — this is Perath of Bursif" (*Ibid.*).[14]

10:12   And Resen, between Ninveh and Kalach; that is the great city.

And Resen - R. Yosef taught: "Resen" — this is Aktispon" (*Ibid.*).[15]

that is the great city - Which is the great city? Ninveh or Resen? The verse (*Jonah* 3:3): "And Ninveh was a great city" would indicate that Ninveh is the "great city" referred to here (*Ibid.*).[16]

10:17   And the Chivi and the Arki and the Sini.

And the Chivi - Why are they called "Chivi"? Because they could "taste" the land as a snake [*chivia* - i.e., they were ultra-sensitive to the qualities and the potentialities of the soil] (*Shabbath* 85a).[17]

10:21   To Shem also, the father of all the children of Ever, the brother of Jefet, the eldest, to him children were born.

the brother of Jefet, the eldest - Jefet was the eldest of the brothers. [The rank order in the verse (6:10): "And Noah begot ... Shem, Cham, and Jefet" is one of wisdom and not of age] (*Sanhedrin* 69b).[18]

11:1   And the whole earth was one language and one speech.

one language - R. Eliezer and R. Yochanan differ on this. One says that they spoke seventy languages; the other, that they spoke the language of the Single One of the World — the holy language (*Yerushalmi, Megillah* 1:9).[1]

11:2   And it was, as they journeyed from the east, that they found a plain in the land of Shinar, and they dwelt there.

and they dwelt [lit., "sat"] **there** - It was taught: "The men of the generation of the Tower of Babel rebelled only out of satiety, as it is written: 'And they sat there,' 'sitting' connoting eating and drinking, as it is written (*Exodus* 32:6): 'And the people sat down to eat and drink, and they arose to disport themselves' " (*Sifrei, Ekev*).[2]

11:3   And they said to one another: "Come, let us make bricks and burn them thoroughly." And they had brick for stone, and they had slime for mortar.

brick for stone - This teaches us that brick and stone are regarded as distinct entities halachically, figured stone being a case in point [it being

permitted to bow down on a floor of brick, but not on one of stone —
see *Leviticus* 26:1] (*Magen Avraham* 131:20).[3]

11:4   And they said: "Come, let us build a city for ourselves and
        a tower, whose top reaches to heaven; and let us make a
        name for ourselves, lest we be scattered abroad upon the
        face of the whole earth."

Come, let us build, etc. - R. Yirmiah b. Elazar said: "They were divided
into three classes: One said: 'Let us go up and dwell there'; another said:
'Let us go up and wage war'; and the third said: 'Let us go up and serve
idols.' The one that said 'Let us go up and dwell there' was scattered by
the L-rd; the one that said 'Let us go up and wage war' was transformed
into apes, spirits, demons, and shades; the one that said 'Let us go up
and serve idols' — 'The L-rd confounded the language of all the land' "
(*Sanhedrin* 109a).[4,5]

Come, let us build - The Holy One Blessed be He said to Israel: "I
desire you, for even when I confer greatness upon you, you humble
yourselves before Me; but the idol worshippers are not like this. I
conferred greatness upon Nimrod, and he said: 'Come, let us build a
city for ourselves' " (*Chullin* 89a).[6,7]

and let us make a name for ourselves - It was taught: "R. Nathan said:
'Did they have anything other than idol worship in mind!' It is written
here: 'And let us make a *name* for ourselves,' and elsewhere (23:13):
'And do not mention the *name* of other gods' " (*Sanhedrin* 109a).[8]

11:7   Let us go down and confound their language there, that
        they may not understand one another's speech.

Let us go down and confound - Once King Ptolemy assembled seventy-
two elders in seventy-two separate houses and said to each of them:
"Transcribe for me [into Greek] the Torah of Moses your teacher." The
Holy One Blessed be He placed goodly counsel into the heart of each of
them, and they all wrote as one: "Let *Me* go down and confound" [so
that Ptolemy would not find support for his polytheistic views]
(*Megillah* 9a).[9]

Let us go down and confound - R. Yochanan said: "Wherever the Sadducees found room for heterodox disputation, they found their answer at their side. They found room for such disputation in: 'Let *us* go down and confound'; and they found their answer at their side: 'And *the L-rd* went down' " (*Sanhedrin* 38b).[10]

11:8   And the L-rd scattered them from there over the face of the whole earth, and they ceased to build the city.

And the L-rd scattered - The generation of the Tower of Babel have no share in the world to come, as it is written: "And the L-rd scattered them from there over the face of the whole earth," and (9): "And from there the L-rd scattered them." "And the L-rd scattered them" — in this world; "And from there the L-rd scattered them" — in respect to the next world (*Ibid.* 107b).[11]

11:9   They, therefore, called its name Babel, because the L-rd confounded there the language of the whole earth; and from there the L-rd scattered them abroad upon the face of all the earth.

called its name Babel - Babel and Borsif are one and the same. Where is this fact of significance? In writs of divorce [a writ in which one of the above names is changed to the other retains its validity] (*Shabbath* 36b).[12]

11:29   And Avram and Nachor took wives for themselves. The name of Avram's wife was Sarai, and the name of Nachor's wife, Milkah, the daughter of Charan, the father of Milkah and the father of Yiskah.

Yiskah - It was taught: " 'Yiskah' is Sarah. Why was she called 'Yiskah'? Because she *saw* [*sachtah*] by means of the holy spirit, as it is written (21:12): 'Everything that Sarah tells you, listen to her voice.' A different view: 'Yiskah' — because everyone *looked* at her beauty" (*Megillah* 14a).[13,14]

11:30 But Sarai was barren; she had no child.

she had no child [valad] - R. Nachman said: "Our mother Sarah was without a womb, as it is written: 'She had no *valad*' — not even a *repository* for a *valad* [child]" (*Yevamoth* 64a).[15]

Lech Lecha

12:1   And the L-rd said to Avram: "Go for your sake, from your land and from your birthplace to the land that I will show you."

Go for your sake - Some say that a change of place rescinds what G-d has decreed for a man, as it is written: "And the L-rd said to Avram: 'Go for your sake, from your land and from your birthplace,' after which it is written: 'And I will make you a great nation' " (*Rosh Hashanah* 16b).[1]

12:2   And I will make you a great nation, and I will bless you and I will make your name great, and you shall be a blessing.

And I will make you - "And I will make you a great nation" — this is the intent [in *Shemoneh Esreh* ("The Eighteen Benedictions")] of "the G—d of Abraham"; "And I will bless you" — this is the intent of "the G—d of Isaac"; "And I will make your name great" — this is the intent of "the G—d of Jacob." One might think that the blessing is concluded with all of their names. We are, therefore, taught: "And *you* shall be a blessing" — the blessing is concluded with your [Abraham's] name alone, and not with all of them (*Pesachim* 117b).[2-4]

12:3   And I will bless those who bless you, and I will curse those who curse you, and there will be blessed in you all the families of the earth.

And I will bless those who bless you - From here it is derived that if one is given the benediction cup [at grace] but declines to make the benediction, his days are shortened, as it is written: "And I will bless those who bless you" (*Berachoth* 55a).[5]

And I will bless those who bless you - R. Yehoshua b. Levi said: "Every Cohain who gives the priestly blessing is blessed, and one who does not, is not blessed, as it is written: 'And I will bless those who bless you' " (*Sotah* 38b).[6]

And I will bless those who bless you - It is written (*Numbers* 6:23): "So shall you bless the children of Israel." This teaches us that non-Cohanim are to be blessed. How do we know that Cohanim are to be blessed? R. Nachman b. Yitzchak said: "It is written: 'I will bless those [the Cohanim] who bless you' " (*Chullin* 49a).[7]

and there will blessed in you - R. Elazar said: " 'And there will be blessed in you all the families of the earth' — the Holy One Blessed be He said to Abraham: 'I have two goodly vines' [same root as "bless"] to entwine in you: Ruth the Moabitess and Na'amah the Ammonitess' " (*Yevamoth* 63a).[8]

all the families of the earth - R. Elazar said: "And there will be blessed in you all the families of the earth" — Even the families that live in the earth [i.e., the entire animal kingdom] are blessed only for the sake of Israel" (*Ibid.*).[9]

12:5   And Avram took Sarai, his wife, and Lot, his brother's son, and all their substance that they had gathered, and the soul that they made in Charan, and they went forth to go to the land of Canaan, and they came to the land of Canaan.

and the soul - It was taught in the forum of Eliyahu: "The world endures for six thousand years: two thousand of void, two thousand of Torah, and two thousand of the days of the Messiah. And when do the two thousand of Torah begin? From: 'And the soul that they made in Charan'" (*Avodah Zarah* 9a).[10]

that they made - Resh Lakish said: "If one teaches his neighbor's son Torah, it is as if he made him, as it is written: 'And the soul that they *made* in Charan' " (*Sanhedrin* 99b).[11]

12:8 And he removed from there to a mountain on the east of Beth-el, and pitched his tent with Beth-el on the west and Ai on the east; and there he built an altar to the L-rd, and he called upon the name of the L-rd.

Beth-el, etc. - R. Elazar said: "One should always pray in advance of affliction, for if Abraham had not prayed in advance of affliction between Beth-el and Ai, not a trace would have been left of the Jews [in the war fought in that spot in the days of Joshua] (*Sanhedrin* 44b).[12]

12:10 And there was a famine in the land, and Avram went down to Egypt, to live there, for the famine was sore in the land of Canaan.

and Avram went down - The Rabbis taught: "If there is a famine in the city, spread your feet [and leave], as it is written: 'And there was a famine in the land, and Avram went down to Egypt, to live there, for the famine was sore in the land of Canaan' " (*Bava Kamma* 60b).[13]

to Egypt [Mitzraymah] - It was taught: "R. Nechemiah said: 'Every word that requires a *lamed* as a prefix [indicating "to"] is written in the Torah with the suffix *heh*, as in *Mitzrayim* [Egypt] - Mitzraym*ah* [*to* Egypt]' " (*Yevamoth* 13b).[14]

12:11 And it was, when he came near to come to Egypt, that he said to Sarai, his wife: "Behold, now I know that you are a beautiful woman."

Behold, now I know - From here we see that Abraham had never looked even upon his own wife, as it is written: "Behold, now I know that you are a beautiful woman" — from which it is to be inferred that until then he did not know (*Bava Bathra* 16a).[15]

12:16 And he benefited Avram for her sake, and he had sheep and oxen, and he-asses and men-servants and maid-servants and she-asses and camels.

And he benefited Avram for her sake - R. Chelbo said: "One should always be solicitous of his wife's honor, for blessing abides in a man's house only for the sake of his wife, as it is written: 'And he benefited Avram for her sake' " (*Bava Metzia* 59a).[16]

12:17   And the L-rd afflicted Pharaoh with great plague spots and, his household, because of Sarai, the wife of Avram.

And the L-rd afflicted, etc. - This teaches us that the transgression of adultery is punishable by plague spots (*Erchin* 16a).[17]

great plague spots - It was taught: "There are twenty-four kinds of boils, none of which is more severe [and more so to the woman than to the man]than *ra-athan*. And it was with these that Pharaoh was afflicted, as it is written: 'And the L-rd afflicted Pharaoh with great plague spots and his *household*' [his *wife*, the connotation being that Pharaoh was afflicted with the type of plague spots which would be grievous in his wife]" (*Yerushalmi, Kethuvoth* 7:9).[18,19]

12:20   And Pharaoh charged men to attend him, and they sent him off, and his wife, and all that he had.

And Pharaoh charged men to attend him, and they sent him off - R. Yehoshua b. Levi said: "Because of the four steps with which Pharaoh accompanied Abraham, he [Pharaoh's descendants] merited keeping Abraham's children in servitude for four hundred years, as it is written (15:13): 'And they will serve them, and they shall afflict them for four hundred years' " (*Sotah* 46b).[20]

13:2   And Avram was very rich in cattle, silver, and gold.

And Avram was very rich, etc. - It was taught: "R. Nehorai said: 'Torah honors a man and preserves him from all ill in his youth and provides him with a goodly end and expectation in his old age. And so we find in respect to our father Abraham, who observed the entire Torah. What is written of him? Of his youth it is stated: 'And Avram was very rich in cattle, silver, and gold'; and of his old age it is stated (24:1): 'And

Abraham was old, well along in days ... and the L-rd blessed Abraham with everything' " (*Yerushalmi, Kiddushin* 4:12).[1]

13:3   And he went to his travels from the Negev until Beth-el, to the place where his tent had been in the beginning: between Beth-el and Ai.

And he went to his travels - R. Yehudah said in the name of Rav: "Whence is it derived that one should not change his accustomed lodging place? From the verse: 'Until the place where his tent was in the beginning.' " R. Yossi b. R. Chanina said: "From the verse: 'And he went to his travels.' " What reflects the difference between the two views? — An incidental lodging place [where one was compelled to stop because of unforseen circumstances. According to the first view, the rule does not apply to such a place, and according to the second view, it does] (*Erchin* 16b).[2]

13:5   And Lot, also, who went with Avram, had sheep and cattle and tents.

And Lot, also, who went, etc. - Rava asked Rabbah b. Mari: "Whence is derived the folk-saying: 'Behind a man of wealth, chips are dragged along'? He answered: "From the verse: 'And Lot, also, who went with Avram, had sheep and cattle and tents' " (*Bava Kamma* 93a).[3,4]

13:10   And Lot lifted up his eyes and beheld all the plain of the Jordan, that it was well watered everywhere, before the L—rd destroyed Sodom and Amorah, as the garden of the L—rd, as the land of Egypt as you come to Tzoar.

And Lot lifted up, etc. - R. Yochanan said: "This entire verse bespeaks transgression: 'And Lot lifted up his eyes' — as in (39:7): 'And the wife of his [Joseph's] master lifted up her eyes [to seduce him]'; 'And he saw' — as in (34:2): 'And Shechem ben Chamor saw her [and ravaged her]'; 'the entire plain [*kikar*] of the Jordan' — as in (*Proverbs* 6:26): 'For the sake of a harlot until a loaf [*kikar*] of bread'; 'for it was all watered' — as in (*Hosea* 2:7): 'I will go up after my lovers, who give me ... my oil and my drink' " (*Nazir* 23a).[5]

as the land of Egypt - It was taught: "There is no land better favored than the land of Egypt, as it is written: 'As the garden of the L-rd, as the land of Egypt' " (*Kethuvoth* 112a).[6]

13:12   Avram dwelt in the land of Canaan, and Lot dwelt in the cities of the plain, and he pitched his tents until Sodom.

And he pitched his tents until Sodom - It was taught: "R. Nehorai said: 'There is no land more fertile than that of Sodom; for we find, with respect to Lot, that he passed through all the cities of the plain and found no land so fertile as that of Sodom, as it is written: 'And he pitched his tents until Sodom' " (*Tosefta, Shabbath* 8).[7]

13:13   And the people of Sodom were evil and sinful to the L-rd exceedingly.

And the people of Sodom were evil - Ravina asked one of the Rabbis: "Whence is derived the formula of the Rabbis: 'May the name of the wicked rot !'" He answered: "From the conjunction of the verse 'And he pitched his tents until *Sodom*' with the verse 'And the people of *Sodom* were evil and sinful to the L-rd exceedingly' " (*Yoma* 38b).[8]

evil and sinful - The people of Sodom have no share in the world to come, as it is written: "And the people of Sodom were exceedingly evil and sinful" — "evil" in this world; "sinful" in respect to the next world" (*Sanhedrin* 107b).[9]

evil and sinful - R. Yehudah said: "evil," in their bodies, as in (39:9): 'How can I do this great *evil* [adultery] and be sinful to G-d!'; "sinful," with respect to their money, as in (*Deuteronomy* 23:22): 'And it [not paying what you owe] will be sinful in you.'" In a *Mishnah* it was taught: "evil," with respect to their money, as it is written (15:9): 'And your eye will be evil against your poor brother'; "sinful," in their bodies, as it is written: ' ... and be *sinful* to G-d' " (*Sanhedrin* 109a).[10,11]

evil and sinful - "evil" to each other; "sinful" through adultery (*Yerushalmi, Sanhedrin* 10:3).[12]

to the L-rd exceedingly - R. Yehudah said: "to the L-rd" — this connotes "blessing" [a euphemism] the name of G-d; "exceedingly" — they sinned with malice. In a *Mishnah* it was taught: "to the L-rd" — this connotes "blessing" the name of G-d; "exceedingly" — this connotes murder, as it is written (II *Kings* 21:16): 'Moreover, Menashe shed innocent blood exceedingly' " (*Sanhedrin* 109a).[13,14]

to the L-rd exceedingly - The people of Sodom have no share in the world to come, as it is written: "And the people of Sodom were evil and sinful to the L-rd exceedingly": "evil and sinful," in relation to this world; "to the L-rd exceedingly," in relation to the world to come" (*Yerushalmi, Sanhedrin* 10:3).[15]

13:14   And the L-rd said to Avram, after Lot was separated from him: "Lift up your eyes and look from the place where you are, northward, and southward, and eastward, and westward."

And the L-rd said - R. Elazar said: "From the curse pronounced against the wicked, we derive blessing for the righteous, it being stated: 'And the people of Sodom were evil and sinful,' after which it is stated: 'And the L—rd said to Avram ... lift up your eyes and look ... for the entire land that you see I have given to you ...' " (*Yoma* 38b).[16]

13:16   And I will make your seed as the dust of the earth, so that if a man can number the dust of the earth, so shall your seed also be numbered.

as the dust of the earth - It was taught: [Though the Torah does occasionally employ hyperbole] "The pronouncement of the Holy One Blessed be He: 'And I will make your seed as the dust of the earth' is not a hyperbolic expression" (*Sifrei, Devarim*).[17,18]

13:17   Arise and walk in the land, along its length and its breadth, for I have given it to you.

Arise and walk - It was taught: "If one sells a path to his neighbor, if the latter walks along it, he is considered to have acquired it. Whence is this derived? From the verse: 'Arise and walk in the land, along its length and its breadth, for I have given it to you' " (*Yerushalmi, Kiddushin* 1:3).[19]

its length and its breadth - It was taught: "The Holy One Blessed be He said to Moses: 'Woe for those who are gone, but not forgotten! I revealed myself several times to the forefathers, and they never doubted me. I said to Abraham: 'Arise and walk in the land, along its length and its breadth, for I have given it to you,' yet when he sought a place to bury Sarah, he could not find one, until he was compelled to buy a plot for four hundred silver shekels — and still he did not doubt me!' " (*Sanhedrin* 111a).[20]

14:1   And it was in the days of Amrafel, king of Shinar, Aryoch, king of Elassar, Kedarlaomer, king of Eilam, and Tidal, king of Goyim,

And it was in the days of Amrafel - R. Levi said (some say R. Jonathan): "The following has been received by tradition from the men of the Great Assembly: "Whenever "And it was in the days" is written, affliction is connoted, as in the case of 'And it was in the days of Amrafel,' after which it is written: 'They waged war' " (*Megillah* 10b).[1]

Amrafel - Rav and Shmuel differ on this, one saying that his name was Nimrod and that he was called Amrafel because he *said* [*amar*] and had our father Abraham *thrown* [*hipil*] into the fiery furnace; and the other, that his name was Amrafel and that he was called Nimrod because he caused the entire world to rebel [*himrid*] against him during his reign (*Eruvin* 53a).[2]

Kedarlaomer - Kedarlaomer is one name [and not a composite], and though the scribe may separate it into two words, he may not write it in parts on two separate lines (*Chullin* 65a).[3]

14:6   And the Chori, in their mount, Seir, until Eil-Paran, which is near the desert.

And the Chori - It was taught: Why are they called "Chori"? R. Shmuel b. Nachmani said in the name of R. Jonathan: "Because they can "smell out" [*merichim*] the land [to determine the relative fertility of the soil.] R. Acha b. Yaakov said: "Because they were "made free" [*bnei chorin*] of their soil" [i.e., it was confiscated from them] (*Shabbath* 85a).[4,5]

14:13   And the survivor came, and told Avram the Hebrew; for he dwelt in the terebinths of Mamre the Emori, brother of Eshkol, and brother of Aner, and these were confederate with Avram.

And the survivor came - R. Yochanan said: "This is Og the king of Bashan, who survived from the generation of the flood" (*Niddah* 61a).[6]

14:14   And Avram heard that his brother was taken captive, and he roused his disciples, who had been reared in his household, three hundred and eighteen, and he pursued them until Dan.

and he roused his disciples - Rav says that he roused them with words of Torah, and Shmuel, that he roused them with gold (*Nedarim* 32a).[7]

and he roused his disciples - R. Avahu said in the name of R. Elazar: "Why was our father Abraham punished and his children enslaved in Egypt for 210 years? Because he pressed Torah scholars into service, as it is written: 'And he roused his disciples, who had been reared in his household' " (*Ibid.*).[8]

three hundred and eighteen - R. Ami b. Abba said: "Eliezer outranked all of them; and others, that he took Eliezer alone; for the *gematria* [numerical equivalent] of Eliezer is 318" (*Ibid.*).[9]

and he pursued them until Dan - R. Yochanan said: "As soon as that righteous one came to Dan, his strength waned, for he saw that his descendants were destined to serve idols in Dan, as it is written (I *Kings* 12:29): 'And he set the one [golden calf] in Bethel and the other in Dan' " (*Sanhedrin* 96a).[10]

14:15   And night descended upon them, he and his servants, and
        he smote them, and he pursued them until Chovah, which
        is to the left of Damascus.

And "lailah" [night] **descended upon them** - R. Yochanan said: "The
angel that was dispatched to Abraham was called "Lailah," as it is
written (*Job* 3:2): 'And Lailah said: "There is a man-child conceived."'
R. Yitzchak Nafcha said: "He performed for his sake the act of night
[i.e., He caused the stars to war for him], as it is written (*Judges* 5:20):
'From the heavens, the stars fought from their courses' " (*Ibid.*).[11,12]

14:18   And Malkitzedek, king of Shalem, brought out bread and
        wine; and he was a priest to the Almighty G-d.

and he was a priest - R. Zechariah said in the name of R. Yishmael:
"The Holy One Blessed be He desired to have the priesthood issue from
Shem [Malkitzedek], but since he put the blessing of Abraham before
that of the Holy One Blessed be He, He made it issue from Abraham. It
is written: 'Blessed is Avram ... and blessed is the Almighty G-d' —
whereupon Abraham said to him: 'Does one place a servant's blessing
before that of his master?' At this juncture, the priesthood was
transferred to Abraham, as it is written: 'And he was a priest to the
Almighty G-d' — *he* was a priest, but not his children" (*Nedarim*
32b).[13,14]

14:19   And he blessed him, and he said: "Blessed is Avram to the
        Almighty G-d, owner of heaven and earth."

owner of heaven and earth - Heaven and earth constitute one of the
acquisitions of the Holy One Blessed be He in His universe, as it is
written: "owner of heaven and earth" (*Pesachim* 87b).[15]

owner of heaven and earth - Abraham is one of the acquisitions of the
Holy One Blessed be He in His universe, as it is written: "Blessed is
Avram to the Almighty G-d, owner of heaven and earth" (*Avoth*
6:10).[16]

14:20 "And blessed is the the Almighty G-d, who has delivered your enemies into your hand." And he gave him a tenth of everything.

And he gave him a tenth - See *Deuteronomy* 14:22.

14:21 And the king of Sodom said to Avram: "Give me the souls, and take the spoil for yourself."

Give me the souls - R. Yochanan said: "Why was Abraham punished, and his children enslaved in Egypt for 210 years? Because he allowed people to be separated from him, whom he could have brought under the wings of the *Shechinah* [the Divine Presence], as it is written: 'And the king of Sodom said to Avram: "Give me the souls, and take the spoil for yourself" ' " (*Nedarim* 32a).[17]

14:22 And Avram said to the king of Sodom: "I have raised my hand to the L-rd, the Almighty G-d, owner of heaven and earth."

owner of heaven and earth - This teaches us that our forefather Abraham acknowledged G-d's sovereignty over heaven and earth (*Sotah* 4b).[18]

14:23 If from a thread until a shoe latchet, and I will not take anything that is yours, lest you say: I have made Avram rich.

If from a thread until a shoe latchet, etc. - Rava expounded: "As a reward for our father Abraham's saying: "If from a thread until a shoe latchet" his children merited two *mitzvoth*: the string of purple thread [*techeleth* in the *tzitzith*,] and the strap of the *tefillin*" (*Sotah* 17a).[19]

14:24 Save only what the youths have eaten, and the share of the men who went with me: Aner, Eshkol, and Mamre — they shall take their share.

only what the youths have eaten - R. Abba said: "How severe is the sin of stealing food and eating it; for even those who are absolutely righteous cannot return it, as it is written: 'save only what the youths have eaten' " [which I cannot return] (*Chullin* 89a).[20]

15:2   And Avram said: "L-rd, G-d, what will You give me, when I go childless? And the steward of my household is Damesek Eliezer."

Damesek Eliezer - R. Elazar said: "'*Damesek* Eliezer' — [acronymically], "he drew forth [*doleh*] and gave others to drink [*mashkeh*]" of the Torah of his master (*Yoma* 28b).[1]

15:5   And He took him outside, and He said: "Look, now, at the heavens, and count the stars if you are able to number them." And He said to him: "So will your children be."

And He took him outside - What is the significance of: "And He took him outside"? R. Yehudah said in the name of Rav: "Abraham said to the Holy One Blessed be He: 'I have looked into my horoscope, and I have seen that I am not to beget children,' whereupon G-d answered: 'Abandon your horoscope, for Israel is not dominated by the stars' " (*Shabbath* 155a).[2]

15:6   And he believed in the L-rd, and He counted it in him for righteousness.

And he believed in the L-rd - The Holy One Blessed be He said to Moses: "The Jews are believers, the sons of believers, the sons of Abraham, of whom it is written: 'And he believed in the L-rd' " (*Shabbath* 97a).[3]

15:8   And he said: "O L-rd G-d, with what shall I know that I will inherit it?"

O L-rd G-d- R. Yochanan said in the name of R. Shimon b. Yochai:

"From the day that the Holy One Blessed be He created the world, no one had ever called Him "L-rd," until Abraham came upon the scene and called him "L-rd," as it is written: 'O L-rd G-d, with what shall I know?' " (*Berachoth* 7b).[4]

with what shall I know - Shmuel said: "Why was Abraham punished and his children enslaved in Egypt for 210 years? Because he presumed to question the Holy One Blessed be He: 'With what shall I know?' " (*Nedarim* 32a).[5]

15:9   Take for Me a heifer of three years old, and a ram of three years old, and a turtledove, and a young pigeon.

Take for me, etc. - Abraham said to the Holy One Blessed be He: "L-rd of the universe, what if Israel sins against You, and You do to them as You did to the generation of the flood and the generation of the Tower of Babel?" G-d answered: "I will not do so," whereupon Abraham asked: "With what shall I know?" To this He replied: "Take for me a heifer of three years old ... " (*Ta'anith* 27b).[6]

15:13   And he said to Avram: "Know that your children will be strangers in a land that is not theirs; and they shall serve them, and they will afflict them four hundred years."

four hundred years - It was taught: "R. Dosa said: 'The days of the Messiah are four hundred years, it being written here: 'And they will afflict them four hundred years, and elsewhere (*Psalms* 90:15): 'Make us rejoice according to the days of our affliction' " (*Sanhedrin* 99a).[7]

15:15   And you will come to your forefathers in peace; you will be buried in a good old age.

to your forefathers in peace - R. Avin Halevi said: "One who takes leave of the dead should not say: 'Go *to* peace' ["*le*shalom"], but "Go *in* peace' ["*be*shalom"], as it is written: 'And you will come to your forefathers *in* peace' " (*Berachoth* 64a).[8]

to your forefathers in peace - It was taught: "Peace is great, for even the dead need peace, as it is written: 'And you will come to your forefathers in peace'" (*Sifrei, Nasso* 6:26).[9]

15:16   And the fourth generation will return here, for the iniquity of the Emori is not yet full.

And the fourth generation - A father imparts to [the credit of] his son the number of generations preceding his redemption, as it is written (*Isaiah* 41:4): "He calls out the generations from the source." Though it is written: "And they will serve them, and they will afflict them four hundred years," it is afterwards written: "And the fourth generation will return here" (*Idiyoth* 2:9).[10]

15:18   On that day, the L-rd made a covenant with Avram, saying: "To your children I have given this land, from the river of Egypt to the great river, the river Euphrates."

To your children I have given - R. Huna said in the name of R. Shmuel b. Nachman: "It is not written here: 'To your children I *will give*,' but 'To your children I *have given*' — I have already given it to them" (*Yerushalmi, Challah* 2:1).[11]

the great river, the river Euphrates - From here R. Shimon b. Tarfon derived: "Get close to an anointed one and the oil will rub off on you." In the forum of R. Yishmael it was taught: "The servant of a king is like a king." The river Euphrates, though the smallest of those mentioned, is yet called "great" because it borders on Eretz Yisroel (*Shevuoth* 47b).[12,13]

15:19   The Keini, the Kenizi, and the Kadmoni.

The Keini, etc. - It was taught (*Deuteronomy* 30:5): "And He will do good for you and multiply you more than your forefathers" — R. Elazar interpreted this as referring to the time to come: "Your forefathers inherited the land of the seven nations, but you are destined to inherit the land of the ten nations. Which are these [in addition to the seven]? The Keini, the Kenizi, and the Kadmoni" (*Yerushalmi, Kiddushin* 1:8).[14]

16:3 And Sarai, Avram's wife, took Hagar, her maid, the
      Egyptian , at the end of ten years of Avram's dwelling in
      the land of Canaan, and she gave her to her husband
      Avram as a wife.

at the end of ten years - The Rabbis taught: "If one were married to a
woman for ten years and she had no children, he should divorce her and
provide her with the amount stipulated in her marriage contract," for
perhaps it has not been granted him to have children with her. And
though there is no proof for this, there is an allusion to it: 'At the end of
ten years of Avram's dwelling in the land of Canaan, he took Hagar as a
wife.' Why emphasize "the land of Canaan"? To teach us that the years
spent outside Eretz Yisroel [Canaan] do not enter into the ten years
mentioned in this connection" [for one might be granted children
through the merit of living in Eretz Yisroel] (*Yevamoth* 64a).[1,2]

16:5 And Sarai said to Avram: "My wrong is upon you. I gave
      my maid into your bosom, and when she saw that she had
      conceived, I was despised in her eyes. May the L-rd judge
      between me and you."

May the L-rd judge - R. Chanan said: "If one calls down heavenly
judgment upon his friend, *he* is punished first, as it is written: 'And
Sarai said: "My wrong is upon you ... may the L-rd judge" ', after which
it is written (23:2): 'And Abraham came to mourn Sarah' " (*Bava
Kamma* 93a).[3,4]

16:8 And he said: "Hagar, maidservant of Sarai, where are you
      coming from and whither are you going?" And she said:
      "I am fleeing from Sarai, my mistress."

from Sarai, my mistress - Ravah said to Rabbah b. Mari: "Whence is
derived the saying: 'If your neighbor calls you an ass, pull the saddle to
your back'? He answered: "From the verse: 'And he said: "Hagar,
maidservant of Sarai, where are you coming from?" ' — to which she
responded: 'I am fleeing from Sarai, my *mistress*' " (*Ibid.* 92b).[5,6]

16:11 And the angel of the L-rd said to her: "Behold, you will conceive and bear a son, and you shall call his name 'Ishmael,' for the L-rd has heard your affliction."

and you shall call his name Ishmael - It was taught: "Ishmael is one of those who were named before they were born, as it is written: 'Behold, you will conceive and bear a son, and you shall call his name "Ishmael"'" (*Yerushalmi, Berachoth* 1:6).[7]

17:1 And when Avram was ninety-nine years old, the L-rd appeared to Avram, and He said to him: "I am the G-d Shakkai; walk before Me and be perfect."

I am the G-d Shakkai ["kk" written as *d*] - Resh Lakish said: " 'I am the G-d Shakkai' — The Holy One Blessed be He said: 'I am the one who told the universe "*Dai!*" ' ["Enough!"] — do not extend yourself any further" (*Chagigah* 12a).[1]

Walk, etc. - R. Simlai expounded (*Psalms* 15:5): " 'O L-rd, who will abide in Your tent ... he who walks in perfection' — "he who walks in perfection": this is Abraham, of whom it is said: 'Walk before Me and be perfect' " (*Makkoth* 24a).[2]

and be perfect - Rabbi [R. Judah Hanasi] said: "Great is the *mitzvah* of circumcision, for with all of the *mitzvoth* that Abraham performed, he was not considered perfect until he circumcised himself, as it is written [in respect to circumcision]: 'Walk before Me and be perfect' " (*Nedarim* 31b).[3]

and be perfect - It was taught: "Rebbe [R. Judah Hanasi] said: 'Great is the *mitzvah* of circumcision, for there was no one who performed *mitzvoth* as our father Abraham did, and yet he was called "perfect" only by virtue of having circumcised himself, as it is written: "Walk before Me and be perfect," immediately after which it is written: "And I shall place My covenant [of circumcision] between Me and you " ' " (*Ibid.* 32a).[4]

and be perfect - R. Yehudah said in the name of Rav: "When the Holy One Blessed be He said to Abraham: 'Walk before Me and be perfect,' he was seized with trembling, saying: 'Is it possible that there is some blemish in me!' But when He said: 'I will place my covenant between Me and you,' his mind was set at rest" (*Ibid.*).[5]

and be perfect - R. Hoshea said: "If one perfects himself, he is granted success, as it is written: 'Walk before me and be perfect,' after which it is written: 'And you will be the father of a multitude of nations.' " (*Ibid.*).[6]

17:5   And your name will no longer be called Avram, and your name shall be Avraham; for I have made you the father of a multitude of nations.

and your name shall be Avraham - It was taught: " 'Avram' has the same general signification as 'Avraham.' It is just that in the beginning he was a father [*av*] to Aram, and in the end he became the father of the entire world" [*av haolam*] (*Berachoth* 13a).[7]

and your name shall be Avraham - Bar Kappara taught: "One who calls Avraham 'Avram' violates a positive commandment, for it is written: 'And your name shall be 'Avraham.' " R. Eliezer said: "He violates a negative commandment, as it is written: 'And your name shall no longer be called 'Avram' " (*Ibid.*).[8]

and your name shall be Avraham - Rami b. Abba said: "It is written: 'Avram' and 'Avraham.' In the beginning the Holy One Blessed be He made him sovereign over 243 organs [the numerical equivalent of 'Avram' is 243], and in the end, over 248 [the numerical equivalent of 'Avraham.'] And these [the additional five] are: two eyes, two ears, and the head of the penis" (*Nedarim* 32b).[9]

the father of a multitude of nations - R. Yochanan said: "Where in the Torah do we see *Notarikon* [acronymics]? In the verse: 'For I have made you the father of a multitude of nations.' ["father of a multitude" = *AV HAMON*]: I have made you a father [*av*] to the nations; I have made you beloved [*haviv*] among the nations; I have made you a king [*melech*] among the nations; I have made you an ancient [*vatik* (*v* and *o* are represented by the same sign)] among the nations; I have made you believed [*ne'eman*] among the nations" (*Shabbath* 105a).[10-16]

the father of a multitude of nations - It was taught in the name of R. Yehudah: "A convert brings first fruits [*bikkurim*] and recites the benediction over them [even though it contains the phrase: 'the land which You promised to *our fathers* ... '] Why so? For it is written: 'For I have made you the father of a multitude of nations.' In the past you were the father of Aram, and now you are the father of all of the nations" (*Yerushalmi, Bikkurim* 1:4).[17,18]

the father of a multitude of nations - If one vows not to derive any benefit from a Jew, he may not derive any benefit from a convert either [for it is written: "For I have made you the father of a multitude of nations"] (*Tosefta, Nedarim* 2).[19]

17:7   And I will establish My covenant between Me and you, and your children after you for their generations for an everlasting covenant, to be a G-d to you and to your children after you.

and to your children after you - Women [who have been divorced or widowed] should not get engaged or married until three months have passed. Why so? R. Nachman said in the name of Shmuel: "Because it is written: 'To be a G-d to you and to your children after you' — [Wait three months] to distinguish between the children of the first husband and that of the second [so that He is definitely a G-d to *your* children]" (*Yevamoth* 42a).[20,21]

and to your children after you - Those who do not fulfill the *mitzvah* of begetting children cause the *Shechinah* [Divine Presence] to depart from Israel, as it is written: "To be a G-d to you and to your children after you" — When there are children after you, the *Shechinah* rests upon them; but when there are not, upon what does it rest? Upon the trees and stones (*Yevamoth* 64a).[22]

and to your children after you - What is signified by "after you"? The Holy One Blessed be He said to Abraham: "Do not marry a gentile woman or a maidservant, so that your children not be accounted hers [as is the *halachah*] (*Yevamoth* 100b).[23]

17:9   And G-d said to Abraham: "And you, heed My covenant,
        you and your children after you, for their generations."

And you, etc. - It was stated: "Whence do we derive that the
circumcision performed by a gentile is invalid? Daro b. Pappa said in
the name of Rav: 'From the verse: "And *you*, heed My covenant" ' "
(*Avodah Zarah* 27a).²⁴

And you, etc. - R. Levi said: "It is written: 'And you, heed My
covenant' — you and all like you [from which it is derived that one who
is uncircumcised may not perform circumcision]" (*Yerushalmi,
Shabbath* 19:2).²⁵

you and your children - [Why is the *mitzvah* of circumcision not
reckoned among the Noachide laws?] Because at the very outset the
mitzvah of circumcision was given only to Abraham. "And you, heed
My covenant; you and your children after you, for all their generations"
— you and your children, not others (*Sanhedrin* 59b).²⁶

17:10   This is My covenant, which you shall keep, between Me
        and you and your children after you; circumcise unto
        yourselves every male.

circumcise unto yourselves - From here we derive that if one's father
does not circumcise him, then *beth din* is obligated to do so (*Kiddushin*
29a).²⁷

every male - "every" — to include a hermaphrodite (*Shabbath* 135a).²⁸

17:11   And you shall circumcise the flesh of your foreskin; and it
        shall be as a sign of the covenant between Me and you.

And you shall circumcise - From here we derive that if one's father [and
beth din] do not circumcise him, then he is obligated to have himself
circumcised (*Yerushalmi, Kiddushin* 1:7).²⁹

as a sign of the covenant - R. Nachman b. Yitzchak said: "In relation to
circumcision it is written: 'sign,' 'covenant,' and 'generations,' and in
relation to the Sabbath it is written: 'sign,' 'covenant,' and

generations.' From here it is derived that the *mitzvah* of circumcision overrides the prohibition against 'labor' on the Sabbath" (*Shabbath* 132a).[30]

17:12   And when he is eight days old, there shall be circumcised among you every male for your generations, born in the house or bought with money, of any stranger who is not of your seed.

And when he is eight days old - From here we derive that circumcision is to be performed in the daytime and not at night (*Ibid.*).[31]

born in the house or bought with money - It was taught: "Who is considered 'born in the house,' and who 'bought with money'? If one acquired a maidservant, and she conceived and gave birth in the house, or if he acquired only the rights to the fetus of a maidservant, this is considered 'born in the house.' If one acquired a pregnant maidservant and she gave birth, or if he acquired a maidservant together with her child, this is considered 'bought with money' " (*Ibid.* 135b).[32,33]

17:13   Circumcise, circumcise, one who is born in your house or bought with money; and My covenant shall be in your flesh for an everlasting covenant.

Circumcise, circumcise - "Circumcise, circumcise" [twice] — to include [the necessity for cutting] shreds of the corona, which make the circumcision invalid (*Yevamoth* 72a).[34]

Circumcise, circumcise - "Circumcise, circumcise" — even one hundred times if necessary. The allusion is to the case of one whose prepuce is drawn forward in such a manner as to conceal the circumcision, in which case it is necessary [by Rabbinical ordinance] to "circumcise" again (*Ibid.* 35).[35]

Circumcise, circumcise - It was taught: "Whence is it derived that circumcision performed by a gentile is invalid? R. Yochanan said: 'From the verse: "Circumcise, circumcise" [connoting that only one who himself requires circumcision may circumcise others]' " (*Avodah Zarah* 27a).[36]

Circumcise, circumcise - From here we derive that two circumcisions are necessary: one, circumcision per se; the other, splitting the membrane and pulling it down (*Yerushalmi, Shabbath* 19:2).[37]

Circumcise, circumcise - From here we derive that if one is born circumcised, it is necessary to cause him to drip the blood of the covenant (*Ibid.*).[38]

Circumcise, circumcise - From here we learn that an uncircumcised Jew may not circumcise another (*Ibid.*).[39]

17:14   And the uncircumcised male, who does not circumcise the flesh of his foreskin, that soul is to be cut off from his people; he has broken My covenant.

And the uncircumcised male - It was taught: 'Whence is it derived that it is the penis which is to be circumcised? R. Nathan said: 'From the verse: "And the uncircumcised *male*, who does not circumcise the flesh of his foreskin" — that skin which indicates the difference between male and female" (*Shabbath* 108a).[40,41]

And the uncircumcised male - The Sabbath is not desecrated for the circumcision of a hermaphrodite, as it is written: "And the uncircumcised male, who does not circumcise the flesh of his foreskin, that soul should be cut off." Why must "male" be stated? To teach us that only one who is *completely* male is to be cut off [if he is not circumcised] (*Yerushalmi, Shabbath* 9:3).[42]

the flesh of his foreskin - It was taught: "Whence is it derived that it is the penis which is to be circumcised? R. Yashiah said: 'It is written here "foreskin" [lit., "uncircumcision"], and elsewhere (*Leviticus* 19:23): "And you shall reckon its fruit as uncircumcised." Just as there, the reference is to something that produces fruit, so here, the reference is to something that produces fruit' " (*Shabbath* 108a).[43]

the flesh of his foreskin - From here we derive that if [one's father] and *beth din* do not circumcise him, then he is obligated to have himself circumcised, as it is written: "And the uncircumcised male, who does not circumcise the flesh of his foreskin, that soul is to be cut off" (*Kiddushin* 29).[44]

he has broken my covenant - This is an allusion to the necessity for "circumcision" in the case of one whose prepuce is drawn forward in such a manner as to conceal the circumcision (*Yevamoth* 72a).[45]

he has broken my covenant - This includes the children of Keturah in the obligation of circumcision (*Sanhedrin* 59b). (See 25:1)[46]

17:15 And G-d said to Abraham: "As for Sarai, your wife, you do not call her name Sarai, for Sarah is her name."

you do not call, etc. - One who calls Sarah "Sarai" does not violate a negative commandment of "Do not call her name Sarai." Why so? For it is written: "*You* do not call." Abraham is being exhorted in this regard, and no others (*Berachoth* 13a).[47]

do not call, etc. - R. Yitzchak said: "A change of name rescinds what G—d has decreed, [in this instance, Sarai's childlessness,] as it is written: 'Do not call her name Sarai, for Sarah is her name' — after which it is written: 'And I have blessed her, and I have also given you a son from her' " (*Rosh Hashanah* 26b).[48]

for Sarah is her name - "Sarai" has the same general signification as "Sarah." It is just that in the beginning she was the princess of her nation, and in the end she became the princess of the entire world (*Berachoth* 13a).[49]

17:19 And G-d said to Abraham: "Sarah your wife will bear you a son, and you shall call his name 'Isaac'; and I will establish My covenant with him for an everlasting covenant, and with his seed after him."

and you shall call, etc. - It was taught: "Isaac was one of those who were given a name before they were born, as it is written: 'Sarah your wife will bear you a son, and you shall call his name "Isaac" ' " (*Yerushalmi, Berachoth* 1:6).[50]

and you shall call, etc. - It was taught: "Why were the names of Abraham and Jacob changed, and not that of Isaac? Because the first were named by their parents, whereas Isaac was named by the Holy One Blessed be He, as it is written: 'And G-d said: "Sarah your wife will bear you a son, and you shall call his name "Isaac" ' " (*Ibid.*).[51]

17:21 And I shall establish My covenant with Isaac, whom Sarah shall bear to you at this time next year.

And I shall establish My covenant - We learned: "R. Yishmael said: "Great is the *mitzvah* of circumcision, over which thirteen covenants were established.' " Which are they? R. Yochanan said: "All those mentioned from (16:18): "On that day the L-rd entered into a covenant with Avram" until: "And I shall establish my covenant with Isaac" ' " (*Yerushalmi, Nedarim* 3:9).[52]

17:26 On this very day, Abraham was circumcised, and Ishmael, his son.

On this very day - On the same day that he was commanded, he circumcised himself (*Tosefoth, Rosh Hashanah* 11a).[53]

Vayera

18:1   And the L-rd appeared to him by the terebinths of
         Mamre, as he sat in the tent door in the heat of the day.

And the L-rd appeared to him - From here we derive that it is among
the attributes of the Holy One Blessed be He to visit the sick. [Abraham
was recovering from his circumcision] (*Sotah* 14a).[1]

And the L-rd appeared to him - R. Chama b.R. Chanina said: "It was
the third day after his circumcision, and the Holy One Blessed be He
came to inquire as to his health" (*Bava Metzia* 86b).[2]

in the heat of the day - What is signified by: "in the heat of the day"? R.
Chama b. R. Chanina said: "It was the third day after Abraham's
circumcision, and the Holy One Blessed be He took the sun out of its
'case' " [and made it beat down so that Abraham would not have to
exert himself in accommodating wayfarers] (*Ibid.*).[3]

18:2   And he lifted up his eyes and he saw, and, behold, three
         people standing over him, and he saw and he ran towards
         them from the tent door, and he bowed to the ground.

and, behold, three people - Who were these three people? Michael,
Gabriel, and Rafael. Michael came to inform Sarah that she would bear
a child; Rafael, to heal Abraham; and Gabriel, to overturn Sodom
(*Ibid.*).[4]

standing over him - If three are walking along the road, the master
should be in the middle, the greater man on his right hand side, and the
lesser, on his left. And so, we find with respect to the three angels who
came to Abraham. Michael was in the middle; Gabriel, on his right; and
Rafael, on his left (*Yoma* 37a).[5]

and he saw, and he ran - What is signified by: "And he saw, and he

ran"'? In the beginning, they came and stood over him. When they saw
that this pained him, they said: 'It is not proper to stand here like this' "
[and when they left, he ran after them] (*Bava Metzia* 86b).[6,7]

18:3   And he said: "My L-rd, if I have found favor in Your eyes,
        do not depart from Your servant."

do not depart - R. Yehudah said in the name of Rav: "Accommodating
guests is greater than receiving the *Shechinah* [the Divine Presence], as
it is written: 'And he said: "My L-rd, if I have found favor in Your eyes,
do not depart" ' " [while I attend to the angels] (*Shabbath* 127a).[8]

do not depart - R. Elazar said: "Come and see that the attributes of
man are not like those of the Holy One Blessed be He. A lesser man
cannot tell a greater one: 'Wait for me until I come to you,' whereas
with respect to the Holy One Blessed be He it is written: 'And he said,
"My L-rd ... do not depart' " (*Ibid.*).[9]

do not depart - What is signified by "Do not depart"? He saw the Holy
One Blessed be He standing in the doorway, and when the Holy One
Blessed be He saw him tying and untying his bandages, He said: "It is
not proper to stand here like this." And in this regard it is written: "Do
not depart from your servant" (*Bava Metzia* 86b).[10,11]

18:4   Let there be taken, I beg you, a little water, and wash your
        feet, and rest under the tree.

Let there be taken, I beg you, etc. - R. Yehudah said in the name of
Rav: "Everything that Abraham did for the angels by himself, the Holy
One Blessed be He did for his children by Himself, and everything that
Abraham did through an intermediary, the Holy One Blessed be He did
for his children through an intermediary: 'And Abraham ran to the
cattle' — (*Numbers* 11:31): 'And a wind went out from the L-rd'; 'And
he took butter and milk' — (*Exodus* 16:4): 'Behold, I will rain bread
from heaven for you'; 'And he stood over them under the tree' —
(*Exodus* 17:6): 'Behold, I will stand before you there upon the rock in
Chorev'; 'And Abraham went with them to see them off' — (*Exodus*
13:21): 'And the L-rd went before them by day'; 'Let there be taken' [by

a messenger], I beg you, a little water' — (*Exodus* 17:6): 'And *you* shall smite the rock, and water will come out of it' " (*Ibid.*).[12,13]

Let there be taken, I beg you, etc. - It was taught in the forum of R. Yishmael: "As a reward for three things, they merited three things: as a reward for 'butter and milk,' they merited the manna; as a reward for 'And he stood over them,' they merited the pillar of cloud; as a reward for 'Let there be taken, I beg you, a little water' they merited Miriam's well" (*Ibid.*).[14,15]

and wash your feet - They said to him: "And do you suspect us of being Arabs, who bow to the dust of their feet [in idol-worship]?" — Ishmael [who would himself serve idols] had already issued from him (*Ibid.*).[16,17]

18:5   And I will take a loaf of bread, and comfort your hearts; and then you may depart, for it is for this that you have passed before your servant. And they said: "Do so, as you have spoken."

And I will take a loaf of bread - And it is written: "And Abraham ran to the *cattle*." R. Elazar said: "From here we see that the righteous say a little, but do a lot" (*Ibid.* 87a).[18]

And then [achar] you may depart - R. Yitzchak said: "Stylistic embellishments were decreed to Moses from Sinai. 'And then [*achar*] you may depart [*ta'avoru*]' is a stylistic embellishment [for it could simply have been written '*veta'avoru*']" (*Nedarim* 37b).[19]

Do so - Why, in relation to Abraham is it written: "Do so, as you have spoken," and, in relation to Lot (19:3): "And he entreated them exceedingly, and they went unto him"? R. Elazar said: "From here we see that a lesser man is to be refused, but not a great one" (*Bava Metzia* 87a).[20]

18:6   And Abraham hastened into the tent to Sarah, and said: "Make ready quickly three measures of flour, fine flour; knead it, and make cakes."

flour, fine flour - It is written "flour," and then "fine flour." R. Yitzchak said: "This [qualification, "fine flour," by or for Sarah] shows us that a woman is more averse to guests than is a man" (*Ibid.*).[21]

18:7   And Abraham ran to the cattle, and took a calf, soft and good; and he gave it to the young man, and he hurried to prepare it.

a calf, etc. - R. Yehudah said in the name of Rav: "a calf" — one; "soft" — two; "and good" — three. Why three if one is sufficient? R. Chanan b. Rava said: "So that he could feed them three tongues with mustard" (*Bava Metzia* 86).[22]

18:8   And he took butter and milk and the calf that he had prepared, and he set it before them; and he stood over them under the tree, and they ate.

And he took butter and milk - But he did not bring bread. [Why so?] Efraim Mikshaah, the disciple of R. Meir, said: "That day Sarah began menstruating, and our father Abraham ate [even] unconsecrated food in purity" (*Ibid.*).[23]

and he stood over them - Once R. Eliezer, R. Yehoshua, and R. Tzadok were seated at the feast of R. Gamliel's son, and R. Gamliel stood and gave them to drink. At this, R. Eliezer said to R. Yehoshua: "What is this, Yehoshua? We are sitting and R. Gamliel b'Rabbi [a title of distinction] is standing over us and giving us to drink!" To this, R. Yehoshua replied: "We find one greater than he who served thus. Abraham was the greatest man of his generation, and yet it is written of him: 'And he stood over them.' Now you may say that they appeared to him as ministering angels, yet the truth is that they appeared to him only as Arabs — and we — R. Gamliel b'Rabbi should not stand over us and give us to drink?" (*Kiddushin* 32b).[24]

and they ate - R. Tanchum b. Chanilai said: "One should never deviate from custom, for when our teacher Moses went to heaven [to receive the Torah] he did not eat bread, and when the ministering angels descended to the earth, they did eat bread, as it is written: 'And they ate' " (*Bava Metzia* 86b).[25]

and they ate - Did they really eat? Say, rather, that it as if they ate and drank (*Ibid.*).[26]

18:9   And they said to him: "Where is Sarah your wife?" And he said: "Behold, she is in the tent."

And they said to him [eilav] - It was taught in the name of R. Yossi: "Why are there dots above the *aleph, yod, vav* in *eilav*? The Torah is hereby teaching us proper conduct — that one should inquire as to the well-being of his host" [*aleph-yod-vav* = "*ayo*" ("Where is he [Abraham]?" — a question the angels asked Sarah, just as they asked Abraham where Sarah was)] (*Ibid.* 87a).[27]

Where is Sarah? - R. Yehudah said in the name of Rav: "The ministering angels knew that our mother Sarah was in the tent. Why, then, did they ask? To endear her to her husband" [knowing he would reply that she was in the tent, in keeping with her modesty.] R. Yossi b. R. Chanina said: "To send her the cup of blessing" (*Ibid.*).[28,29]

Behold, she is in the tent - [From here it is to be derived that it is a woman's honor to remain at home] (*Yevamoth* 77a).[30]

Behold, she is in the tent - This is to show us the modesty of our mother Sarah (*Bava Metzia* 87a).[31]

18:12   And Sarah laughed within her, saying: "After I have become old, I have been rejuvenated, and my lord is old."

within her [bekirbah] - Once King Ptolemy assembled seventy-two elders in seventy-two different houses and told each of them: "Transcribe for me [into Greek] the Torah of Moses your teacher." The Holy One Blessed be He placed goodly counsel into the heart of each of them, and they all wrote as one: "And Sarah laughed among her neighbors" [*bikrovehah* - so that he would not question why Sarah should be punished for laughing, and not Abraham, if they both laughed inwardly] (*Megillah* 9a).[32]

After I have become old, etc. - R. Chisda said: "'After I have become old, I have been rejuvenated' — after my flesh has become worn and my wrinkles have multiplied, my flesh has been rejuvenated and my wrinkles smoothed out, and my former beauty has been restored" (*Bava Metzia* 87a).[33]

18:13 And the L-rd said to Avraham: "Why did Sarah laugh, saying: 'Shall I really give birth, and I am old!'?"

and I am old - It was taught in the forum of R. Yishmael: "Great is peace, for the Holy One Blessed be He Himself deviated from the truth for its sake, as it is written: 'And Sarah laughed, saying: "And *my lord* is old," ' yet subsequently it is written: 'And the L-rd said to Abraham: "Why did Sarah laugh, saying: '*I* am old'?" ' " (*Ibid.*).[34]

18:14 Is anything withheld from the L-rd? At this time [next year] I will return to you, as you now live, and Sarah shall have a son.

At this time [next year] **I will return to you** - From here we derive that Isaac was born on Pesach, for it was on Pesach that the angel was standing there and telling her: "At this time [next year] I will return to you, as you now live, and Sarah shall have a son" (*Rosh Hashanah* 11a).[35]

18:15 Then Sarah denied, saying: "I did *not* laugh," for she was afraid. And He said: "No, you *did* laugh."

And He said, etc. - R. Yochanan said in the name of R. Eliezer b. R. Shimon: "We do not find the Holy One Blessed be He speaking with a woman, except with Sarah alone, as it is written: 'And He said: "No, you *did* laugh!" ' " (*Yerushalmi, Sotah* 7:1). [36]

And He said, etc. - R. Biri said: "How many circuits the L-rd made in order to hear the speech of righteous women, as it is written [after all the goings back and forth (from angel, to Sarah, to the L-rd, to Abraham, to Sarah, to the L-rd)] : 'No, you *did* laugh!' " (*Ibid.*).[37]

18:17   And the L-rd said: "Shall I conceal from Abraham what I
        do?"

Shall I conceal, etc. - Ravina asked one of the Rabbis: "Whence is
derived the formula of the Rabbis: 'The remembrance of the righteous is
for blessing'?" The latter answered: "From the fact that it is written:
'Shall I conceal from Abraham,' and, immediately thereafter: 'And
Abraham will be a great nation' " (*Yoma* 38b).[38]

18:18   And Abraham will be a great and mighty nation, and in
        him will be blessed all the nations of the earth.

And Abraham will be [hayo yihiyeh] - R. Nachman said in the name of
R. Manna: "The world cannot endure with fewer than thirty righteous
men like our father Abraham. Whence is this derived? — 'And
Abraham *hayo yihiyeh.*' The *gematria* [numerical equivalent] of *yihiyeh*
[which is superfluous] is thirty" (*Yerushalmi, Avodah Zarah* 2:1).[39]

and in him will be blessed - R. Elazar said: "What is the intent of 'And
in him will be blessed all the nations of the earth'? Even ships going
from Gaul to Spain are blessed [i.e., are granted a safe voyage] only for
the sake of Israel" (*Yevamoth* 63a).[40]

18:19   For I have known him so that he may command his sons
        and his household after him to heed the way of the L-rd,
        to do righteousness and justice, so that the L-rd may bring
        upon Abraham what He has spoken concerning him.

For I have known him - R. Elazar said - "From the blessing of the
righteous, you infer the curse [the sin] of the wicked. It is written: 'For I
have known him so that he may command his sons and his household
after him to heed the way of the L-rd, to do righteousness and justice,'
after which it is written: 'And the L-rd said: "The outcry of Sodom and
Gemorrah, because it is great" ' " [from which it may be inferred that
their sin was perverting righteousness and justice] (*Yoma* 38b).[41]

his sons, etc. - "His sons and his household ... to do righteousness and
justice" — his sons, to do justice, and his household, [connoting

"women"] to do righteousness, for women are not commanded to administer justice (*Sanhedrin* 57b).[42]

righteousness and justice - It was taught: "There are three identifying characteristics of the Jewish nation: mercifulness, shamefacedness, and lovingkindness. Lovingkindness — as it is written: "For I have known him so that he may command his sons and his household after him to heed the way of the L-rd, to do *righteousness* [synonymous with "lovingkindness"] and justice.'" (*Yevamoth* 79a).[43]

righteousness and justice - A certain translator began his discourse by saying: "Our brothers, men of lovingkindness, the sons of men of lovingkindness, who abide by the covenant of our father Abraham, of whom it is written: 'For I have known him so that he may command his sons and his household after him to heed the way of the L-rd, to do *righteousness* and justice ...' " (*Kethuvoth* 8b).[44]

righteousness and justice - R. Simlai expounded (*Isaiah* 33:15): "He that walks righteously, and speaks uprightly": "He that walks righteously" — this refers to Abraham, of whom it is written: 'For I have known him so that he may command his sons and his household after him to heed the way of the L-rd, to do righteousness and justice' " (*Makkoth* 24a).[45]

18:20   And the L-rd said: "The outcry of Sodom and Gemorrah, because it is great and their sin is very severe."

because it is great [*rabbah* - similar to **ribbah** (young girl)] - There was a certain young girl in Sodom who took out some bread for a poor man in a pitcher. She was discovered, however, and was smeared over with honey and placed atop the city wall [so all could see.] The bees came and devoured her — and this is what is alluded to in: "And the L-rd said: 'The outcry of Sodom and Gemorrah *ki rabbah*' " — "in respect to *ribbah* [the young girl]" (*Sanhedrin* 109b).[46,47]

because it is great - [In respect to Sodom it is written: "The outcry of Sodom and Gemorrah, because it is *great*," and in respect to the generation of the flood it is written (6:5): "And G-d saw that the evil of man is *great*.]" This teaches us that their actions were similar (*Yerushalmi, Bava Metzia* 1:21).[48]

18:25 Far be it from You to do a thing like this, to kill a
       righteous man together with an evildoer. Far be it from
       You. Shall the Judge of all the earth not do justice?

Far be it from You [chalilah] - R. Abba b. R. Kahana expounded: "Far
be it from You to do a thing like this, to kill a righteous man together
with an evildoer." "Abraham said before the Holy One Blessed be He:
"L-rd of the universe, it would be profane [*chullin* - like "*chalila*"] in
You to kill a righteous man together with an evildoer' " (*Avodah Zarah*
4a).[49]

18:26 And the L-rd said: "If I find in Sodom fifty righteous men
       in the midst of the city, I will spare the entire place for
       their sake."

for their sake - This teaches us that the righteous shield the world
(*Sanhedrin* 99b).[50]

18:27 And Abraham answered and he said: "Behold, now, I
       have taken upon me to speak to the L-rd, and I am dust
       and ashes."

dust and ashes - Rava expounded: "As a reward for Abraham's saying
'And I am dust and ashes,' his children merited two *mitzvoth*: the ashes
of the red heifer (*Numbers* 19:10), and the dust of *sotah* [in the instance
of a woman accused of faithlessness (*Numbers* 5:17)]." Why is the dust
used for covering the blood after ritual slaughtering not also
mentioned? — For in that instance the dust serves only as a complement
to the *mitzvah*, but does not provide benefit for its performer [for the
flesh may be eaten even if the blood is not covered] (*Sotah* 17a).[51]

dust and ashes - Rava said: "Why did the Torah institute dust for a
sotah? For if she is vindicated, there will issue from her a son like our
father Abraham, of whom it is written: 'And I am dust and ashes,' and
if not, she returns to her dust" (*Ibid.*).[52]

dust and ashes - The Holy One Blessed be He said to Israel: I desire
you, for even when I accord greatness to you, you humble yourselves. I
gave greatness to Abraham, and he said: 'And I am dust and ashes' "
(*Chullin* 89a).[53]

dust and ashes - The order of fast days: The ark is taken into the city thoroughfare, and burnt ashes are placed upon it, upon the head of the Nasi, and upon the head of the chief of *bet din*. Why burnt ashes? To bring to mind the merit of Abraham, who said: "And I am dust and ashes" (*Yerushalmi, Ta'anith* 2:1).[54]

18:33   And the L-rd went when He finished speaking to Abraham, and Abraham returned to his place.

And the L-rd went - It was taught: "One should never take leave of his master or his neighbor without asking leave to do so. In this regard, we learn proper conduct from the Holy One Blessed be He, of whom it is written: 'And the L-rd went when He finished speaking to Abraham.' He said to him, as it were: 'I would like to take leave of you' " (*Derech Eretz* 5).[55]

19:1   And the two angels came to Sodom in the evening, and Lot sat in the gate of Sodom, and Lot saw, and he rose to meet them, and he bowed with his face to the ground.

And the two angels came - And further (25) it is written: "And *he* overturned the cities:" How is this to be understood? — Gabriel went to destroy Sodom, and Michael to save Lot (*Bava Metzia* 86b).[1,2]

19:15   And when the morning star rose, the angels hastened Lot, saying: "Arise, take your wife and your two daughters, who are found, lest you be consumed in the sin of the city."

And when the morning star rose - Rabbah b. Bar Chanah said in the name of R. Yochanan: "From the rising of the morning star until sunrise a man can walk a distance of five miles, as it is written: 'And when the morning star rose, the angels hastened Lot, saying: "Arise, etc.,"' after which it is written (23): 'And when the sun came out upon the earth, Lot arrived in Tzoar.'" And R. Chanina said: "I saw that area, and it is a distance of five miles between the two cities" (*Pesachim* 93b).[3]

who are found - Rava expounded (*Psalms* 40:8): "Then I said: 'Behold, I have come in the scroll of the book written about me' — David said: 'I said I have come now [into royalty], but I did not know that it [my ascension to royalty] had already been written of [i.e., foreshadowed] in the scroll of the book [the Torah].' There [in respect to the daughters of Lot] it is written 'who are *found*,' and here it is written (*Psalms* 89:21): 'I have *found* David My servant; with My holy oil have I anointed him.' " [David descended from Ruth the Moabitess, so-called because she descended from Moab, the son of Lot by his elder daughter. She was "found" there for the purpose of making David king] (*Yevamoth* 77a).[4,5]

19:17 And it was, when they had brought them outside, that he said: "Run for your life; do not look behind you, and do not stay in the plain. Escape to the mountain lest you be consumed."

Run for your life - The angel said to Lot: "It is enough that you save your *life*." This teaches us that Lot ran out with his hands on his head, saving nothing of his possessions (*Yerushalmi, Sanhedrin* 10:8).[6]

19:18 And Lot said to them: "Not so, my L-rd."

Not so, my L-rd - All of the names ["lord"] mentioned in the episode of Lot are profane [referring to the angels] except for this one [which refers to G-d]: "And he said: 'Not so, my L-rd; your servant has found favor in Your eyes, and *You* have spared my life' " — He who has it in His power to kill and to grant life — the Holy One Blessed be He (*Shevuoth* 35b).[7]

19:19 Your servant has found favor in Your eyes, and You have magnified Your kindness which You have shown to me in saving my life. I cannot escape to the mountain lest evil overtake me and I die.

lest evil overtake me - A man may not compel his wife to move from one place to another and even from a less desirable location to a better one; for relocation, even to a better place, puts one's body to a test, as it is written: "Lest evil overtake me" (*Yerushalmi, Kethuvoth* 13:10).[8]

19:20   Behold, this city is close to flee there, and it is small. Let me run there, I beg you. Is it not small? And my soul shall live.

close, etc. - R. Chama b. Guria said in the name of Rav: "One should always seek to live in a city that has been newly settled; for since it has been newly settled, its transgressions are fewer, as it is written: 'Behold, this city is close to flee there, and it is small.' What is signified by 'close' and 'small'? If the words are to be understood in their literal sense, can the angel not see this for himself? We must say, then, that the meaning is: in view of the fact that the city is 'close' [newly settled], its transgressions are 'small' [few]" (*Shabbath* 10b).[9-11]

Let me run there, I beg you [na] - R. Yitzchak said: "Tzoar had been settled for fifty-one years, as it is written: 'Let me run there *na.*' The *gematria* [numerical equivalent] of *na* is fifty-one. Sodom had been settled for fifty-two years, and had been at peace for twenty-six, as it is written (14:4): 'For twelve years they had served Kedarlaomer and for thirteen years they had rebelled, and in the fourteenth year Kedarlaomer came ... ' " [after which (the remaining twenty-six years) they were at peace] (*Ibid.*).[12]

19:24   And the L-rd rained down on Sodom and Gemorrah brimstone and fire from the L-rd, from heaven.

And the L-rd rained down on Sodom - And in respect to Jerusalem it is written (*Lamentations* 1:13): "From above, He sent fire." And it is written (*Ibid.* 4:6): "For the transgression of My people is greater than the sin of Sodom." Now, does G-d play favorites! [Why did He wait until Jerusalem's sin was greater?] Rabbah said in the name of R. Yochanan: "There was a quality in Jerusalem, which did not exist in Sodom: for concerning Sodom it is written (*Ezekiel* 16:49): 'Behold, this was the iniquity of your sister, Sodom: grandeur, surfeit of bread ... yet she did not strengthen the hand of the poor and needy,' whereas of Jerusalem it is written (*Lamentations* 4:10): 'The hands of [normally] *merciful* women boiled their children' " (*Sanhedrin* 104b).[13,14]

from the L-rd - We would expect "from *Him*," but this is the way Scripture speaks. Similarly, we have (4:23): "And Lemech said to his wives, Addah and Tzilah: 'Hear my voice, wives of Lemech!' " We would expect "*my* wives," but this is the way Scripture speaks (*Ibid.* 38b).[15]

19:27   And Abraham arose in the morning to the place where he had stood there before the L-rd.

And Abraham arose, etc. - It was taught: "Abraham instituted the morning prayer, as it is written: 'And Abraham arose in the morning to the place where he had *stood*,' and 'standing' connotes praying, as it is written (*Psalms* 106:30); 'Then Pinchas *stood up* and prayed'" (*Berachoth* 26b).[16]

where he had stood - It was taught: " 'Standing' connotes praying, as it is written (*Psalms* 106:30): 'And Pinchas stood up and prayed.' This teaches us that our father Abraham set aside a place for praying" (*Ibid.* 6b).[17]

19:28   And he looked at the face of Sodom and Gemorrah, and at the face of the entire plain, and he saw, and, behold, the smoke of the land arose as the smoke of a furnace.

as the smoke of a furnace - This teaches us that a furnace does not produce smoke until the flame takes hold of its contents. [This has certain halachic implications] (*Menachoth* 26b).[18]

19:29   And it was, when G-d destroyed the cities of the plain, that G-d remembered Abraham, and He sent Lot from the midst of the overthrow, when He overthrew the cities in which Lot sat.

that G-d remembered - R. Yochanan said: "Even in the midst of His
anger the Holy One Blessed be He remembers the righteous, as it is
written: 'And it was, when G-d destroyed the cities of the plain, that
G—d remembered Abraham, and He sent Lot from the midst of the
overthrow' " (*Berachoth* 43b).[19]

19:33   And they gave to drink — their father — wine, that night.
        And the elder daughter came and she lay with her father;
        and he did not know in her lying down and in her getting
        up.

And they gave to drink, etc. - Where did they find wine in the cave? —
It was presented to them [by G-d] for the occasion (*Sifrei, Ekev* 43).[20]

And the elder daughter came - R. Chiyya b. Avin said in the name of R.
Yehoshua b. Karcha: "One should always take the initiative in the
doing of a *mitzvah*, for because of the one night in which the elder sister
preceded the younger [in living with their father for the perpetuation of
mankind], she merited putting forward four generations of royalty in
Israel before her sister" [Oved (son of Ruth the Moabitess), Yishai,
David, Solomon — her sister not entering royalty until Rechovom, the
son of Solomon by Na'amah the Ammonitess] (*Nazir* 23b).[21]

in her lying down and in her getting up - It was taught in the name of R.
Yossi b. R. Choni: "Why is there a dot over the [middle] *vav* in
uvekumah ['and in her getting up'] — to intimate to us that he was not
aware of her lying down, but he was aware of her getting up [and should
not have allowed the younger daughter to inebriate him]" (*Ibid.* 23a).[22]

19:38   And the younger daughter, also, bore a son, and she called
        his name "Ben Ami." He is the father of the children of
        Ammon to this day.

Ben Ami ["the son of my nation"] - It was taught: "R. Chiyya b. Abba
said in the name of R. Yochanan: 'Whence do we derive that the Holy
One Blessed be He does not withhold reward even for discretion in the
use of words? For in relation to the elder daughter, who called her son
'Moav' [lit., 'from my father'], the Holy One Blessed be He commanded

(*Deuteronomy* 2:9): 'Do not besiege Moav, nor incite a war against them' — it is not permitted to *war* against them, but it is permitted to subjugate them; whereas in relation to the younger daughter, who called her son [euphemistically] 'Ben Ami' ['son of my nation'], the Holy One Blessed be He commanded Moses (*Deuteronomy* 2:19): 'Do not besiege them [Ammon] and do not incite them [*at all*]' — it is not even permitted to *subjugate* them" (*Ibid.*).[23-27]

20:3   And G-d came to Avimelech in a dream at night, and He said to him: "You deserve to die because of the woman that you have taken; she is a man's wife."

You deserve to die - At the hands of man. And though it is written (6): "And I also withheld you from sinning against *Me*," even so, his sin is subject to human justice. This is similar to the case of Joseph, where even though he says (39:9): "And I will sin to *G-d*" [by living with the wife of Potiphar], [it is obvious that] his sin is subject to human justice. [From here it is to be derived that one who commits a sin, assuming (consciously) that he is not sinning, is close to sinning intentionally] (*Makkoth* 9a).[1,2]

a man's wife [beulath baal] - "a woman with her husband" — she rises with him [to a higher status], but does not fall with him [to be reduced to a lower status]. Whence is this derived? R. Huna said: "And she is *beulath baal*" — with the rising [*bealiyatho* - similar to *beulath*] of the husband [*baal*], and not with his falling" (*Kethuvoth* 61a).[3]

beulath baal - R. Chanina taught: "And she is *beulath baal*" [lit., having had intercourse with the husband] — With the Noachides, a woman's having lived with her husband is the criterion for establishing future intimacy with another as adultery, but not the exchanging of marriage vows [*chupah*] without intercourse" (*Sanhedrin* 57b).[4]

beulath baal - R. Avahu taught in the name of R. Elazar: "And she is *beulath baal*" — One is liable [for adultery] only with those who are legally married [as opposed to those who had been intimate without intending marriage]; and one is not liable [for adultery] with those who are only engaged to be married" (*Yerushalmi, Kiddushin* 1:1).[5]

20:7   And, now, return the wife of the man, for he is a prophet,
        and he will pray for you; and if you do not return her,
        know that you will surely die — you and all that is yours.

for he is a prophet - And if he were not a prophet, it would not be
necessary to return her? — This is the meaning: "Return the wife of the
man," and as to your saying: "Did he not say to me: 'She is my sister'?
he is a prophet and has divined your motives from your deportment. If a
visitor comes to a city, is it customary to ask him: "Is she your wife or
your sister"! From here it is to be derived that a Noachide incurs the
death penalty in such instances of capital offense where he could have
learned the truth and did not (*Makkoth* 96).[6]

and he will pray for you - If one strikes his friend, even though he
recompenses him for his injury, his pain, his medical expenses, his
unemployment, and his shame, he is not forgiven until he asks him for
forgiveness, as it is written: "And now, return the wife of the man, for
he is a prophet, and he will pray for you" [that you be forgiven] (*Bava
Kamma* 92a).[7]

20:12   And, in truth, she is my sister, the daughter of my father,
        but not the daughter of my mother, and she became my
        wife.

my sister, the daughter of my father - This teaches us that a sister from
one's mother is forbidden to a Noachide (*Sanhedrin* 58b).[8]

20:13   And it was when they made me go astray — G-d — from
        the house of my father, I said to her: "This is your
        kindness that you shall do with me. In every place that we
        come, say: 'He is my brother.' "

made me go astray — G-d - All of the names [of the L-rd] mentioned
with respect to Abraham are sacred, including this: "When they made
me go astray — G-d." The meaning is: "If not for G-d [who
strengthened me], idol-worshippers would have made me go astray"
(*Yerushalmi, Megillah* 1:9).[9]

20:16   And to Sarah he said: "Behold, I have given your brother
a thousand pieces of silver. Let it be a covering of the eyes
for you, to all that are with you, and to all others." Thus
she was reproved.

a covering of the eyes - R. Yitzchak said: "Let the benediction of a
common person never be light in your eyes; for Avimelech *cursed* Sarah
[and G-d fulfills blessings more readily than curses] and his malediction
was fulfilled in her children, as it is written: 'Let it be a covering of the
eyes for you.' He said to her: 'Since you concealed from me the fact that
he is your husband, and you caused me this suffering, may it be His will
that you have children whose eyes are covered [blind].' And this curse
was fulfilled in her children, as it is written of Isaac (27:1): 'And his eyes
became dulled from sight' " (*Bava Kamma* 93a).[10]

20:17   And Abraham prayed to G-d, and G-d healed Avimelech,
and his wife, and his maidservants, and they bore
children.

And Abraham prayed - Whence is it derived that if one asks his friend
for forgiveness the latter is considered cruel if he does not forgive him?
From the verse: "And Abraham prayed to G-d" [that Avimelech be
forgiven] (*Ibid.* 92a).[11]

20:18   For the L-rd had closed up every womb in the house of
Avimelech because of Sarah, the wife of Abraham.

for the L-rd had closed up [lit., "closed up, closed up"] - Why "closed
up" twice? R. Elazar said: "One for the males, in respect to semen, and
the other for the females, in respect to ovulation and parturition" (*Ibid.*
92a).[12]

every womb - It was said in the forum of R. Yanai: "This teaches us that
even the hens in Avimelech's palace did not lay eggs" (*Ibid.* 92a).[13]

21:1   And the L-rd remembered Sarah as he said, and the L-rd
did to Sarah as He had spoken.

And the L-rd remembered - Sarah was remembered on Rosh Hashanah [i.e., G-d decreed on Rosh Hashanah that Sarah would bear a child.] It is written here: "And the L-rd *remembered* Sarah," and elsewhere (I*Samuel*2:21): "And the L-rd *remembered* Channah." Just as Channah was remembered on Rosh Hashanah, so Sarah was remembered on Rosh Hashanah (*Rosh Hashanah* 11a).[1]

as he said - Rava said to Rabbah b. Mari: "Whence do the Rabbis derive their formula: 'If one prays for his friend, and he is in need of the same thing himself, he is answered first'? — From the verse (20:17): 'And Abraham prayed [for Avimelech],' after which it is written: 'And the L-rd remembered Sarah as he said' — as Abraham said on behalf of Avimelech" (*Bava Kamma* 92a).[2]

21:4   And Abraham circumcised Isaac, his son, when he was eight days old, as G-d had commanded him.

And Abraham circumcised - A father is obligated to circumcise his son, as it is written: "And Abraham circumcised Isaac, his son, as G-d had commanded him." This would account for the instance at hand. How do we know that the same applies for future generations? It was taught in the forum of R. Yishmael: "Wherever 'command' is stated, the connotation is one of 'impelling,' both in respect to the situation under consideration and in respect to future generations" [and here it is written: "as G-d had commanded him"] (*Kiddushin* 29a).[3-5]

as G-d had commanded him - A woman is not obligated to circumcise her child, for it is written: "As G-d has commanded *him*" — *him* and not her (*Ibid.*).[6]

21:7   And she said: "Who would have said to Abraham: 'Sarah nursed children'? For I have borne him a son in his old age."

Sarah nursed children - Now, how many children did Sarah nurse? R. Levi said: "Because the gentiles sneered: 'Do you see this old man and old woman, who brought a foundling from the market-place and said: "It is our son"!' — What did Abraham do? He invited all of the great men of the generation, and Sarah invited all of their wives, and each one brought her child with her, without its nursemaid. A miracle was performed for our mother Sarah: her breasts opened like two fountains, and she nursed them all" (*Bava Metzia* 87a).[7]

21:8   And the child grew and he was weaned, and Abraham made a great feast on the day that Isaac was weaned.

and he was weaned - R. Avira expounded: " 'And the child grew and he was weaned' — the Holy One Blessed be He is destined to make a feast for the righteous when His lovingkindness to the seed of Isaac shall have been consummated" (*Pesachim* 119b).[8]

21:9   And Sarah saw the son of Hagar the Egyptian, that she had borne to Abraham, making sport.

making sport - It was taught: R. Shimon b. Yochai said: "R. Akiva expounded: 'The "sport" referred to here is nothing other than idol worship, as it is written [with respect to the golden calf] (*Exodus* 32:6): "And they rose up to make sport." ' R. Eliezer said: 'It refers to adultery, as it is written (39:17): "This Hebrew servant came to me to make sport with me." ' R. Yehoshua said: 'It refers to murder, as it is written (II *Samuel* 2:14): "Let the young men arise and make sport ... and thrust his sword in his fellow's side." ' But I say, G-d forbid that there should be in the household of that righteous one anyone who would do so. But 'making sport', in this case, refers to the inheritance. Ishmael would laugh and say: 'I am the first-born and I will take a double portion of the inheritance' — and I find my view more tenable than R. Akiva's" (*Tosefta, Sotah* 6).[9]

hearken to her voice - This teaches us that Sarah our mother was a prophetess (*Megillah* 14a).[10]

for in Isaac, etc. - If one vows to derive no benefit from the seed of Abraham, he is forbidden to derive benefit from Jews, but permitted to derive benefit from gentiles. But is Ishmael not his seed? — "For in *Isaac* shall there be called seed to you." But is Esau not his [Isaac's] seed? — "*In* Isaac," and not *all* of Isaac (*Nedarim* 31a).[11]

for in Isaac, etc. - Why is circumcision not binding upon the sons of Ishmael? Is it not written (17:9): "And you, heed My covenant — you and your children after you according to your generations"? Because of: "For in *Isaac* shall there be called seed to you." If so, let circumcision be binding upon the children of Esau! *"In* Isaac," and not *all* of Isaac (*Sanhedrin* 59b).[12]

21:17 And G-d heard the voice of the youth, and an angel of G—d called to Hagar from heaven and said to her: "What troubles you, Hagar? Do not fear, for G-d has heard the voice of the youth in the place that he is."

in the place that he is - R. Yitzchak said: "A man is judged only in respect to his state at the moment [and not in respect to G-d's foreknowledge of his future acts], as it is written: 'For G-d has heard the voice of the youth in the place that he is' " [and will help him even though he is destined to be an evil-doer] (*Rosh Hashanah* 16b).[13]

21:23 And now, swear to me by G-d that you will not deal falsely with me, nor with my son, nor with my son's son; but according to the kindness that I have done with you, you will do with me, and with the land in which you have sojourned.

swear to me - R. Chamma b. R. Chanina said: "In the days of Samson, the oath of Avimelech was voided, because the Philistines were the first to break the agreement, as it is written (*Judges* 13:5): 'And he, [fig.,] "because of the voiding of the oath," helped Israel from the hands of the Philistines'" (*Sotah* 10a).[14]

21:25 And Abraham reproved Avimelech because of the well of water which the servants of Avimelech had stolen.

And Abraham reproved - And afterwards it is written (27): "And they both entered into a covenant." This teaches us that reproof leads to peace (*Sifrei, Devarim*).[15]

21:33 And he planted an *eshel* in Beersheva, and he called there
       in the name of the L-rd, the L-rd of the Universe.

And he planted an eshel - R. Yehudah and R. Nechemiah are at
variance here. One says that *eshel* is an orchard, and the other, that it is
an inn. According to him who says "orchard," we can understand the
use of the word "planted"; but according to him who says "inn," how is
"planted" to be understood? — As in the verse (*Daniel* 11:45): "And he
shall *plant* the tents of his palace" (*Sotah* 10a).[16]

And he planted an eshel - Resh Lakish said: "This teaches us that he
cultivated an orchard and planted in it all kinds of fruit trees" (*Ibid.*).[17]

and he called - Read it not *Vayikra* ["and he called"], but *Vayakri*
["and he made to call."] We are hereby taught that our father Abraham
made every wayfarer call out in the name of the Holy One Blessed be
He. How so? After they had eaten and drunk, they would stand up to
bless him — at which he would say to them: "Have you eaten what is
mine? Have you not eaten of the fare of the L-rd of the Universe?" At
this, they would thank, praise, and bless Him who spoke and caused the
world to come into being (*Ibid.*).[18]

22:1   And it came to pass after these things that G-d tested
       Abraham. He said to him: "Abraham," and he said:
       "Here I am."

after these things [devarim] - After what? R. Yochanan said in the
name of R. Yossi b. Zimra: "After the words [*devarim* can mean
"words" as well as "things"] of Satan. It is written: 'And the child grew,
and he was weaned, and Abraham made a feast.' Satan said to the Holy
One Blessed be He: 'You blessed this old man with a child at the age of
one hundred, and yet, from every feast that he made, could he not spare
one dove or pigeon to sacrifice to You?' To this the Holy One Blessed be
He replied: 'Is there anything he would not do for his son? Yet, if I
asked him to sacrifice his son to Me, he would do so immediately' —
whereupon: 'And the L-rd tried Abraham' " (*Sanhedrin* 89b).[1]

after these things - R. Levi said: " 'After these things' — after the
words of Ishmael to Isaac, viz.: 'I am greater than you, for I was

circumcised at thirteen, and you only at eight days [when you had no say in the matter].' Yitzchak replied: 'You taunt me in respect to only one organ? If the Holy One Blessed be He were to tell me: 'Sacrifice yourself before Me, I would do so immediately!' — whereupon: 'And the L-rd tried Abraham' " (*Ibid.*).[2]

22:2   And He said: "Take, I beg you, your son, your only one, that you love — Isaac — to the land of Moriah, and offer him up there as a burnt-offering on one of the mountains that I shall tell you of."

Take, I beg you [na] - R. Shimon b. R. Abba said: " '*Na*' connotes imploration. The Holy One Blessed be He said to Abraham: 'I have exposed you to many trials, and you have withstood them all. Now [I implore you] withstand this one, so that it not be said that the former trials were insignificant' " (*Sanhedrin* 89b).[3]

your son, etc. - Abraham replied: "I have two sons": "Your only son"; "This is the only son of his mother, and so is the other"; "that you love"; "I love both"; "Isaac." Why all this? So that Abraham would not be overwhelmed with the sudden shock [of being commanded to sacrifice Isaac] (*Ibid.*).[4]

to the land of Moriah - What is the signification of Mount *Moriah*? R. Levi b. Chamma and R. Chanina differ on this question. One says: "The mountain from which instruction [*hora'ah*] went forth to Israel." The other says: "The mountain from which fear [*mora*] went forth to the nations of the world" (*Ta'anith* 16a).[5]

and offer him up - It was taught: "Abraham said to the Holy One Blessed be He: 'L-rd of the Universe: it is clear to You that when You told me: "Offer him up as a burnt-offering," I could have retorted: "Yesterday You told me: 'For in Isaac shall there be called seed to you,' and now You tell me: 'Offer him up as a burnt-offering!' " But I restrained myself from doing so in order to do Your will. In like manner, may it be Your will that when the seed of Isaac are being afflicted, and there is no one who can say anything in their defense, that *You* speak in their defense' " (*Yerushalmi, Ta'anith* 2:4).[6]

22:3 And Abraham arose early in the morning and he saddled his ass, and he took his two young men with him, and Isaac his son, and he split wood for the burnt-offering, and he arose, and he went to the place that G-d had told him.

And Abraham arose early - It was taught: "Circumcision may be performed the entire day, but the zealous make haste to do *mitzvoth*, as it is written: 'And Abraham arose early in the morning' " (*Pesachim* 4a).[7]

in the morning - R. Avahu said: "It is to be derived from here that a Torah scholar should not go out alone at night" (*Chullin* 91b).[8]

and he saddled his ass - It was taught in the name of R. Shimon b. Elazar: "Love [in this case, of a *mitzvah*] upsets the protocols of greatness." Whence is this derived? From the deportment of Abraham, as it is written: 'And he [not his servant] saddled his ass' " (*Sanhedrin* 105b).[9]

22:5 And Abraham said to his young men: "Sit here with the ass, and the youth and I will go until there, and we shall bow down, and we shall return to you."

with the ass - Rav said: "All agree that servants are not considered as having parentage, as it is written: 'Sit here with [*im*] the ass' — a people ["*am*" (similar to '*im*')] that is like the ass" (*Yevamoth* 62a).[10,11]

with the ass - R. Avahu said: "Even a Canaanite maidservant in Eretz Yisrael is assured of the world to come, it being written here (*Isaiah* 42:5): 'He gives soul to the people [*am*] upon it [Eretz Yisroel],' and there: 'Sit here with ["*im*"] the ass' — "*am* [a people] like the ass" (*Kethuvoth* 111a).[12]

with the ass - a people like the ass. From here it is to be derived that there is no halachic marriage with a Canaanite maidservant (*Kiddushin* 68a).[13]

with the ass - R. Pappa said: "If an ox gored a maidservant and she miscarried, the owner must pay the value of the fetuses. Why so? Because it is considered as if a pregnant ass had been gored, it being written: 'Sit here with the ass' — a people like the ass" (*Bava Kamma* 49a).[14,15]

and we shall return to you - R. Yochanan said: "Whence do we derive that "there is a 'covenant sealed with the lips'?" From the verse: 'And we shall return to you.' The statement took effect, and they both returned" (*Moed Katan* 18a).[16]

22:8   And Abraham said: "G-d will provide Himself with the lamb for the burnt-offering, my son," and both of them went together.

the lamb for the burnt-offering - Satan waylaid Abraham on the road and said to him (*Job* 4:2): "Is it right of G-d to try you and weary you like this? ... You instructed many, and you strengthened the weak hands; your words ... and now this should come upon you and you should be wearied!" Abraham replied: "I shall persist in my innocence." Satan countered: (*Ibid.* 4:12): "Now a word came stealthily to me" — so have I heard from behind the Divine Curtain: 'The lamb for the burnt-offering, and not Isaac for the burnt-offering'! "Abraham responded: "Yours is the punishment of the inveterate liar. Even if he were to tell the truth, he would not be believed" (*Sanhedrin* 89b).[17,18]

22:10   And Abraham stretched forth his hand, and he took the knife to slaughter his son.

and he took the knife - From here it is to be derived that a burnt-offering requires a knife for its slaughtering, for in this instance we are dealing with a burnt-offering, as it is written: "And he offered him up as a burnt-offering" (*Zevachim* 97b).[19]

and he took the knife - Rebbi [R. Judah Hanasi] stated: "Whence is it derived that ritual slaughter is not to be performed with a fixed instrument? From the verse: 'And he *took* the knife to slaughter' " (*Chullin* 16a).[20]

22:11   And an angel of the L-rd called to him from heaven and said to him: "Abraham, Abraham," and he said: "Here I am."

Abraham, Abraham - The connotation is one of love and of impelling (*Torath Cohanim, Vayikra*).[21]

22:12   And he said: "Do not stretch your hand out to the youth, and do not do anything to him, for now I know that you fear G-d, and you have not withheld your son, your only one, from Me."

that you fear G-d - It was taught: "R. Meir said: 'Abraham's fear of G—d was fear proceeding from love, as it is written (*Isaiah* 41:8): 'The seed of Abraham, my lover' " (*Sotah* 31a).[22]

that you fear G-d - R. Yochanan said: "What is stated of Job is greater than what is stated of Abraham; for of Abraham it is stated: 'that you fear G-d,' whereas of Job it is stated (*Job* 1:1): 'A man that was perfect and upright, that feared G-d and turned away from evil' " (*Bava Bathra* 15b).[23]

that you fear G-d - R. Abba said: "What is stated of Ovadiah is greater than what is stated of Abraham; for of Abraham it is stated: 'that you fear G-d' whereas of Ovadiah it is stated (I *Kings* 18:3): 'And Ovadiah feared the L-rd greatly'" (*Sanhedrin* 39b).[24]

22:13   And Abraham lifted his eyes, and, behold, a ram after, caught in the thicket by his thorns, and he took the ram and he offered it up as a burnt-offering in place of his son.

a ram after - What is the intent of "after"? R. Yuda b. Simon said [The Holy One Blessed be He said to Abraham]: "After all of the generations, your children are destined to be caught up in transgression and enmeshed in affliction, and in the end, they will be redeemed through the horns of this ram, as it is written (*Zechariah* 9:14): 'And the L-rd G-d shall blow the shofar' " (*Yerushalmi, Ta'anith* 2:4).[25,26]

22:14   And Abraham called that place "The L-rd will see," as it
is said to this day: "In the mount, the L-rd will be seen."

And Abraham called - This teaches us that our father Abraham saw the
Temple built, destroyed, and rebuilt: "And Abraham called that place
'The L-rd will see' " — built; "as it is said to this day in the mount of the
L—rd" — destroyed; "the L-rd will be seen" — rebuilt in time to come
(*Sifrei, Deuteronomy* 352).[27]

In the mount, the L-rd will be seen - It is written (I *Chronicles* 21:15):
"And as He was about to destroy, the L-rd saw, and He relented."
What did He see? R. Yochanan said: "He saw the Temple, as it is
written: 'As it is said to this day: "In the mount, the L-rd will be seen"'"
(*Berachoth* 62b).[28,29]

22:21   Utz, his first-born, and Buz, his brother, and Kemuel, the
father of Aram.

Utz, his first-born - It was taught: "Bar Kappara said: 'Job lived in the
days of Abraham, as it is written (*Job* 1:1): "There was a man in the
land of Utz by the name of Job," and [in the days of Abraham]: "Utz,
his [Nachor's] first-born" ' " (*Yerushalmi, Sotah* 5:6).[30]

Chayei Sarah

23:2   And Sarah died in Kiryat Arbah, which is Chevron, in the land of Canaan; and Abraham came to mourn Sarah and to weep for her.

in Kirayt Arbah - What is signified by "*Arbah*"? ["four"] R. Yitzchak said: "Four pairs: Adam and Eve, Abraham and Sarah, Isaac and Rivkah, Jacob and Leah" (*Eruvin* 53a).[1]

and Abraham came to mourn - [This teaches us that a eulogy is for the honor of the dead] for if it were for the honor of the living, would Sarah's burial have been delayed for Abraham's honor? (*Sanhedrin* 46b).[2]

23:4   I am a stranger and a sojourner with you. Give me possession of a burying place with you, and I will bury my dead one from before me.

and I will bury my dead one from before me - One whose dead one is before him is exempt from all of the *mitzvoth* of the Torah. And though the body may not actually be in front of him, still, since it is incumbent upon him to bury it, it is considered as lying in front of him, as it is written: "And I will bury my dead one from *before* me" (*Berachoth* 18a).[3]

23:9   And he shall give me the doubled cave which he has, which is in the end of his field; for the full price he shall give it to me in your midst for possession of a burying place.

Me'arat Hamachpelah [the doubled cave] - Rav and Shmuel differ on this. One says there were two chambers, one inside the other, and that "doubled" denotes the doubling of the pairs [See (1) above]. The other says there were two chambers, one on top of the other, and that this is what "doubled" refers to (*Eruvin* 53a).[4,5]

23:13 And he spoke to Efron in the hearing of the people of the land, saying: "But if you would, I pray you, hear me, I have given the money for the field. Take it from me, and I will bury my dead there."

I have given the money for the field - Our bills of sale, though they may be written thus: "I have sold," "I have given," are not proof [of the sales] having been transacted in the past], for "I have given" may also refer to a forthcoming transaction, as in: "I have given the money for the field; take it from me" (*Ran, Kiddushin* I).[6]

Take it from me - And further on it is written (25:10): "The field that Abraham acquired." This teaches us that "taking" is called "acquiring," and that "taking" is effected through money alone. [This has certain halachic implications] (*Kiddushin* 2a).[7]

23:16 And Abraham listened to Efron, and Abraham weighed out to Efron the silver which he had named in the hearing of the sons of Chet, four hundred silver shekels current with the merchant.

current with the merchant - R. Elazar said: "The wicked say much, and do not do even a little. How do we know this? From Efron. In the beginning it is written: "four hundred silver shekels," and in the end: "four hundred silver shekels current with the merchant," Efron refusing to take anything but centenaria of far greater value than standard shekels (*Bava Metzia* 87a).[8]

current with the merchant - R. Chanina said: "Whenever silver currency is referred to in the Torah, a *sela* is intended, except in the case of Efron, where even though "silver" alone is written, even so, the intent is centenaria, as it is written: "four hundred shekels of silver, current with the merchant" — there being a place where centenaria are referred to as shekels" (*Bechoroth* 50a).[9,10]

23:17   And the field of Efron was acquired, which was at the doubled cave, which was before Mamre; the field, and the cave which was in it, and all the trees that were in the field, which were in all its borders round about.

in all its borders round about - One who sells a "field" is not understood to be selling a grafted carob or the trunk of a sycamore within it, as it is written: "And the field of Efron was acquired ... and all the trees ... which were in all its borders round about" — Only those trees which require a border round about [to indicate ownership] are acquired with the purchase of the field, and not those [as the aforementioned, whose special nature makes their ownership well known] and which do not require a border to indicate ownership (*Bava Bathra* 69b).[11,12]

in all its borders round about - What is signified by "round about" ? R. Mesharshia said: "Here we find the institution of boundary markers in the Torah" (*Ibid.*).[13]

24:1   And Abraham became old, hoar with age, and the L-rd blessed Abraham with everything.

And Abraham became old - R. Chamma b. R. Chanina said: "All the days of our fathers, learning did not cease from them. Abraham became old and dwelt in the tents of learning, as it is written: ' "And Abraham became old [in wisdom]' " (*Yoma* 28b).[1]

And Abraham became old - Until the time of Abraham, there was no visible old age, so that if one wished to speak to Abraham, he might mistakenly speak to Isaac, and if he wished to speak to Isaac, he might mistakenly speak to Abraham [See 25:19] (*Bava Metzia* 87a).[2]

and the L-rd blessed, etc. - The Torah protects a man from all manner of evil in his youth, and provides him with a goodly end and expectation in his old age, as it is written: "And Abraham became old, and the L-rd blessed Abraham with everything" (*Kiddushin* 22a).[3]

with everything [bakol] - R. Avira expounded: "One who is haughty and repents of it lives out all of his years, as our father Abraham lived out all of his, as it is written (*Job* 24:24): 'And if they humble themselves, they will die as *kol*' — as Abraham, Isaac, and Jacob, of whom it is written, respectively: '*bakol*' [with everything], '*mikol*' [from everything], '*kol*' [everything]" (*Sotah* 5a).[4,5]

with everything [bakol] - It was taught: R. Meir said: "*Bakol* — because he had no daughters." R. Yehudah said: "*Bakol* — because he had a daughter." Others say that "Bakol" was her name. R. Eliezer Hamodai said: "Abraham had astrological powers so great that all the kings of east and west paid attendance at his door." R. Shimon b. Yochai said: "There was a precious gem hanging from Abraham's neck, and any sick person who beheld it was immediately cured" (*Bava Bathra* 16b).[6-8]

with everything - It was taught: "And the L-rd blessed Abraham with everything" — even Esau did not rebel in Abraham's lifetime. Another interpretation of "with everything": Ishmael repented in Abraham's lifetime (*Ibid.*).[9]

with everything - The Rabbis taught: "The Holy One Blessed be He caused Abraham to taste of what resembled the world to come, and he was not vulnerable to the evil inclination, the angel of death, or worms and maggots, as it is written: 'And the L-rd blessed Abraham with everything' " (*Ibid.*).[10]

24:2   And Abraham said to his servant, the elder of his house, who ruled over everything that was his: "Place, I pray you, your hand under my thigh."

who ruled, etc. - R. Elazar said: " 'Who ruled over all that was his' — he ruled over [mastered] the Torah of his master. This teaches us that Eliezer, Abraham's servant, was a scholar who dwelt in the tents of learning" (*Yoma* 28b).[11]

who ruled, etc. - If one writes to another that he should rule over and govern all that is his, he is not making him a gift of his possessions, but appointing him a caretaker over them, as we find in respect to Abraham's servant, Eliezer, concerning whom it is written: "who ruled over all that was his" (*Responsa, Rosh* 84).[12]

place your hand, etc. - From here it is derived that one who swears must hold an object in his hand (*Shevuoth* 38b).[13]

24:3   And I will make you swear by the L-rd, the G—d of the heavens and the G—d of the earth, that you not take a wife to my son of the daughters of the Canaanites, in whose midst I dwell.

and the G-d of the earth - Before Abraham, the Holy One Blessed be He was G-d of the heavens only, and when Abraham came upon the scene, he made Him sovereign over heaven and earth, as it is written: "And I will make you swear by the L-rd, the G-d of the heavens and the G-d of the earth" (*Sifrei, Ha'azinu*).[14]

24:8   And if the woman does not desire to go with you, then you shall be clean of this oath; only my son do not return there.

And if the woman does not desire - R. Meir said: "Any condition which is not like that of the sons of Gad and the sons of Reuven [i.e., containing both the positive and the negative element ("if ... and if not") See Numbers 32:39] is not a condition. This is the intent of: 'And if the woman does not desire to go with you, then you shall be clean of this oath' " (*Kiddushin* 61b).[15]

24:14   And it will be, the maiden to whom I will say: "Incline your pitcher and I will drink," and she will say: "Drink, and also your camels will I give to drink," she have You designated for your servant Isaac, and thereby shall I know that You have done kindness with my master.

And it will be, the maiden, etc. - R. Shmuel b. Nachmani said in the name of R. Jonathan: "Eliezer, the servant of Abraham, though he did not ask correctly, was answered correctly: 'And it will be, the maiden to whom I will say: "Incline your pitcher and I will drink"' — this would permit [for presentation to him] even one who was lame or blind — yet *Rivkah* was presented to him" (*Ta'anith* 4a).[16]

And it will be, the maiden, etc. - Rav said: "Any divining which is not [implicitly believed in] as that of Eliezer, the servant of Abraham, [who *committed himself* to his divining] is not considered divining [in the sense in which the Torah forbids it]" (*Chullin* 95b).[17]

Drink, and also your camels - From here it is to be derived that even though one is forbidden to partake of anything before he feeds his animals, this applies to food; but as regards drink, man takes precedence, as we find with Rivkah, who said: "Drink, and also your camels will I give to drink" (*Magen Avraham* 167:18).[18]

24:16   And the maiden was of very goodly appearance, a virgin, whom no man had known; and she went down to the well, and she filled her pitcher, and she came up.

And the maiden, etc. - It was taught: "*Bethulah* [a virgin] connotes a maiden, as it is written: 'And the maiden was of very goodly appearance, a *bethulah*' " (*Yevamoth* 61b).[19]

a virgin, whom no man had known - "A virgin" — not having been lived with in the normal manner; "whom no man had known" — in an abnormal manner (*Yerushalmi, Kethuvoth* 81:3).[20]

24:17   And the servant ran towards her and he said: "Give me to drink a little water from your pitcher."

Give me to drink [hagmi'ini] - From here [the fact that "hagmi'ini" is spelled with an *aleph*] we can see that "gemiah" in "One who carries out the amount of a *gemiah* of milk on Shabbath is liable" is to be spelled with an *aleph* and not with an *ayin* (*Shabbath* 77a).[21]

24:21   And the man wondered her, keeping silent to know if the L—rd had prospered his way or not.

And the man wondered - R. Yitzchak said: "The Torah speaks in all languages, as it is written: 'And the man [lit.,] *wondered* her.' " (*Yerushalmi, Rosh Hashanah* 1:8).[22]

24:27   And he said: "Blessed is the L-rd, G-d of my master Abraham, who did not withhold His kindness and His truth from my master. As for me, the L-rd has guided me in the way to the house of my master's brethren."

Blessed is the L-rd - From here we learn the formula for blessings (*Rokeach* 363).[23]

24:31   And he said: "Come, blessed is the L-rd. Why do you stand outside? For I have prepared the house and a place for the camels."

and a place for the camels - This teaches us that the camels would not enter until all of the idols had been removed from their presence (*Avoth d'R. Nathan* 28).[24]

24:32   And the man came into the house and he undid the camels, and he gave straw and provender for the camels, and water to wash his feet and the men's feet that were with him.

and he undid the camels - He untied their muzzles [their having been muzzled so as not to graze in the fields of others] (*Yerushalmi, Shekalim*).[25]

24:33   And he set before him to eat, and he said: "I will not eat until I have spoken my words"; and he said: "Speak."

I will not eat - From here it is to be derived that if food is set before one, he need not wait to be told to eat, for Eliezer said: "I will not eat until I have spoken my words" — and he had not yet been asked to eat. But since food had been set before him, asking was not necessary (*Magen Avraham* 107:18).[26]

24:34   And he said: "I am Abraham's servant."

I am Abraham's servant - Rava said to Rabbah b. Mari: "Whence is derived the folk-saying: 'If there is something that might lower you in men's eyes, mention it [before others do]' "? He answered: "From the verse: 'I am Abraham's servant'" (*Bava Kamma* 92b).[27]

24:42   And I came this day to the well and said: "O L-rd, G-d of my master Abraham; if now You prosper my way which I go,"

And I came this day - The Rabbis taught: "The road 'quickened' for Eliezer, Abraham's servant, as it is written: 'And I came this day' — the same day that he had left" (*Sanhedrin* 95a).[28]

24:50   Then Lavan and Betuel answered and said: "This thing has gone forth from the L-rd; we cannot speak to you bad or good."

This thing has gone forth from the L-rd - Rav said in the name of R. Reuven b. Itztrobli: "From *Pentateuch, Prophets,* and *Hagiographa* we learn: 'It is by the L-rd that a woman is given to a man.' From *Pentateuch* — as it is written: 'This thing has gone forth from the L-rd' " (*Moed Katan* 18b).[29]

24:55   And her brother and her mother said: "Let the maiden stay with us days or ten, and then she may go."

days or ten - What is meant by "days"? If "two days," do people speak thus? They tell him: "Two days." He says: "No." And they say "Ten days"! What, then, is meant by "days"? A year, as it is written (*Leviticus* 25:29): "Within a year (lit., "days") he may redeem it." This teaches us that a virgin is given twelve months from the time she is engaged to prepare what she needs for her marriage (*Kethuvoth* 57b).[30]

and then she may go - R. Yitzchak said: "Stylistic embellishments were decreed to Moses from Sinai. 'And then [*achar*] she may go [*telech*] is a stylistic embellishment [for it could simply have been written *vatelech* ('and she will go')]" (*Nedarim* 37b).[31]

24:60   And they blessed Rivkah and they said to her: "Our sister, may you be to thousands of ten thousands, and may your seed inherit the gate of its haters."

And they blessed Rivkah - It was taught: "From where in the Torah do we derive the institution of the wedding blessings? From the verse: 'And they blessed Rivkah' " (*Kallah* I).[32]

24:61   And Rivkah and her maidens arose and rode on the camels, and they went behind the man; and the servant took Rivkah and went.

and they rode - It was taught in the forum of R. Yishmael: "One should always speak 'cleanly,' for in relation to a *zav* [a man afflicted with a genital flow] the Torah referred to his seat as *merkav* [connoting straddling with the legs], whereas in relation to a *zavah* [a woman so afflicted], her seat is referred to as *moshav* [connoting a side-saddle position.] But is it not written: 'And Rivkah and her maidens arose and rode [*vatirkavnah* (straddling)] on the camels'! — Because of their fear of [being thrown from] the camels, this position was considered natural [and not immodest]" (*Pesachim* 3a).[33,34]

behind the man - behind the man, and not in front of him. This teaches us that a man should not walk behind a woman (*Berachoth* 61a).[35]

24:63   And Isaac went to pray in the field towards evening, and he lifted up his eyes, and he saw, and, behold, camels were coming.

to pray [lasuach] in the field - It was taught: "Isaac went *lasuach* in the field towards evening." "*Sichah*" connotes prayer, as it is written (*Psalms* 102:1): 'A prayer for the afflicted, when he faints, and before the L-rd pours out his prayer [*sicho*]' " (*Ibid.* 26b).[36]

25:1   And Abraham took another wife, whose name was Keturah.

and he took a woman - Rava said to Rabbah b. Mari: "Whence is derived the folk-saying: 'Sixty-one afflictions visit the tooth of one who hears someone eating and does not eat himself'? From the verse: 'And Isaac brought her into the tent' after which it is written: 'And Abraham took another wife' " (*Bava Kamma* 92b).[1,2]

25:5   And Abraham gave all that was his to Isaac.

all that was his to Isaac - The Rabbis taught: 'When the sons of Ishmael and of Keturah came to contend with Israel, they said: 'The land of Canaan belongs to us and to you, for it is written: "And these are the generations of Ishmael the son of Abraham," and "And these are the generations of Isasac the son of Abraham." Geviha b. Pesisa answered them: 'But it is written: "And he gave all that was his to Isaac, and to the sons of the concubines he gave gifts." If a father made a bequest to his children in his life-time, and sent them away from each other, can they have any claims against each other?' They could not answer, and fled" (*Sanhedrin* 91a).[3,4]

25:6   And to the sons of the concubines, which Abraham possessed, Abraham gave gifts; and he sent them away from Isaac his son, while he yet lived, eastward, to the east country.

gifts - What kind of gifts? R. Yirmiah b. Abbah said: "This teaches us that he gave them 'the name of uncleanliness' " [probably, potent charms] (*Ibid.*).[5]

25:9   And Isaac and Ishmael his sons buried him in the doubled cave in the field of Efron the son of Tzochar the Hittite, which is before Mamre.

Isaac and Ishmael - R. Yochanan said: "Ishmael repented in his father's life-time, as it is written: 'And Isaac and Ishmael his sons buried him.'

Ishmael allowed Isaac to precede him, by way of honoring him, and his honoring him indicates that he had repented in his father's life-time" (*Bava Bathra* 16b).[6,7]

25:11   And it was after the death of Abraham, and G-d blessed Isaac his son, and Isaac dwelt by Beer Lachai Roi.

and G-d blessed, etc. - [He comforted him in his mourning. This teaches us that it is among the attributes of the Holy One Blessed be He to comfort mourners] (*Sotah* 14a).[8]

25:17   And these are the years of the life of Ishmael, one hundred and thirty-seven years; and he died and he was gathered unto his people.

the years of the life of Ishmael - R. Chiyya b. Abba asked: "Why were the years of Ishmael enumerated? — To reckon, by means of them, the years of Jacob" (*Megillah* 17a).[9]

Toldoth

25:19   And these are the generations of Isaac, the son of Abraham. Abraham begot Isasac.

Abraham begot Isaac - When Sarah gave birth to Isaac, people began sneering: "Can Abraham, a one-hundred-year-old man, beget children?" Hereupon, Isaac's appearance immediately changed to that of Abraham, at which all admitted in one voice: "Abraham begot Isaac" (*Bava Metzia* 87a).[10]

25:21   And Isaac prayed opposite his wife, for she was barren; and the L-rd was entreated of him, and Rivkah his wife conceived.

And Isaac prayed [vaye'etar] - R. Yitzchak said: "Why are the prayers of the righteous compared to a pitch-fork [*eter*]? For just as a pitch-fork turns the stalks from place to place, so the prayers of the righteous turn the disposition of the L-rd from severity to mercy (*Yevamoth* 64a).[11,12]

opposite his wife - It is not written "*for* his wife," but "*opposite* [i.e., "on the same plane as"] his wife." This teaches us that both of them were unable to beget children. And why were our forefathers unable to beget children? Because the Holy One Blessed be He desires the prayers of the righteous [in imploration for children] (*Ibid.*).[13]

and the L-rd was entreated of him - Why not "of *them*"? For the prayers of a righteous one whose father is righteous are greater than the prayers of a righteous one whose father is wicked.(*Ibid.*).[14]

25:23   And the L-rd told her: "Two nations are in your womb, and two peoples will depart from your innards; and one nation shall grow stronger than the other nation, and the elder shall serve the younger."

And the L-rd told her - through an interpreter (*Yerushalmi, Sotah* 7:1).[15]

two GYM - R. Yehudah said in the name of Rav: "Read it not '*goyim*' [nations], but '*gayim*' [great ones.] This refers to Antoninus [descended from Esau] and Rebbi [R. Judah Hanasi, descended from Jacob], from whose tables there was never lacking neither radishes nor lettuce, summer or winter" (*Avodah Zarah* 11a).[16,17]

and one nation, etc. - R. Nachman b. Yitzchak said: "If someone tells you that Caesaria [the domain of Esau] and Jerusalem [the domain of Jacob] have been destroyed, or that Caesaria and Jerusalem have been settled, do not believe him. If he tells you that Caesaria has been destroyed and Jerusalem settled, or that Jerusalem has been destroyed and Caesaria settled, believe him, as it is written: 'And one nation shall grow stronger than the other nation' [the implication is: when the other nation is weak]" (*Megillah* 6a).[18]

Uleom mileom, etc. - R. Elazar said: "Even fetuses in their mothers' womb curse the flatterer, as it is written (*Proverbs* 24:24): 'He who says to the evil-doer: "You are righteous," will be cursed by the nations, will be abhorred by the *leumim*' and '*leum*' means a fetus, as it is written: '*Uleom* mi*leom ye'ematz*' " ["*leom*" in this context being understood as a fetus]" (*Sotah* 41b).[19]

Uleom, etc. - R. Shimon Chasida said: "A teacher who withholds a *halachah* from his student is cursed even by fetuses in their mothers' womb, as it is written (*Proverbs* 11:26): 'He who withholds *bar* shall be cursed by *leom*.' '*Leom*' signifies a fetus, as it is written: '*Uleom* mi*leom ye'ematz*,' and '*bar*' connotes Torah, as it is written (*Psalms* 2:12): 'Desire *bar*' [in context, 'Torah']" (*Sanhedrin* 92a).[20]

Uleom, etc. - R. Chanina b. Pappa expounded: "In time to come, the Holy One Blessed be He will say: 'Let all who occupied themselves with Torah come and receive their reward' — whereupon the gentiles will congregate in a mixed multitude. The Holy One Blessed be He will then say: 'Let each nation and its king come forward, as it is written (*Isaiah* 43:9): 'And let the *leumim* be assembled,' "*leum*" signifying "a nation," as it is written: '*Uleom* mi*leom ye'ematz*' " (*Avodah Zarah* 2b).[21,22]

25:24 And her days were filled to give birth, and, behold, there were twins in her belly.

And her days were filled - R. Nachman b. Yitzchak said: "If one places his bed between north and south, his wife will not miscarry, it being written here (*Psalms* 17:14): 'And Your "north" will *fill* their bellies,' and there: 'And her days were *filled* to give birth, and, behold, there were twins in her belly' " (*Berachoth* 5b).[23]

25:25 And the first one went out ruddy, all over as a hairy cloak, and they called his name "Esau."

And the first one went out - It was taught in the forum of R. Yishmael: "As a reward for three 'firsts' [stated in relation to the festivals], the Jews merited three 'firsts': to cut off the seed of Esau, to build the holy Temple, and to be graced with the name of the Messiah. To cut off the seed of Esau — as it is written: 'And the *first* one went out ruddy' " (*Pesachim* 5a).[24]

25:27 And Jacob was a complete man, a dweller of tents.

And Jacob was a complete man - This teaches us that our father Jacob was born circumcised (*Avoth d'R. Nathan* 2).[25]

25:29 And Jacob cooked pottage, and Esau came from the field, and he was tired.

and Esau came, etc. - It was taught: "So long as Abraham was alive, Esau did not rebel, as it is written: 'And Esau came from the field, etc.' And it was taught: 'That day Abraham died, and Esau committed five transgressions' " (*Bava Bathra* 16b).[26]

and Esau came, etc. - R. Yochanan said: "That evil-doer Esau committed five transgressions on that day: He violated an engaged maiden; he murdered; he denied the resurrection; he denied the L-rd; he despised the birth-right. He violated an engaged maiden — it is written here: 'And Esau came from the *field*,' and elsewhere (*Deuteronomy* 22:27): 'For he found her in the *field*.' He murdered — it is written here:

'And he was *tired*,' and elsewhere (*Jeremiah* 4:31): 'My soul is *tired* with killing.' He denied the resurrection — as it is written: 'Behold, I am going to die.' He denied the L-rd — it is written here: 'What is *this* to me,' and elsewhere (*Exodus* 15:2): '*This* is my G-d, and I will praise Him.' He despised the birth-right — as it is written: 'And Esau despised the birth-right' " (*Ibid.*).[27-31]

26:3   Live in this land, and I will be with you, and I will bless you. For to you and to your children will I give all of these lands. And I will fulfill the oath that I swore to Abraham your father.

Live in this land - The Holy One Blessed be He said to Moses: "Woe for those who have departed ! I revealed myself to the forefathers on several occasions, and they never doubted Me. I said to Isaac: 'Live in this land, and I will bless you,' and yet, his servants desired to drink water, and they could not find any until they became embroiled in a dispute, as it is written (20): 'And the shepherds of Gerar quarreled with the shepherds of Isaac' — and, still, he did not doubt Me" (*Sanhedrin* 111a).[1]

26:5   Because Abraham hearkened to My voice and he heeded My charge, My mitzvoth, My statutes and My laws.

Because [ekev] he heeded - R. Ami b. Abba said: "Abraham was three years old when he recognized his Creator. The numerical equivalent of '*ekev*' is 172, and Abraham lived 175 years altogether" (*Nedarim* 32a).[2]

My mitzvoth, My statutes, and My laws - Rav said: "Our father Abraham fulfilled the entire Torah, as it is written: 'Because Abraham hearkened to My voice and heeded My charge, My *mitzvoth*, My statues, and My laws.' — Now, may this not refer to the seven Noachide commandments? — If so, why is it necessary to state 'My *mitzvoth*' and 'My laws' [which connote a greater number]?" (*Yoma* 28b).[3]

and My laws - Rava said - "Abraham fulfilled even the ordinance of *eruv tavshilin*, as it is written: 'and My *laws*' [plural] — both the written and the oral laws" (*Ibid.*).[4]

26:12   And Isaac sowed in that land, and he found in that year a
        hundredfold; and the L-rd blessed him.

And Isaac sowed - Dostai b. R. Yanai said in the name of R. Meir: "It is
stated in respect to Isaac (24): 'And I will bless you, and I will multiply
your seed.' Isaac reasoned: 'G-d's blessing rests only upon my acts,' and
he arose and sowed: 'And Isaac sowed in that land ... and he found ... a
hundredfold'" (*Tosefta Berachoth* 6).[5]

and he found ... a hundredfold - The Rabbis taught: "In the blessings of
Eretz Yisroel, one *beth sa'ah* produces fifty thousand *kurim* [the normal
yield being five hundred], as it is written: 'And Isaac sowed in that land
... and he found ... a hundredfold' " (*Kethuvoth* 112a).[6]

26:19   And Isaac's servants dug in the valley, and they found
        there a well of living waters.

a well of living waters - R. Chanina said: "One who sees a well in a
dream will see peace, as it is written: 'And Isaac's servants dug in the
valley, and they found there a well of living waters.'" R. Nathan says:
"He will find Torah, as it is written (*Proverbs* 8:35): 'For whoever finds
me [Torah] finds *life*,' and here: 'a well of *living* waters'" (*Berachoth*
56b).[7,8]

a well of living waters - R. Yehoshua b. Levi said: "One who sees a well
in a dream should arise and say: 'a well of living waters,' before a
different verse comes to the fore, viz. (*Jeremiah* 6:7): 'As a well keeps its
water fresh, so she keeps fresh her wickedness' " (*Ibid.*).[9]

26:31   And they rose early in the morning, and they swore one to
        another, and Isaac sent them away, and they went from
        him in peace.

and they went from him in peace - This teaches us that reproof leads to
peace (*Sifrei, Devarim*).[10]

27:1   And it was, when Isaac became old, that his eyes became

dim from seeing, and he called Esau his elder son, and he
said to him: "My son," and he answered: "Here I am."

when Isaac became old - R. Chama b. R. Chanina said: "All the days of
our forefathers, they never stopped learning. Isaac continued learning in
his old age, as it is written: 'And it was, when Isaac became old' [*zaken* -
connoting old in learning]" (*Yoma* 28b).[1]

that his eyes became dim - R. Elazar said: "All who gaze upon the
features of an evildoer, their eyes become dim, as it is written: 'And it
was, when Isaac became old, that his eyes became dim *from seeing*', i.e.,
from looking upon the evil-doer, Esau" (*Megillah* 28a).[2]

27:4   And make me savory food, as I love, and bring it to me,
        and I will eat, so that my soul will bless you before I die.

and I will eat, so that my soul will bless you - From here it is derived
that he who makes a benediction must be in a joyful state (*Responsa,
Maharam* 354).[3]

27:9   Go to the flock, and take for me from there two good kids
        of goats, and I will make of them savory food for your
        father, as he loves.

kids of goats - From the verse: "Go to the flock and take for me from
there two good kids of goats," it may be derived that goats, too, can be
included in the designation "flock" [this has certain halachic
implications] (*Chullin* 137a, see *Tosefoth*).[4]

27:12   Perhaps my father will feel me, and I will be a deceiver in
        his eyes, and I will bring upon myself a curse and not a
        blessing.

Perhaps my father will feel me - R. Simlai expounded (*Proverbs* 15:1):
"'L-rd, who shall abide in Your tent? ... he who walks uprightly, and
acts justly, and speaks the truth in his heart, he whose tongue is not
habituated [to lying]' — this refers to our father Jacob, who said [in

aversion to dissimulation]: 'Perhaps my father will feel me' "
(*Makkoth*24a).[5]

a deceiver - R. Elazar said: "Those who are deceptive in their speech are
akin to idol-worshippers. It is written here: 'And I will be a *deceiver* in
his eyes, and elsewhere [in respect to idols] (*Jeremiah* 10:15): 'They are
vanity, the work of *deception* [... the portion of Jacob is not as these']"
(*Sanhedrin* 92a).[6]

27:15   And Rivkah took the choice garments of Esau, her elder
        son, which were with her in the house, and she clothed
        with them Jacob, her younger son.

the choice garments of Esau, her elder son - "Choice" in what respect?
He officiated in them in the high-priesthood (*Yerushalmi, Megillah*
1:11).[7]

27:16   And the skins of the kids of goats, she put upon his hands
        and upon the smooth of his neck.

kids of goats - The phrase implies that in this instance they are kids of
goats, from which we may infer that where "kids" in general are
mentioned, the reference may also be to the young of cows or of sheep
(*Chullin* 113b).[8]

27:22   And Jacob came near to Isaac his father, and he felt him.
        And he said: "The voice is the voice of Jacob, but the
        hands are the hands of Esau."

The voice, etc. - "The voice" [connoting Jacob's cry of pain] — this
relates to Andryonus Caesar, who killed in Alexandria, Egypt, six
hundred thousand 'on top of' six hundred thousand Jews, twice the
number of the Jews of the exodus. "The voice of Jacob" — this relates
to Aspasyanus Caesar, who killed in the city of Betar four million —
others say, forty million Jews. "And the hands are the hands of Esau"
— this relates to the kingdom of Rome, that destroyed our Temple, and
burned our sanctuary, and exiled us from our land (*Gittin* 57b).[9]

The voice, etc. - "The voice is the voice of Jacob" — there is no answered prayer wherein the seed of Jacob are not involved; "and the hands are the hands of Esau" — there is no military victory wherein the seed of Esau are not involved (*Ibid.*).[10]

The voice, etc. - It was taught: "Rebbe [R. Judah Hanasi] expounded: 'The voice of Jacob cried out at what was done to him at Betar by the hands of Esau' " (*Yerushalmi, Ta'anith* 4:5).[11]

27:27 And he drew near and he kissed him, and he smelled the odor of his garments, and he blessed him, saying: "See the odor of my son as the smell of a field that the L-rd has blessed."

the odor of his garments - R. Zeira said: "Read it not '*begadav*' ['garments'] but '*bogdav*' ['rebellers']" [i.e., even those Jews who are not entirely loyal give off a sweet savor because of the *mitzvoth* that they do observe] (*Sanhedrin* 37a).[12]

See the odor, etc. - This teaches us that Isaac saw the Temple built, destroyed, and rebuilt: "See the odor of my son" — built, as it is written [of the sacrifices]: "for a fragrant odor"; "as the smell of a field" — destroyed, as it is written (*Jeremiah* 26:18): "Zion shall be plowed as a field"; "that the L-rd has blessed" — rebuilt in time to come, as it is written (*Psalms* 133:3): "For there has the L-rd commanded blessing, life for evermore" (*Sifrei, Deuteronomy* 352).[13]

as the smell of a field - R. Yehudah said in the name of Rav: "As the smell of a field of apples" (*Ta'anith* 29b).[14]

27:28 And G-d will give you of the dew of heaven and of the fatness of the earth, and an abundance of corn and wine.

And G-d will give you - Isaac said to him: "What G-d gave to Abraham as a bequest is now given to you" (*Yerushalmi, Berachoth* 1:2).[15]

and wine - R. Kahana asked: "It ['wine']is written '*tirash*,' and we pronounce it '*tirosh*.' If one is judicious [in his drinking of wine], he becomes a *rosh* [head, chief]; if not, he becomes a *rash* [pauper]" (*Yoma* 76b).[16]

27:29   Peoples will serve you and nations will bow down to you; be a lord to your brothers, and there will bow down to you the sons of your mother. Those who curse you will be cursed, and those who bless you will be blessed.

Those who curse you will be cursed - A certain gentile once met R. Yishmael and blessed him. R. Yishmael responded: "What applies to you has already been said." A different gentile met him and cursed him: He responded: "What applies to you has already been said." At this, his students said to him: "Our master, you answered the second just as you answered the first!" To this he said: "But so it is written! 'Those who curse you will be cursed, and those who bless you will be blessed' " (*Yerushalmi, Berachoth* 8:8).[17]

27:33   And Isaac trembled a great trembling, and he said:"Who, then, is it who hunted venison, and brought it to me, and I ate of all before you came? And I blessed him, and he shall, indeed, be blessed."

and I ate of all - The Rabbis taught: "The Holy One Blessed be He caused Isaac to taste of what resembled the world to come, and he was not vulnerable to the evil inclination, the angel of death, or worms and maggots — it being said concerning him 'of *all*' " (*Bava Bathra* 17a).[18]

27:38   And Esau said to his father: "Do you have only one blessing, my father? Bless me, also, my father." And Esau lifted his voice, and he cried.

Do you have only one blessing? - The Rabbis taught: "Esau came with an irrefutable claim, as it is written: 'Do you have only one blessing, my father?' " (*Sanhedrin* 101b).[19]

27:41   And Esau hated Jacob because of the blessing that his father had blessed him. And Esau said in his heart: "When the days of mourning for my father are at hand, then I will kill Jacob my brother."

And Esau hated - The Saturnalia is a festival of the idol worshippers. What is signified by "*Saturnalia*"? *S*inah *t*munah, *s*onai, *n*okeim, ve*n*oteir [an acronymic for hidden hatred, hatred, revenge, and grudge-bearing], as it is written: "And Esau hated [Vayi*stom*] Jacob." And in Rome they call it the "Saturnalia of Esau" (*Yerushalmi, Avodah Zarah* 1:2).[20]

27:45 Until your brother's anger turns away from you, and he forgets what you have done to him. Then I will send and take you from there. Why should I lose both of you in one day?

in one day - [When Jacob was brought to be buried in the *Me'arat Hamachpelah*] Esau came and attempted to prevent the burial, at which Chushim, the son of Dan, took a pole and hit him over the head. The eyes of Esau came out and fell at the feet of Jacob. At that moment the prophecy of Rivkah was fulfilled, viz.: "Why should I lose both of you in one day" (*Sotah* 13a).[21]

28:9 And Esau went to Ishmael, and he took Machlath the daughter of Ishmael the son of Abraham, the sister of Nevayoth, in addition to his wives, for himself as a wife.

And Esau went to Ishmael - Rava said to Rabbah b. Mari: "Whence is derived the folk saying: 'The barren trees go to [i.e., grow alongside of] the barren reeds'?" He answered: "It is written in the Torah: 'And Esau went to Ishmael and took Machlath the daughter of Ishmael as a wife' " (*Bava Kamma* 92b).[1,2]

and he took Machlath - Now, was her name Machlath? Was it not Basmath? This teaches us that all of Esau's transgressions were forgiven [*nimchelu* (same root as *Machlath*)]. From here it is derived that a bridegroom's sins are forgiven (*Yerushalmi, Bikkurim* 3:3).[3]

the sister of Nevayoth - Do I not know that she was the sister of Nevayoth from "Machlath the daughter of Ishmael"? Why, then, "the sister of Nevayoth"? This teaches us that Ishmael [her father] betrothed her to Esau and died, so that Nevayoth [her brother] gave her in marriage to Esau (*Megillah* 17a).[4]

Vayetze

28:11 And he reached the place and he slept there, for the sun had set. And he took some stones from the place and put them by his head, and he slept in that place.

vayifga bamakom - It was taught: "Jacob instituted the evening prayer, as it is written: '*Vayifga bamakom* ["in that place"] and he slept there.' '*Pegiyah*' [as in*Vayifga*] connotes prayer, as it is written (*Jeremiah* 7:16): 'Therefore, do not pray ... and do not make intercession [*al tifgu*] to Me' " (*Berachoth* 26b).[5]

And he reached the place - The Rabbis taught: "The road 'quickened' for our father Jacob. It is written: 'And Jacob went out of Beersheva and he went to [arrived at] Charan,' and yet, it is afterwards written: 'And he reached the place' [Beth-el, which is before Charan]! — When he came to Charan, he said: 'Is it possible that I have passed the place where my father prayed [Beth-el] without praying there myself!' At this, he thought of returning there. As the thought of returning there went through his mind, immediately, the road 'quickened' for him, and 'He reached the place' " (*Sanhedrin* 95b).[6,7]

for the sun had set - After he had prayed, he sought to return to Charan, at which the Holy One Blessed be He said: "Can this righteous one come to My 'inn' and be allowed to leave without spending the night there! — whereupon, immediately, the sun set (*Ibid.*).[8]

some stones from the place - But further on, it is written (18): "And he took *the* stone"! How can this be? R. Yitzchak said: "This teaches us that all of the stones converged at one place [his head], each one saying: 'Let the righteous one place his head upon me!' And it was taught: 'They all fused into one stone' " (*Chullin* 91b).[9]

28:12 And he dreamed a dream, and, behold, a ladder set upon

the earth and its top reaching heaven, and, behold, angels
of G-d, ascending and descending upon it.

ascending and descending - It was taught: "How broad was the ladder?
Eight thousand parasangs. For it is written: 'And, behold, angels of
G—d, ascending and descending upon it' — two ascending and two
descending, making for four meeting at its breadth. And it is written of
an angel (*Daniel* 10:6): 'And his body was like the beryl,' and we learned
that the beryl is two thousand parasangs" (*Ibid.*).[10,11]

ascending and descending - It was taught: "They ascended and gazed at
the Heavenly 'image,' and then descended and gazed at the earthly
image [Jacob] and wanted to kill him [out of envy], whereupon,
immediately: 'And, behold, the L-rd was standing above him.' R.
Shimon b. Levi said: 'If it were not stated explicitly, it would be
impossible to say it — as a man who wards off adverse elements from
his son' " (*Ibid.*).[12]

28:13   And, behold, the L-rd was standing upon it, and He said:
"I am the L-rd, the G-d of Abraham your father and the
G-d of Isaac. The land that you are lying upon, I will give
it to you and to your children."

the G-d of Abraham, etc. - It was taught: "Why do we recite the
eighteen benedictions [*shemoneh esreh*] each day? R. Chanina said in
the name of R. Pinchas: 'Because of the eighteen times that our
forefathers, Abraham, Isaac, and Jacob are mentioned conjointly in the
Torah.' And if anyone will say to you: 'But they are so mentioned
nineteen times!' answer him that 'And let my name be called upon
them, and that of my father, Abraham and Isaac' is not included,
["Jacob" not being specifically mentioned here]" (*Yerushalmi,
Berachoth* 4:3][13,14]

that you are lying upon - What does this teach us? R. Yitzchak said:
"This teaches us that the Holy One Blessed be He folded up all of Eretz
Yisroel and placed it under our father Jacob, so that it would be easy for
his descendants to conquer it" (*Chullin* 91b).[15]

I will give it to you - It was taught: "The Holy One Blessed be He said to Moses: 'Woe for those who are lost but not forgotten! On several occasions I appeared to the forefathers, and they never doubted Me. I said to Jacob: 'The land that you are lying upon, I will give to you.' He desired to pitch his tent, but could find no land until he bought it for a hundred *kesitah*: and yet, he never doubted Me' " (*Sanhedrin* 111a).[16]

28:14   And your children will be as the dust of the earth, and you shall spread abroad, to the west and to the east, and to the north and to the south.

west and east - R. Yochanan said in the name of R. Yossi: "All who rejoice upon the Sabbath are given an unbounded inheritance, as it is written (*Isaiah* 58:14): 'Then you will rejoice in the L-rd, and He will feed you the inheritance of Jacob your father' — that [inheritance] of Jacob, concerning which it is written: 'And you shall spread abroad: to the west and to the east, and to the north and to the south' " (*Shabbath* 118b).[17]

28:17   And he was afraid, and he said: "How awesome is this place; this is not, none other than the house of G-d, and this is the gate of heaven."

How awesome, etc. - We are hereby taught that our father Jacob saw the Temple built, destroyed, and rebuilt in time to come. "How awesome is this place" — built; "this is not" — destroyed; "none other than the house of G-d" — rebuilt in time to come (*Sifrei, Devarim* 354).[18]

Beth-el ["the house of G-d"] - R. Elazar asked: "Why is it written (*Isaiah* 2:3): 'And many nations shall go and say: "Come, let us go up to the mountain of the L-rd, to the house of the G-d of Jacob"'? Why not 'the G—d of Abraham and Isaac'? — Not as Abraham, who called it a mountain, as it is written (22:14): 'In the mountain, the L-rd will be seen,' and not as Isaac, who saw it as a field, as it is written (24:63): 'And Isaac went out to pray in the field,' but as Jacob, who called it a house, as it is written: 'And he called the name of the place *Beth-el* ["the house of G-d"]' " (*Pesachim* 88a).[19]

28:20   And Jacob vowed a vow, saying: "If G-d will be with me, and will keep me in this way that I go, and give me bread to eat and clothing to wear,"

a vow, saying - What is the intent of "saying"? — Saying to future generations that they should offer vows in times of affliction (*Tosefoth Chullin* 2b, according to *Medrash Rabbah*).[20]

If G-d will be with me - Rabbeinu Meir ruled that a vow, an oath, and a handshake are binding even if they are conditional; for most of them are, indeed, of this conditional nature, viz.: "*If* G-d will be with me," and, similarly (*Numbers* 21:2): "*If* you give this people into my hands" (*Mordecai, Bava Kamma* IV).[21]

28:22   And this stone, which I have set up for a pillar, shall be the house of G-d, and all that You give me I will tithe unto You.

all that You give me - Though a man consecrate something which has not yet entered the world, still, if he says: "I take it upon myself to consecrate it," he must, because of this vow, consecrate it when it does materialize, as is borne out in the case of Jacob, who said: "And all that You give me I will tithe unto You," after which it is written (31:13): "which you vowed there unto Me as a vow" (*Rambam, Erchin* 6:31-33).[22]

I will tithe [lit., "I will tenth; I will tenth"] - It was taught: "One who gives more than the required amount of charity should not exceed that amount by more than a fifth, for he might come to be beholden to his fellows. Whence is this derived? From the verse: 'And all that You give me, I will tenth; I will tenth it [(two-tenths, or, one-fifth)] to You' " (*Kethuvoth* 50a).[23]

29:5   And he said to them: "Do you know Lavan the son of Nachor?" And they said: "We know."

Lavan the son of Nachor - From here [from the fact that he is called Lavan the son of Nachor (his grandfather) rather than Lavan the son of

Bethuel (his father)] it is derived that if one's father is a heretic he is called up for the Torah reading by his grandfather's name, and not by his name, alone, so that he not be humiliated [by the omission of a paternal name] (*Terumath Hadeshen* 51).[1]

29:12   And Jacob told Rachel that he is her father's brother, and that he is the son of Rivkah, and she ran and told her father.

that he is her father's brother - Now, was he her father's brother? Was he not the son of her father's sister [Rivkah]? — He asked her: "Will you marry me?" She answered: "Yes, but my father is a deceiver, and you will not be able to contend with him." At this, he said: "I am his brother [his equal] in deception" (*Megillah* 13b).[2]

29:17   And the eyes of Leah were worn, and Rachel was beautiful and well favored.

And the eyes of Leah were worn [lit., soft] - What is the intent of "worn"? If, literally, "worn," is it conceivable that the Torah would resort to circumlocution in order to avoid the degrading phrase "unclean beasts," as it is written (7:8) "and from the beasts that are not clean," and allow itself to speak degradingly of the righteous ones? How, then, is "worn" to be understood? Rav said: "She heard people saying: 'Rivkah has two sons, and Lavan, two daughters; the older son is intended for the older daughter, and the younger son for the younger daughter' " — whereupon she asked: "What is the older son like?" They replied: "He is a wicked man, who robs people." "And the younger one?" "He is an upright man, who resides in the tents [of learning]." She cried until the lids fell from her eyes (*Bava Bathra* 123a).[3]

29:25   And it was in the morning, and, behold, she was Leah. And he said to Lavan: "What did you do to me? Did I not serve you for Rachel? Why did you fool me?"

and, behold, she was Leah - And was she not Leah until now? —

Because of the tokens that Jacob had given to Rachel [so that Lavan not substitute Leah in the darkness], and which she, in turn, had given to Leah [so that she not be shamed in the situation she had been placed into], he had not recognized her until that time [when it became light] (*Megillah* 13b).[4]

29:27   Complete these seven days, and this one, too, will be given to you for the work with which you serve me seven additional years.

Complete these seven days - [of festivity in celebration of Leah's marriage]: It was taught: "Women are not married on the festival, so as not to intermix one rejoicing [that of the festival] with another [that of the marriage.] R. Yaakov derived this principle [of non-intermixture] from here: 'Complete these seven days [and only *then*] and this one [Rachel] too, will be given to you' " (*Yerushalmi, Moed Katan* 1:7).[5]

29:31   And the L-rd saw that Leah was hated, and He opened her womb, and Rachel was barren.

that Leah was hated - What is the intent of "was hated"? If it is to be understood literally, is it conceivable that the Torah would resort to circumlocution to avoid the degrading phrase "unclean beasts," as it is written (7:8): "and from the beasts that are not clean," and allow itself to speak degradingly of the righteous ones? But the meaning is, rather: that the Holy One Blessed be He saw that the deeds of Esau were hateful in her eyes [See 29:17], "and He opened her womb" (*Bava Bathra* 123a).[6]

and He opened her womb - It was taught: "R. Akiva said: 'Just as there is a key to a house, so there is a key to a woman, as it is written: 'And He opened her womb' " (*Bechoroth* 45a).[7]

29:32   And Leah conceived and bore a son, and she called him Reuven, saying: "For the L-rd has seen my affliction, and now my husband will love me."

and she called him "Reuven" [lit., "See the son"] - What is signified by the name "Reuven"? Leah said: "See the difference between my son and the son [Esau] of my father-in-law [Isaac.] For the son of my father-in-law, though he sold his birth-right willingly, it is written about him (27:41): 'And Esau hated Jacob,' whereas my son, though Joseph forcibly took the birth-right from him, as it is written (I *Chronicles* 5:1): 'But since he defiled his father's bed, his birth-right was given to the sons of Joseph' — still, he was not envious of him, as it is written (37:21): 'And Reuven heard, and he rescued him [Joseph] from their hands' " (*Berachoth* 7b).[8]

29:35   And she conceived again, and she bore a son, and she said: "This time I will thank the L-rd." Therefore, she called his name Yehudah, and she left off bearing.

I will thank the L-rd - R. Yochanan said in the name of R. Shimon b. Yochai: "From the day that the Holy One Blessed be He created the universe, no one had ever thanked Him, until Leah arrived upon the scene and thanked Him, as it is written: '*This time,* I will thank the L—rd' " (*Ibid.*).[9]

30:1   And Rachel saw that she had not borne to Jacob, and Rachel envied her sister, and she said to Jacob: "Give me children, and if not, I am dead."

and if not, I am dead - R. Yehoshua b. Levi said: "If one has no children, it is as if he is dead, as it is written: 'And if not, I am dead' " (*Nedarim* 64b).[1]

30:14   And Reuven went in the days of the wheat harvest and he found *dudaim* in the field, and he brought them to Leah his mother, and Rachel said to Leah: "Give me some of the *dudaim* of your son."

in the days of the wheat harvest - Of what significance is this? Rava b. R. Yitzchak said in the name of Rav: "We are hereby shown that the righteous ones do not stretch out their hands to take what is not theirs" [for only after the fields have been harvested is it permitted to glean from them] (*Sanhedrin* 99b).[2]

and he found dudaim - What are "*dudaim*"? Rav said: "Yavruchi"; Levi said: "Sigli"; R. Jonathan said: "Sviski" [all fragrant flowers] (*Ibid.*).[3]

30:16   And Jacob came from the field in the evening, and Leah went out to him, and she said: "Come to me, for I have hired you with my son's "*dudaim*"; and he lived with her that night.

and Leah went out to him - R. Shmuel b. Nachman said in the name of R. Jonathan: "A woman who solicits her husband [to live with her] for the sake of a *mitzvah* is rewarded with sons, the like of which did not exist even in the generation of Moses: for in relation to the generation of Moses it is written (*Deuteronomy* 1:13): 'Take for yourselves wise, understanding, well-known men,' after which it is written (15): 'And I took .. wise, well-known men,' — but he could not find 'understanding' men. In relation to Leah, however, concerning whom it is written: 'And Leah went out to him and said: 'Come to me' — of her children it is written (I *Chronicles* 12:33): 'And of the children of Issachar, knowers of *understanding* for the times, to know what Israel should do' " (*Eruvin* 100b).[4]

that night [lit., "in the night, He"] - What is the intent of: "And He lived with her in the night, He"? This teaches that the Holy One Blessed be He assisted in that union, as it is written (49:14): "*Issachar, chamor garem*" ["an ass brought about the birth of Issachar" (Jacob pursued a stray ass to the tent of Leah)] (*Niddah* 31a).[5]

that night [lit., "in the night, He"] - What is the intent of: "And He lived with her in the night, He"? In thought, as it were. He, alone, was privy to the fact that she did so only for the sake of establishing tribes (*Yerushalmi, Sotah* 3:4).[6]

30:21   And after, she bore a daughter, and she called her name Dinah.

And after, she bore a daughter - What is the intent of "and after"? After Leah had ruled in judgment over herself, saying: "Twelve tribes are destined to issue from Jacob. Six have issued from me, and four from the maidservants, so that there are now ten; and if this one I am bearing will be a male, my sister, Rachel, will not be on a par with one of the maidservants!" — whereupon, immediately, the fetus was transformed to a female, as it is written: "And she called her name *Dinah*" [judgment] (*Berachoth* 60a).[7]

30:22 And G-d remembered Rachel, and G-d listened to her, and He opened her womb.

And G-d remembered Rachel - It is written here: "And G-d *remembered*," and, in relation to Rosh Hashanah (*Leviticus* 23:24): "A *remembrance* of the shofar-blast" — whence it is derived that Rachel was remembered [for the bearing of children] on Rosh Hashanah (*Rosh Hashanah* 11a).[8]

and He opened her womb - R. Yochanan said: "The key of childbearing is in the hands of the Holy One Blessed be He, and is not given to a messenger, as it is written: 'And G-d remembered Rachel, and G-d listened to her and He opened her womb' " (*Ta'anith* 2a).[9]

30:24 And she called his name Joseph, saying: "The L-rd will add to me another son."

another son - She did not say "other sons," but "another son." It is seen from here that our mother Rachel was one of the first prophetesses, prophesying that she would bear only one more son [Benjamin] (*Yerushalmi, Berachoth* 9:5).[10]

30:25 And it was when Rachel had borne Joseph that Jacob said to Lavan: "Send me away, and I will go to my place and to my land."

when Rachel had borne, etc. - Why only after Joseph had been born did Jacob depart from Lavan's house? R. Shmuel b. Nachmani said:

"Because our father Jacob saw that Esau's children would be subdued only by those of Joseph, as it is written (*Ovadiah* 1:18): 'And the house of Jacob shall be fire; and the house of Joseph, a flame; and the house of Esau, stubble' " (*Bava Bathra* 123b).[11]

30:27   And Lavan said to him: "If I have found favor in your eyes, I have learned of signs that the L-rd blessed me for your sake."

that the L-rd blessed me for your sake - "Blessing follows upon the heels of Torah scholars, as it is written: 'I have learned of signs that the L-rd blessed me for your [Jacob's] sake' " (*Berachoth* 42a).[12]

31:4   And Jacob sent, and he called Rachel and Leah to the field, to his flock.

to the field - It was taught: R. Akiva said: 'I love the Medes [for their discretion], for when they take counsel with each other, they do so only in the field [where they cannot be overheard.]' R. Adda b. Ahava said: "Where in Scripture is this seen to be a desirable practice? — 'And Jacob sent, and called Rachel and Leah to the field' " (*Berachoth* 8b).[1]

31:6   And you know that I served your father with all my strength.

I served with all my strength - A worker must work with all his strength, for the righteous one, Jacob, said: "For I served your father with all my strength." He, therefore, was rewarded for his labors in this world, too, as it is written (30:43): "And the man [Jacob] prospered exceedingly" (*Rambam, Sechiruth* 13:17).[2]

31:24   And G-d came to Lavan the Aramite in a dream at night, and He said to him: "Take heed that you do not speak with Jacob from good to evil."

from good to evil - We can understand that Lavan should not speak evil to Jacob, but why not good? This teaches us that the good of the wicked is evil to the righteous. And what evil can arise here? He might promise him good in the name of his gods (*Yevamoth* 103b).[3]

31:35   And she said to her father: "Let it not anger my lord that I cannot rise before you, for I am in the way of women." And he searched, and he did not find the images.

the way of women [derech nashim] - Whence is derived the Persian term for a menstruating woman ["*dishtana*"]? From this verse: "For I am in the way of women" [*derech nashim* - giving the acronym "*dishtana*"] (*Avodah Zarah* 24b).[4]

31:38   This twenty years have I been with you. Your yews and she-goats have not cast their young, and the rams of your flock I have not eaten.

and the rams of your flock - Can the meaning be that he did not eat rams but he ate lambs! — The word "rams" is used to teach us that a one-day-old male sheep can be called a ram [for certain legal or ritual purposes] (*Bava Kamma* 65b).[5]

31:40   Thus I was: In the day, the drought consumed me, and in the night, the frost, and my sleep departed from my eyes.

Thus I was: In the day, the drought consumed me, etc. - It was taught: "Until what point is a hired watchman required to watch? Until the point of: 'Thus I was: In the day, the drought consumed me, and in the night, the frost' " (*Bava Metzia* 93b).[6]

31:43   And Lavan answered and he said to Jacob: "The daughters are my daughters and the sons are my sons and the sheep are my sheep, and all that you see belongs to me. And as to my daughters, what can I do for these today or for the children that they have borne?"

and the sons are my sons - "The sons are my sons and the sheep are my sheep" — "Just as the sheep are my sheep — for you bought them from me — so the sons are my sons — for you bought them from me [i.e., they were owned by me]" (*Yevamoth* 62b).[7]

31:47 And Lavan called it *Yegar Sehadutha*, and Jacob called it *galed.*

Yegar Sehadutha ["the heap of witness"] - It was taught: "The Targum in the Torah [as opposed to secular writings] must be rescued from a fire on the Sabbath. What is the "Targum in the Torah"? *"Yegar Sehadutha"* (*Shabbath* 115b).[8]

Yegar Sehadutha - If the Targum in the Torah is written in Hebrew, it does not cause ritual uncleanliness. Which Targum? *"Yegar Sehadutha."* [To end the practice of secreting *terumah* in the holy writings, and thus exposing them to desecration by rodents, the sages decreed that these writings produce ritual uncleanliness upon contact] (*Megillah* 9a).[9]

Yegar Sehadutha - R. Shmuel b. Nachmani said in the name of R. Jonathan: "Do not hold the Syrian tongue lightly, for it appears in the Torah. Where? '*Yegar Sehadutha*' " (*Yerushalmi, Sotah* 7:7).[10]

31:50 If you afflict my daughters, and if you take wives beside my daughters, no man is with us. See, G-d is witness between you and me.

If you afflict, etc. - "If you afflict" — by withholding their conjugal requirements: "And if you take" — rivals. From here it is derived that the withholding of the conjugal requirement is considered "affliction" (*Yoma* 77b).[11,12]

Vayishlach

32:8   And Jacob was greatly afraid, and he was distressed; and
he divided the people that were with him, and the flocks
and the cattle and the camels, into two camps.

And Jacob was afraid - R. Yaakov b. Iddi asked: "In one place it is
written (28:15): 'And I shall be with you [Jacob] and keep watch over
you wherever you go,' and, in another: 'And Jacob was afraid!' — He
thought to himself: 'Perhaps G-d's assurance is not fulfilled if I sin
afterwards' " (*Berachoth* 4a).[1]

32:9   And he said: "If Esau comes to the one camp and he
smites it, then the remaining camp will escape."

then the remaining camp will escape - It is written (I *Kings* 18:14):
"And it was, when Izevel cut off the prophets of the L-rd, that
Ovadyahu took a hundred prophets and hid fifty in a cave." Why fifty
[and not all in one cave]? R. Elazar answered: "He learned from Jacob,
as it is written: 'Then the remaining camp will escape' " (*Sanhedrin*
39b).[2,3]

32:11   I have become small from all of the lovingkindness and
from all of the truth that you have done with Your
servant. For with my staff I passed over this Jordan, and
now I have become two camps.

I have become small, etc. - R. Yanai said: "Let a man never put himself in a place of danger, and say that a miracle will be performed for him. Perhaps a miracle will not be performed for him; and if it is, it will be deducted from his merits. Whence is this derived? '*I have become small* from all of the lovingkindness and from all of the truth' " (*Shabbath* 31a).[4]

32:15   Two hundred she-goats and twenty he-goats, two hundred
        ewes and twenty rams.

Two hundred she-goats, etc. - R. Eliezer said: "He sent them according to the ability of the males to mate without becoming fatigued: two hundred she-goats and twenty he-goats — one for ten; two hundred ewes and twenty rams — one for ten; forty kine and ten bulls — one for four; twenty she-asses and ten foals — one for two, for the latter become more quickly fatigued" (*Yerushalmi, Kethuvoth* 3:7).[5,6]

two hundred ewes [rechelim] - Issi b. Hinni found R. Yochanan teaching his son: "The *halachah* of the first shorn wool [the priest's gift] obtains only in respect to *rechelim* [here used generically, as "sheep"]." Thereupon, Issi said to him: "Say '*recheloth.*' " R. Yochanan rejoined: "But is it not written: 'two hundred *rechelim*'?" Whereupon Issi replied: "Even so — the Torah speaks *its* language, and the sages, their own" (*Chullin* 137b).[7]

32:16   Thirty milch camels with their colts, forty cows and ten
        bulls, twenty she-asses and ten foals.

Thirty milch camels, etc. - [Why are the male camels not enumerated?] R. Berechyah said: "Because camels are modest in their copulation, the Torah did not speak of them openly in this respect" (*Yerushalmi, Kethuvoth* 5:7).[8]

32:25   And Jacob remained alone, and a man wrestled with him
        until the break of day.

And Jacob remained alone - R. Elazar said: "He remained to gather up some small utensils. From here we derive that the righteous value their possessions more than their persons [for he endangered himself by remaining there alone.] And why so? Because they recoil from stretching out their hand to steal" (*Chullin* 91a).[9]

and a man wrestled with him - R. Yitzchak said: "From here it is to be derived that a Torah scholar should not go out alone at night" (*Ibid.*).[10]

32:26 And he saw that he could not prevail against him, and he touched the hollow of his thigh, and the hollow of Jacob's thigh was put out of joint in wrestling with him.

in wrestling with him - R. Yehoshua b. Levi said: "This [the fact that the root of the word *beheavko* ("in wrestling") is *avak* (dust)] teaches us that the dust of their feet ascended to the Throne of Glory — it being written here '*beheavko immo*,' and elsewhere (*Nachum* 1:3): 'And the clouds are the dust [*avak*] of His feet' " (*Ibid.*).[11]

32:27 And he said: "Send me away, for the morning star has risen." And he said: "I will not send you unless you bless me."

for the morning star has risen - Jacob said to him: "Are you a thief or a gambler that you fear the morning star?" To this he answered: "I am an angel, and from the day that I was created, my time to sing praise to the L—rd did not arrive, until this moment" (*Chullin* 91b).[12]

32:29 And he said: "Your name will no longer be called Jacob, but Israel, for you have wrestled with G-d and with men, and you have overcome."

with G-d [Elokim] and with men [anashim] - He intimated to Jacob that two regents were destined to descend from him — the Chief of the Exile in Babylonia [alluded to by "*Elokim*"] and the *Nassi* in Eretz Yisroel [alluded to by "anashim."] The future exile was thus intimated to him (*Chullin* 92a).[13]

32:32   And the sun shone for him as he passed over Penuel, and
he limped on his thigh.

And the sun shone for him - Rav said: From here it is derived that a
Torah scholar should not go out alone at night (*Ibid.* 91b).[14]

And the sun shone for him - Did the sun shine for him alone? Did it not
shine for the whole world? R. Yitzchak answered: "The sun that had set
for him [so that he would abide there, viz. (28:11): "And he reclined
there for the sun had set"] now shone for him [to heal the wound he had
sustained] (*Chullin* 91b).[15]

32:33   Therefore, the children of Israel may not eat the thigh
sinew, which is upon the hollow of the thigh, to this day;
because he touched the hollow of Jacob's thigh in the
thigh sinew.

they may not not eat - R. Avahu said: "Wherever it is written: 'It may
not be eaten, etc.,' a prohibition both against eating and against the
derivation of benefit is implied." But is it not written with respect to the
thigh sinew: "They may not eat," in spite of which we learn: "A man
may send to a gentile a thigh containing the sinew because its location is
readily apparent [and it can be seen whether or not the sinew is
present]?" — R. Avahu holds that when the Torah permitted derivation
of benefit from *nevelah* [an animal not ritually slaughtered], it likewise
permitted such derivation of benefit from its fat and from its thigh sinew
(*Pesachim* 22a).[16,17]

they may not eat - The Rabbis taught: "The thigh sinew is considered
an organ. Therefore, if one eats it, even if it is not the size of an olive, he
is liable. And, even so, if it is the size of five or six olives and he eats the
size of but one olive from it, he is still responsible. Why? "Eating" is
written in relation to it, and the size of an olive constitutes eating
(*Chullin* 96b).[18]

the Children of Israel - R. Huna said: "The thigh sinew of a burnt
offering is extracted and flung onto the ash pile of the altar, for it is
written: 'The Children of Israel may not eat the thigh sinew,' and
elsewhere it is written (*Ezekiel* 45:15): 'From the well-watered pastures

of *Israel* [for a meal offering and for a *burnt offering* ... '] — from which it is derived that only what is permitted to be eaten by a Jew may be a burnt offering" (*Chullin* 90b).[19,20]

the Children of Israel - The Rabbis taught: "The prohibition against the thigh sinew obtains only in a clean animal and not in an unclean one. And though it was prohibited to the children of Jacob, at which time an unclean animal was permitted, even so, it was reiterated at Mount Sinai, at which time unclean animals were forbidden. It was written in its place only to teach us the *reason* for which it was prohibited. Know this to be true, for it is not written: 'Therefore, the children of *Jacob* may not eat,' but 'the Children of Israel' and they were not called 'the Children of *Israel*', until Sinai" (*Ibid.* 91a).[21]

the thigh sinew - R. Yehoshua b. Levi asked: "Why is the thigh sinew called '*gid hanasheh*' ["the sinew of slipping"]? Because it slipped from its place and went up, as it is written (*Jeremiah* 50:30): 'Their strength slipped away [*nashethah*]; they have become like women' " (*Ibid.* 91a).[22]

the thigh sinew - The Rabbis taught: "One who eats of the thigh sinew of an unclean animal is not liable, for it is written: 'The Children of Israel may not eat the thigh sinew.' This implies an animal whose thigh sinew would be forbidden though its flesh is permitted, and excludes an unclean animal, whose thigh sinew would be forbidden and its flesh forbidden" (*Ibid.* 101a).[23]

which is upon the hollow of the thigh - Shmuel said: "The Torah forbade only that which is on the hollow alone [and not that part of the sinew which extends beyond it], as it is written: 'which is upon the hollow of the thigh' " (*Ibid.*).[24]

the hollow of the thigh - It was taught: "The prohibition of the thigh sinew obtains in a *kowi* [an animal of doubtful genus]. Why so? The Torah made the thigh sinew the criterion for prohibition, and it *does* possess a thigh sinew (*Krituth* 21a).[25]

the thigh - Why "*the* thigh"? This teaches us that only that sinew is meant which extends over the entire thigh — to exclude the outer sinew, which is not forbidden (*Chullin* 91a).[26]

because he touched the hollow - It was taught [that the thigh sinew of a bird is permitted] Why so? Because it is written: "the hollow" — to exclude a bird, which has no hollow (*Ibid.* 96b).[27]

33:2   And he put the handmaids and their children first, and Leah and her children after, and Rachel and Joseph after.

Leah and her children [acharonim] - From here it is to be derived that it is the custom of Scripture to refer to the middle ones, too, as "*acharonim*" [lit., "the last"], for after Leah and her children it is written: "And Joseph and Rachel" (*Tosefoth Yomtov, Demai* 7:3).[1]

33:3   And he passed before them, and he bowed down to the ground seven times until he drew near to his brother.

And he passed before them - R. Yehudah said in the name of Shmuel: "The benedictions for all *mitzvoth* are to be recited immediately before ["*over*"] performing them." How do we know that "*over*" has the sense of "immediately before"? Abbaye answered: "For it is written: 'And he passed ["*over*"] before them' " (*Pesachim* 7b).[2]

33:10   And Jacob said: "I beg you, no. If I have found favor in your eyes, then take my present from my hand; for I have, therefore, seen your face as one sees the face of G-d, and you have favored me."

as one sees the face of G-d - R. Shimon b. Lakish expounded: "It is permitted to flatter the wicked in this world, as it is written: 'For I have, therefore, seen your face as one sees the face of G-d' " (*Sotah* 41b).[3]

as one sees the face of G-d - What is the intent of "as one sees the face of G-d"? R. Levi said: "This is analogous to the situation of a man who was invited to the home of his friend, and who perceived that the latter sought to kill him — whereupon he said to him: 'This dish tastes like the one I ate in the king's palace.' The latter, upon hearing this said to himself: 'He is acquainted with the king,' and, fearing him, did not kill him" (*Ibid.*).[4]

33:11   Take my blessing that is brought to you, for G-d has been
gracious to me and because I have everything. And he
urged him, and he took it.

and because I have everything - The Rabbis taught: "The Holy One
Blessed be He caused Jacob to taste of what resembled the World to
Come, and he was not vulnerable to the evil inclination, the Angel of
Death, or worms and maggots — as it is written of him: 'And because I
have *everything'* " (*Bava Bathra* 17a).[5]

33:12   And he said: "Come, let us go, and I will walk alongside
you."

and I will walk alongside you - When R. Yehoshua b. Chanina was on
his death-bed the Rabbis asked him: "What will now become of us at
the hands of the Sadducees?" Whereupon he answered: "When counsel
departs from Israel, wisdom departs from the gentiles, as it is written:
'And he [Esau] said: "Come, let us go, and I will walk alongside
you"'" [the implication being that they parallel each other] (*Chagigah*
5b).[6,7]

and I will walk alongside you - It was taught: "For twenty-two years the
Romans kept their faith with the Jews, and in the end, they subjugated
them — in the beginning, abiding by 'Come, let us go, and I will walk
alongside you,' and in the end, by (14): 'Let my lord [Esau] pass before
his servant [Jacob]' " (*Avodah Zarah* 8b).[8]

33:14   Let my lord, I pray you, pass before his servant; and I will
lead on slowly according to the pace of the cattle that goes
before me and according to the children, until I come to
my lord, to Seir.

to my lord, to Seir - The Rabbis taught: "If a Jew meets a gentile on the
way, and the latter asks him where he is going, let the Jew 'widen the
way' for him, as Jacob our father did with Esau — as it is written: 'Until
I come to my lord, to Seir' — whereas it is later written (*Ibid.* 17): 'And
Jacob traveled to Succoth' " [and not so far as Seir] (*Ibid. 25b*).[9]

to my lord, to Seir - R. Huna said: "But we do not find that Jacob our father went to Seir!" It is, however, as R. Yuden said in the name of Rav: "Jacob was intimating to Esau what would come to pass in time to come, as it is written (*Ovadiah* 1:21): 'And liberators shall ascend to Mount Zion to judge the mountain of Esau [*Seir*]' " (*Yerushalmi, Avodah Zarah* 2:1).[10]

33:17   And Jacob traveled to Succoth, and he built a house for himself; and for his cattle he made booths. Therefore, the place is called Succoth.

And Jacob traveled, etc. - It was taught: "He left Aram Naharayim and came to Succoth, where he sojourned eighteen months, as it is written: 'And Jacob traveled to Succoth [lit., "booths", intimating a six-month summer residence] and he built a *house* for himself [intimating a six-month winter residence] and for his cattle he made booths [intimating an addtional six-month summer residence]' " (*Megillah* 17a).[11]

33:18   And Jacob came complete to the city of Shechem, which is in the land of Canaan, and he encamped before the city.

And Jacob came complete - Rav said: "Complete in his body, complete in his wealth, complete in his Torah" (*Shabbath* 33a).[12]

and he encamped - What is the intent of "and he encamped"? Rav said: "He instituted currency for them." Shmuel said: "He instituted market-places for them." R. Yochanan said: "He instituted bath-houses for them" (*Ibid.*).[13]

and he encamped - What did he do? He set up shops and sold cheap. From this it is to be dervied that we are obligated to make improvements [in our host community], as our forefathers did (*Yerushalmi, Shevi'ith* 9:1).[14,15]

33:19   And he bought the piece of land on which he had pitched his tent from the sons of Chamor, the father of Shechem, for one hundred *kesitah*.

for one hundred kesitah - R. Akiva said: "When I went to Africa, they called a *ma'ah* a *kesitah*." What difference does this make? To interpret the "one hundred *kesitah*" of Scripture as one hundred *danki (Rosh Hashanah* 26a).[16]

33:20   And he erected there an altar, and He called him "powerful one" — the G-d of Israel.

powerful one, the G-d of Israel - R. Elazar said: "How do we know that the Holy One Blessed be He called Yaakov "*el*" ["powerful one"]? Because it is written: '*Vayikra lo el Elokei Yisroel*.' For if you assume that Yaakov called the altar "*El*", we should have: "*Vayikra lo Yaakov* ... " ["And *Yaakov* called it ... "] The meaning then must be that He called Yaakov "*el*." And who called him "*el*"? "*Elokei Yisroel*" [the G—d of Israel]" (*Megillah* 18a).[17]

34:1   And Dinah, the daughter of Leah, went out to see the daughters of the land.

And Dinah, the daughter of Leah, went out - Now was our mother Leah a harlot [that she is brought into this context of rape?] — But because it is written (30:16): "*And Leah went out to him*," we relate Dinah's going out to Leah's going out (*Yerushalmi, Sanhedrin* 2:6).[1,2]

34:2   And Shechem, the son of Chamor the Hittite, the prince of the land, saw her, and he took her, and he lay with her, and he afflicted her.

and he afflicted her - What is the intent of "And he afflicted her"? He afflicted her through abnormal intercourse (*Yoma* 77b).[3]

34:7   And the sons of Jacob came from the field when they heard. And the men were saddened, and it angered them greatly, because he had done a vile thing in Israel, to lie with the daughter of Jacob, and such could not be done.

when they heard - R. Tanchum said: "This verse is not explicit: 'And the sons of Jacob came from the field when they heard'? Or 'When they heard, the men were saddened'?" (*Yerushalmi, Avodah Zarah* 2:7).[4]

because he had done a vile thing - There are some who say that Job lived in the days of Jacob and married Dinah, Jacob's daughter; for it is written (*Job* 2:10): "You speak as one of the vile women," and here: "Because he had done a vile thing" (*Bava Bathra* 15b).[5]

34:15   Only with this we will satisfy you, if you will be as we are, to circumcise all of your males.

we will satisfy you ["naoth lachem"] - From here we can deduce that the correct reading is: "The benediction over the *havdalah* candle of Sabbath is not made until satisfaction may be derived ["sheyaotho" (with an *aleph*)] from its light, and not with an *ayin* [which would connote: "until the time difference between day and night would be discernible"] (*Yerushalmi, Berachoth* 8:6).[6]

34:25   And it was on the third day, when they were in pain, that the sons of Jacob, Shimon and Levi, the brothers of Dinah, took each man his sword and came into the city secure, and slew all the males.

on the third day - Whence is it deduced that a child is bathed on the third day of its circumcision, even if it falls on the Sabbath? From the verse: "And it was on the third day, when they were in pain" (*Shabbath* 86a).[7]

when they were in pain - We do not have "behiyotham *coaiv*" [singular, "when they were in *pain*"], but "behiyotham *coavim*" [plural, lit., "when they were in *pains*."] This teaches us that all of their limbs were in pain. We thus bathe the entire body of a child on the third day after its circumcision, even if it falls on the Sabbath (*Yerushalmi, Shabbath* 13:3).[8]

Shimon and Levi, each man his sword - Nowhere in the Torah do we find anyone under thirteen being referred to as "*ish*," ["a man"]; but we do find a thirteen-year-old being referred to as "a man," for it is written: "Shimon and Levi, each *man*, his sword" — and we have learned that at that time they were thirteen [that is, Levi, the younger brother, was thirteen] (*Nazir* 29b, see Rashi).[9]

35:2   And Jacob said to his household and all that were with him: "Remove the strange gods that are in your midst, and purify yourselves, and change your garments."

and purify yourselves - This teaches us that idols produce uncleanliness, and that one who separates himself from them requires ritual immersion (*Semag* 2:240).[1]

35:3   And let us arise and go up to Beth-el, and I will make there an altar to the Almighty, who answers me in the day of my affliction, and who was with me in the way in which I went.

to the Almighty [El] who answers me - R. Yochanan said: "Wherever the Sadducees find room for heretical questioning, their answer is at their side. They questioned heretically in relation to the verse (*Ibid.* 7): 'For there *Elokim* [lit., plural of *El*] revealed Himself to him.' Their answer is at their side: 'To the Almighty ["*El*," singular], who answers me' " (*Sanhedrin* 38b).[2]

35:4   And they gave to Jacob all of the strange gods that were in their hands and the rings that were in their ears, and Jacob hid them under the terebinth which is near Shechem.

and Jacob hid them - R. Yishmael b. R. Yossi went to a certain mountain. When some Cuthites approached him, he said to them: "You are not bowing down to the mountain, but to the images beneath it, as it is written: 'And Jacob hid them under the terebinth which is near Shechem' " (*Yerushalmi, Avodah Zarah* 5:4).[3]

35:10   And G-d said to him: "Your name will no longer be called

Yaakov, but Yisrael will be your name"; and He called his name Yisrael.

will no longer be called, etc. - It was taught: "Your name will no longer be called 'Yaakov,' but 'Yisrael' will be your name" — not that "Yaakov" is to be entirely eliminated, but that "Yisrael" is to be primary and "Yaakov" secondary (*Berachoth* 13a).[4]

will no longer be called, etc. - It was taught: "One who calls Jacob "Yaakov" does not, thereby, violate a negative commandment of: 'Your name will no longer be called Yaakov.' Why so? Because Scripture itself reverts to it, as it is written (46:2): 'And G-d spoke to Yisrael in a vision of the night, and He said: "Yaakov, Yaakov" ' " (*Ibid.*).[5]

35:11   And G-d said to him: "I am the Almighty G-d; be fruitful and multiply. A nation and a congregation of nations shall issue from you, and kings shall come forth from your loins."

I am the Almighty G-d ["Shakkai"] (actually written with *d* in place of *k*) - Resh Lakish said: "What is the intent of 'I am the Almighty G-d [Shakkai]'? The Holy One Blessed be He said: 'I am the one who said to the universe: "Dai!" ' ["Enough!", i.e., Extend yourself no further] (*Chagigah* 12a).[6]

be fruitful and multiply - It was taught: "The *mitzvah* of procreation attaches to the man and not to the woman. Whence do we derive this? R. Yosef said: From the verse: 'And G-d said to him: "Be fruitful and multiply" [*preh ureveh*, (singular), and not *pruh urevuh* (plural)]' " (*Yevamoth* 65b).[7]

35:18   And it was as her soul departed in death that she called his name Ben-oni; and his father called him Binyamin.

Binyamin - Throughout the Torah Binyamin is written defective [without the *yod* before the final *nun*], except here, where it is written *plene* (*Sotah* 36b).[8]

35:22   And it was, when Israel dwelt in that land that Reuven
went and lay with Bilhah, his father's concubine, and
Israel heard, and the sons of Jacob were twelve.

And it was, when Israel dwelt - The episode of Reuven is read, but not
translated for the congregation. Once, when R. Chanina b. Gamliel
went to Cubul, and the reader read: "And it was when Israel dwelt," he
said to the translator, translate the last phrase only ["And the sons of
Jacob were twelve"] — and the sages praised him for this (*Megillah* 25
b).[9,10]

and he lay, etc. - R. Shmuel b. Nachmani said in the name of R.
Jonathan: "Anyone who says that Reuven sinned is making a mistake.
How, then, are we to understand: 'And he lay with Bilhah, his father's
concubine'? This teaches us that he transfered his father's bed [from the
tent of Bilhah to that of his mother, Leah], and the Torah considers this
as if he had lived with her" (*Shabbath* 55b).[11,12]

and he lay, etc. - It was taught: "R. Shimon b. Elazar said: 'That
righteous one [Reuven] was spared from that sin. How, then, are we to
understand: 'And he lay with Bilhah his father's concubine'? He stood
up against his mother's shame, saying: 'If my mother's sister [Rachel]
was my mother's rival, must the maidservant of my mother's sister
[Bilhah] also be my mother's rival!' — whereupon he arose, and
transfered her bed" (*Ibid.*).[13,14]

and he lay, etc. - It was taught: "Others say: "He transfered two beds —
one, that of the *Shechinah* [the Divine Presence]; the other, that of his
father, as it is written (49:4): 'Then you defiled my bed by ascending it.'
Read it not *yetzui* [my *bed*] but *yetzuai* [my *beds*]" (*Ibid.*).[15]

and the sons of Jacob were twelve - R. Shmuel b. Nachmani said in the
name of R. Jonathan: "Anyone who says that Reuven sinned is making
a mistake, for it is written: 'And the sons of Jacob were twelve,' which
teaches us that they were all considered as one [in holiness]" (*Ibid.*).[16]

36:12   And Timna was a concubine to Elifaz the son of Esau, and
she bore to Elifaz, Amalek. These are the sons of Addah,
Esau's wife.

And Timna was a concubine to Elifaz - What is the significance of this? Timna was a daughter of royalty, as it is written: "The chief of Lotan was Timna," and every "chief" connotes a king-without-crown. Desiring to become a convert, she went to Abraham, Isaac, and Jacob; but they did not accept her. She thereupon went and became the concubine of Elifaz, son of Esau, saying: "Better be a maidservant to this nation than a princess to another." In the end, Amalek issued from her. Why so? Because they should not have rejected her (*Sanhedrin* 99b).[1,2]

36:20   These are the sons of Seir the Chori, the inhabitants of the land: Lotan and Shoval and Tzivon and Anah.

the inhabitants of the land - Were all the others the inhabitants of heaven? The intent is that they were expert in all that related to the habitation of the land, being able to say: "This plot of land is suitable for olives; this, for grapes; this, for figs" (*Shabbath* 85a).[3]

36:24   These are the sons of Tzivon: Ayah and Anah. He is Anah, who found the mules in the wilderness as he grazed the asses of Tzivon his father.

These are the sons of Tzivon: Ayah and Anah - Here it is written: "And these are the sons of Tzivon: Ayah and Anah," and elsewhere (*Ibid.* 20): "And these are the sons of Seir: Tzivon and Anah" [implying that Anah was Tzivon's brother and *not* his son.] How can this be? This teaches us that Tzivon lived with his mother and begot Anah. But may it not be that there were two Anahs? No, for the verse states: "He is Anah," i.e., the same Anah mentioned before (*Bava Bathra* 115b).[4-6]

He is Anah, etc. - It was taught: "R. Shimon b. Gamliel said: 'There were mules in the days of Anah, as it is written: "He is Anah, who found the mules in the wilderness." ' " The exegetes of obscure verses said: "Anah himself was the issue of incest, and he, therefore, brought such a creature into the world [a mule being the offspring of a horse and an ass]" (*Pesachim* 54a).[7-9]

the mules [yemim] - R. Yehoshua b. Levi said: "Why are mules called '*yemim*'? Because they cast fear [*eimah*] upon all men. As R. Chanina said: 'No one who ever consulted me about the blow of a white mule recovered' " (*Chullin* 7b).[10]

the mules [yemim] - What are *yemim*? R. Yehudah b. Simon said: "*Hemyonus*" [Gr., a mule], and the Rabbis said: "*Hemisu*", half horse-half ass" (*Yerushalmi, Berachoth* 8:5).[11]

36:43 The chief Magdiel, the chief Iram. These are the chiefs of Edom according to their settlements in the land of their possession. He is Esau the father of Edom.

He is Esau - He persists in his wickedness, from the beginning until the end (*Megillah* 11a).[12]

Vayeshev

37:1   And Jacob dwelt in the land of his father's sojournings, in the land of Canaan.

And Jacob dwelt - R. Yochanan said: "Wherever '*Vayeshev*' ["and he dwelt"] is written, it connotes distress, viz.: 'And Jaob dwelt in the land of his father's sojourning'; — after which it is written: 'And Joseph brought evil reports of them ... ' " (*Sanhedrin* 106a).[1]

37:2   These are the generations of Jacob. Joseph was seventeen years old, and he grazed the flock with his brothers. And the lad was with the sons of Bilhah and the sons of Zilpah, the wives of his father. And Joseph brought evil report of them to their father.

These are the generations, etc. — It was taught: "Joseph was great enough to have twelve tribes issue from him, just as they issued from Jacob, as it is written: 'These are the generations of Jacob - Joseph' [indicating an equality between Joseph and Jacob], but semen issued from between the [ten] fingers of his hands [accounting for a reduction of ten tribes, leaving only two, Joseph's sons, Ephraim and Menashe (See commentary on 49:24)]. Notwithstanding this, however, they [the other ten] issued from his brother, Benjamin, and all were called by his name" [See commentary on 46:21] (*Sotah* 36b).[2-4]

These are the generations, etc. - R. Jonathan said: "It would have been befitting for the first-born to issue from Rachel, for it is written: 'These are the generations of Jacob - Joseph,' but Leah pre-empted her through her implorations" (*Bava Bathra* 123a).[5]

These are the generations, etc. - Should it not have been written: 'These are the generations of Jacob - Reuven'? Why 'Joseph'? But, just as Jacob was born circumcised [see commentary on 25:27], so Joseph was born circumcised (*Avoth d'R. Nathan* 2).[6]

seventeen years old - R. Levi said: "One should sustain hope for as long as twenty-two years for the materialization of a good dream; for it is written: 'Joseph was seventeen years old,' then (41:46): 'Joseph was thirty years old when he stood before Pharaoh,' giving us thirteen years, which, together with the seven years of plenty and two years of famine [(45:6): 'For two years the famine has been in the land'] give us twenty-two [at which time Joseph revealed himself to his brothers and the dream was fulfilled]" (*Berachoth* 55b).[7]

evil report of them - What did he say? R. Meir said: "He said: 'They are to be suspected of eating meat torn from living animals [*eiver min hachai*].' R. Yehudah said: "He said: 'They are demeaning the children of the maidservants and treating them as slaves.' R. Shimon said: "He said: 'They are gazing at the daughters of the land.' R. Yehudah b. Pazzi said: "It is written (*Proverbs* 16:11): 'A just weight and balance ["measure for measure"] are the L-rd's' — The Holy One Blessed be He said: 'He says they are to be suspected of eating meat torn from living animals - I will demonstrate otherwise (37:31): "And they *slaughtered* a he-goat"; he says that they demean the children of the maidservants — (*Psalms* 105:17): "Joseph was sold for a servant"; he says that they gaze at the daughters of the land — "The 'bear' will be loosed against you," as it is written (39:7): "And the wife of his master lifted her eyes to Joseph""" (*Yerushalmi, Peah* 1:1).[8,9]

37:3   And Israel loved Joseph more than all his sons, for he was the son of his old age, and he made him a coat of many colors.

a coat of many colors - R. Chama b. Guria said in the name of Rav: "One should never show favoritism to one son above the other, for because of the additional expenditure of the weight of two coins of fine wool for the many-colored coat that Jacob made for Joseph, beyond what he spent for his other sons, his brothers envied him, and the end result was that our forefathers went down to Egypt" (*Shabbath* 10b).[10,11]

37:9   And he dreamed yet another dream, and he told it to his brothers, saying: "Behold, I dreamed another dream, and, behold, the sun and the moon and eleven stars bowed down to me."

and, behold, the sun and the moon - R. Berechyah said: "Though part of a dream is substantiated, the entire dream is not. Whence is this derived? From Joseph, in respect to whom it is written: 'And, behold, the sun and the moon bowed down to me'; and at that time, his mother [symbolized by the moon] was not alive" (*Berachoth* 55a).[12]

37:10   And he told it to his father and to his brothers, and his father rebuked him and said to him: "What is this dream that you have dreamed? Shall I and your mother and your brothers, indeed, come to bow down to you upon the earth?"

to bow down to you, upon the earth - The Rabbis taught "*Hishtachavaah* [bowing down] connotes prostration upon the earth with outstretched hands and feet, as it is written: 'to bow down [*lehishtachavoth*] to you, upon the earth' " (*Ibid.* 34b).[13]

37:12   And his brothers went to graze the sheep of their father in Shechem.

to graze the sheep [eth hatzon] - There are dots on the word "*eth*", to teach us that they did not go to graze the sheep, but to eat, and drink, and indulge themselves (*Avoth d'R. Nathan* 34).[14]

37:14   And he said to him: "Go and see the peace of your brothers and the peace of the sheep, and return word to me." And he sent him from the valley of Chevron and he came to Shechem.

Go and see - The Rabbis taught: "Go and see [when it is possible to see, i.e., by day] the peace of your brothers" — this teaches us that a Torah scholar should not go out alone at night" (*Chullin* 91b).[15]

And he sent him from the valley [lit., "depth"] **of Chevron** - R. Chanina b. Pappa said: "Through the deep counsel of that righteous one [Abraham] who was buried in Chevron — as it is written (15:13): 'You will, indeed, know that your children will be strangers in a foreign land'" (*Sotah* 11a).[16]

and he came to Shechem - It was taught in the name of R. Yossi: "A place set aside for trouble: in Shechem, Dinah was violated; in Shechem, Joseph was sold; in Shechem, the kingdom of David was divided" (*Sanhedrin* 107a).[17]

37:21   And Reuven heard and rescued him from their hands, and he said: "Let us not kill him."

And Reuven heard - R. Tanchum b. Chanilai said: "Why did the tribe of Reuven merit being reckoned first [for the cities of refuge]? Because Reuven initiated the rescue, as it is written: 'And Reuven heard, and rescued him from their hands' " (*Makkoth* 10a).[18]

37:22   And Reuven said to them: "Do not spill blood. Cast him into this pit, which is in the desert; but do not send a hand against him," to rescue him from their hands, to return him to his father.

to rescue him - From this it is to be derived that it is proper to write about and publicize the doer of a *mitzvah*, for the Torah publicized the *mitzvah* of Reuven, who thought to rescue Joseph and return him to his father (*Responsa, Rashba* 981).[19]

37:24   And they took him, and they cast him into the pit. And the pit was empty; it contained no water.

And the pit was empty; it contained no water - R. Nathan b. Minyumi expounded in the name of R. Tanchum: " 'And the pit was empty; it contained no water' — From the phrase: 'and the pit was empty,' can I not myself infer that it contained no water? Why must the Torah tell me: 'it contained no water'? This is to teach us that it contained no water, but it did contain snakes and scorpions" (*Shabbath* 22a).[20]

37:26   And Judah said to his brothers: "What profit is there in killing our brother and covering his blood?"

What profit - It was taught: "R. Meir said: 'Anyone who blesses Judah, who said: "What profit is there in killing our brother", rebuffs the L-rd; and in this regard it is written (*Psalms* 10:3); 'And he who blesses the compromiser rebuffs the L-rd' " (*Sanhedrin* 6b).[21]

37:28   Then there passed by Midianite men, merchants; and they pulled and they raised Joseph from the pit. And they sold Joseph to the Ishmaelites for twenty pieces of silver, and they brought Joseph to Egypt.

and they pulled and they raised - From here it is to be derived that pulling does not effect acquisition until the object is removed from its place (*Gates of R. Hai Gaon, Gate* 16).[22]

for twenty pieces of silver - R. Shimon b. Lakish said [Why did the Torah require five *shekalim* for the redemption of the first-born?]: "Because the first-born of Rachel was sold for twenty pieces of silver [the equivalent of five *shekalim*.] Therefore, everyone redeems his first-born son with twenty pieces of silver" (*Yerushalmi, Shekalim* 2:3).[23]

for twenty pieces of silver - R. Levi said: "How much fell to the lot of each of them? A *taba'ah*, the equivalent of half a *shekel*. The Torah, therefore, required that each one give his half-*shekel taba'ah* [as an atonement when Israel is counted (see *Exodus* 30:15)]" (*Ibid.*).[24]

37:35   And all his sons and all his daughters arose to comfort him, but he refused to be comforted, and he said: "For I will go down to my son mourning into Sheol." And his father cried over him.

but he refused to be comforted - Why so? Because one does not "assimilate" consolation for a living person; but a dead person is [eventually] forgotten from one's heart, as it is written (*Psalms* 31:13): "I have been forgotten, as a dead man, from the heart" (*Soferim* 21).[25]

37:36   And the Midianites sold him to Egypt, to Potiphar, Pharaoh's chamberlain, the chief steward.

And the Midianites sold him - It was taught; "Not for naught did Pinchas go out [as commander] to war against the Midianites [*Numbers* 31:6], but in order to exact payment for what they did to his mother's father, as it is written: 'And the Midianites sold him' " (*Sotah* 43a).[26]

38:1   And it was at that time that Judah went down from his brothers, and he turned to an Adulamite man whose name was Chirah.

And it was at that time - "And it was at that time that Judah went down from his brothers." It was taught in the name of R. Yossi: "It was a time set aside for distress" (*Sanhedrin* 102a).[1]

that Judah went down - R. Elazar said: "If someone does a *mitzvah* and does not finish it, and someone else comes and finishes it, he [the first] is brought down from his greatness, as it is written: 'And it was at that time that Judah 'went down from his brothers [having initiated Joseph's rescue, but not having consummated it]' " (*Sotah* 13b).[2]

38:2   And Judah saw there the daughter of a Canaanite, whose name was Shua, and he took her and lived with her.

the daughter of a Canaanite - What is meant by "Canaanite"? If, literally, a Canaanite, is it possible that after Abraham had warned Isaac [against marrying a Canaanite] and Isaac had warned Jacob, that Judah would go and marry a Canaanite! The meaning must be, then, "the daughter of a merchant," as we find (*Isaiah* 23:8): "whose dealers are princes, whose merchants [*kinanehah* (from "Canaan")] are the honorable men of the earth" (*Pesachim* 50a).[3]

38:7   And Er, the first-born of Judah, was evil in the sight of the L-rd, and the L-rd killed him.

and the L-rd killed him - It was taught: "Er, too, destroyed his semen":

How do we know this? R. Nachman b. Yitzchak said: "For it is written (*Ibid.* 10): 'And He killed him [Onan] *too*' — the implication being that Onan incurred the death penalty for the same reason as Er" [and since, in relation to Onan, we have (9): "And he destroyed [his semen] upon the ground," we deduce that Er was guilty of the same offense (*Yevamoth* 34b).[4]

38:9   And Onan knew that the seed would not be his, and it was when he came to his brother's wife that he destroyed [his semen] upon the ground.

he destroyed [his semen] upon the ground - He "threshed" inside [in the womb] and "winnowed" outside [upon the ground] (*Ibid.*)[5]

38:10   And it was evil in the eyes of the L-rd, what he had done, and He killed him, too.

And it was evil in the eyes of the L-rd - R. Ami said: "Whoever arouses licentious thought in himself is not admitted into the domain of the Holy One Blessed be He, it being written here: 'And it was evil in the eyes of the L-rd,' and elsewhere (*Psalms* 5:4): 'For You are not a G-d who desires evildoers; evil shall not dwell with You' " (*Niddah* 13b).[6]

and He killed him, too - R. Yochanan said: "One who emits semen in vain incurs the penalty of death, as it is written: 'And what he did was evil in the eyes of the L-rd, and He killed him, too' " (*Ibid.*).[7]

38:11   And Judah said to Tamar, his daughter-in-law: "Remain a widow in your father's house until Shelah, my son, is grown." For he said: "Lest he, too, die, as his brothers." And she sat in her father's house.

Remain a widow [almanah] - Why is she called "*almanah*"? R. Chama of Bagdath said: "Because the Rabbis were destined to institute a *kethubah* [marriage contract] of a *manah* [one hundred gold pieces] for a widow [*Kethuvoth* 10b).[8]

your father's house - This teaches us that the term "father's house" applies to all who issue from the father, even after his death; for Tamar was the daughter of Shem, and Shem had already died, notwithstanding which Judah said: "Remain a widow in your father's house" (*Tosefoth, Kiddushin* 5a).[9]

38:12   And time passed, and Shua's daughter died, the wife of Judah. And Judah was comforted, and he went up to his sheep shearers, he and his friend, Chirah the Adulamite, to Timnah.

and Shua's daughter died - R. Shmuel b. Nachmani said: "If someone begins a *mitzvah* and does not finish it, and someone else comes along and finishes it, he buries his wife and sons, as it is written: 'And Shua's daughter died,' and Er and Onan had died [See commentary (2) above]" (*Sotah* 13b).[10]

38:13   And it was thus told to Tamar: "Behold, your father-in-law is going up to Timnah to shear his sheep."

is going up to Timnah - But concerning Samson it is written (*Judges* 14:1): "And Samson went *down* to Timnah!" R. Elazar said: "In respect to Samson, who was demeaned by it, it is written that he went *down*; in respect to Judah, who was ennobled by it, it is written that he went *up*." R. Shmuel b. Nachmani said: "There was one Timnah — coming from one side, one went down; coming from the other side, he went up" (*Sotah* 10a).[11,12]

38:14   And she put off her widow's garments and covered herself with a veil, and she enwrapped herself, and she sat at the entrance of Enayim, which is on the road to Timnah. For she saw that Shelah had grown up and she had not been given to him as a wife.

and she sat at the entrance of Enayim [petach enayim] - R. Alexandrai said: "This teaches us that she went and sat at the door [*petach*] of our father Abraham, a place that all eyes [*enayim*] aspire to see." R. Chanin said in the name of Rav: "There is a place called *Enayim*, as it is written (*Joshua* 15:33): 'Tappuach and Enayim' [place names]." R. Shmuel b. Nachmani said: "She gave *enayim* ["plausibility"] to her words when he solicited her. He said to her: 'Perhaps you are an idolator.' She answered: 'I am single.' 'Perhaps your father accepted a marriage offer on your behalf.' She answered: 'I am an orphan.' 'Perhaps you are unclean [menstruating].' She answered: 'I am clean' " (*Ibid.*).[13-15]

and she sat at the entrance of Enayim - Is this possible! Even the worst of harlots do not do this [out in the open]! The meaning is that she turned her eyes [*enayim*] to the portal [*petach*] towards which all eyes look, and said before Him: "L-rd of the Universe: let me not leave this household, childless!" (*Yerushalmi, Sotah* 1:4).[16,17]

38:15   And Judah saw her and thought her to be a harlot because she covered her face.

because she covered her face - He thought her a harlot because she covered her face? R. Elazar said: "Because she had kept her face covered in her father-in-law's house [which explains why Judah did not recognize her now]," as R. Shmuel b. Nachmani said in the name of R. Jonathan: "Every daughter-in-law who is modest in her father-in-law's house merits that kings and prophets descend from her. Whence is this derived? From Tamar [king - David; prophet - Isaiah]" (*Sotah* 10b).[18,19]

38:20   And Judah sent the kid of the goats by the hand of his friend the Adulamite to take the pledge from the hand of the woman, but he could not find her.

the kid of the goats - Since it is written here: "the kid of the goats," the implication is that here, specifically, the kid is "of the goats," and that where the word "kid" [*gedi*] appears elsewhere, it may refer even to the young of a cow or of a sheep [this has certain halachic implications] (*Chullin* 113b).[20]

38:24   And it came to pass, about three months after, that it was told to Judah: "Tamar, your daughter-in-law, has played the harlot, and, behold, she has conceived by harlotry," and Judah said: "Take her out and burn her."

And it came to pass, about three months after - It was taught: "Somchos said in the name of R. Meir: 'A pregnancy is recognizable after three months: and though we have no proof for this, there is an allusion to it, as it is written: "And it came to pass, about three months after, that it was told to Judah: 'Tamar, your daughter-in-law, has played the harlot, and, behold, she has conceived' " ' " (*Niddah* 8b).[21]

And Judah said - [Why was Judah's judgment (instead of that of the greater men of the generation) sought first? Because in capital cases the opinion of the lesser judges is first secured. And according to that authority who holds that our laws are at variance with theirs (the sons of Noah), how is Judah's judging to be understood? — Although higher opinions were first secured, his was considered most acceptable, and the judgment was recorded in his name] (*Yerushalmi, Sanhedrin* 84:7).[22-24]

Take her out and burn her - From here it is to be derived that the death penalty for adultery with an idolator was decreed by the *beth din* of Shem (*Avodah Zarah* 36b).[25]

38:25 She was taken out, and she sent to her father-in-law, saying: "By the man whose these are am I with child," and she said: "Recognize, I beseech you, whose are these signet, cords, and staff?"

She was taken out [*hi mutzait*, lit., "It was found"] - Should it not have been written "*hi mitotzaat*" [lit., "She was taken out"]? — R. Elazar explained: "After her signs [given her by Judah] were found. Samael [the guardian angel of Esau] came and removed them [so that she would be burned], and Gabriel came and retrieved them" (*Sotah* 10b).[26,27]

and she said: "Recognize" - R. Chama b. Chanina said: "*He* [Judah] accosted his father with 'Recognize' (37:32): 'Recognize! Is this the coat of your son?' and he was accosted with 'Recognize': 'Recognize! Whose are these, the signet and the cords' " (*Ibid.*).[28-30]

and she said: "Recognize na" - "*Na*" is a term of beseeching. She said to him: "I beseech you; recognize your Creator, and do not avert your eyes from me" (*Ibid.*).[31]

38:26 And he said: "She is right; it is by me. For because of this
I did not give her to Shelah, my son." And he did not live
with her anymore.

She is right; it is by me - R. Chanin b. Bizna said in the name of R.
Shimon Chasida: "Joseph, who sanctified the name of heaven in private
[with the wife of Potiphar] merited that one letter [*h*] of G-d's name be
added to his, as it is written (*Psalms* 81:6): 'He placed testimony in
Ye*h*osef'; Judah, who sanctified the name of Heaven in public, merited
that he be called entirely by the name of the L-rd" [See 29:35] (*Ibid.*).[32]

She is right; it is by me - How did he know? Is it not possible that just
as *he* went to her, others did, too? Rava answered: "He reckoned the
number of months and days, and they corresponded — What we see, we
entertain [as an explanation]; what we do not see, we do not entertain"
(*Makkoth* 23b).[33]

and he did not "yasaf" - Shmuel Sava said in the name of R. Shmuel b.
Ami: "Once he had lived with her, he did not '*cease*' from her; for it is
written here: "And he did not *yasaf* to live with her," and elsewhere
(*Deuteronomy* 5:19): "a great voice, which did not *cease* [*yasaf*]" (*Sotah*
10b).[34]

and he did not live with her anymore - Three verses are stated in one
connection. The speaker in one is not the speaker in the other, and the
speaker of the second is not the speaker in the last. "Recognize whose is
the signet" was stated by Tamar: "And he said: 'She is right; it is by
me'" — the speaker is Judah; and the Holy Spirit pronounced: "And he
did not live with her anymore" (*Yerushalmi, Sotah* 9:6).[35]

38:28 And it was, as she was giving birth, that he put forth a
hand; and the midwife took and bound upon his hand a
scarlet thread, saying: "This one came out first."

that he put forth a hand - R. Huna said: "If the fetus put forth a hand
and retracted it, the mother assumes the ritual uncleanliness of child-
birth, as it is written: 'And it was when she *gave birth*, that he put forth a
hand'" (*Niddah* 28b).[36]

This one came out first- From here it is dervied that a midwife is believed to testify about a child that he is the first-born (*Yerushalmi, Bava Bathra* 3:1).³⁷

39:1   And Joseph was brought down to Egypt, and Potiphar, Pharaoh's chamberlain, the chief steward, an Egyptian, bought him from the hands of the Ishmaelites who brought him down there.

And Joseph was brought down to Egypt - R. Elazar said: "Read it not '*hurad*' [was brought down] but '*horid*' [he brought down], for he brought down Pharaoh's magicians from their glory" (*Sotah* 13b).¹

and Potiphar bought him - Rav said: "He bought him for himself [for sodomy] and Gabriel came and emasculated him. How is this seen? In the beginning his name is written 'Potiphar,' and in the end (45:41): '*Poti-fera*' ['*fera*' connoting emasculation]" (*Ibid.*).²

39:5   And it was, from the time he had appointed him over his house and over all his possessions, that the L-rd blessed the house of the Egyptian for the sake of Joseph: and the blessing of the L-rd was with all that was with him in the house and in the field.

for the sake of Joseph - Abbaye said: "Upon the heels of Torah scholars comes blessing, as it is written: 'And the L-rd blessed the house of the Egyptian for the sake of Joseph' " (*Berachoth* 42a).³

39:9   There is no one greater in this house than I, and he has kept back nothing from me but you, for you are his wife. And how can I do this great evil, and I will sin to G-d.

this great evil - In relation to adultery it is written "this *great* [(one)] evil," and in relation to slander (*Psalms* 12:4): "the tongue that speaks *great* [(many)] things." This teaches us that the slanderer's transgression exceeds even the adulterer's (*Erchin* 15b).⁴

and I will sin to G-d - Adultery is one of those sins for which punishment is exacted in this world, with the core remaining for punishment in the world to come, as it is written: "And how can I do this great evil *and* I will sin to G-d" (*Yerushalmi, Peah* 1:1).[5]

39:10   And it was, when she spoke to Joseph day after day, and he did not listen to her, to lie with her, to live with her.

day after day - It was taught: "Every day she would assail him with words: 'I will have you imprisoned [(if you do not lie with me)]!' He answered (*Psalms* 146:8): 'The L-rd looses the prisoners.' She said to him: 'I will have you bowed down!' He answered (*Ibid.*): 'The L-rd raises those who are bowed down.' She said to him: 'I will blind your eyes!' He answered (*Ibid.*): 'The L-rd opens the eyes of the blind.' She gave him a thousand pieces of silver to consent to her, and he refused" (*Yoma* 35b).[6]

to lie, etc. - "to lie with her" — in this world; "to be with her" — in the next world. From this R. Eliezer concluded: "If someone commits a transgression [of this kind] it is tied to him like a dog" (*Avodah Zarah* 5a).[7]

39:11   And it came to pass about this time that he came home to do his work, and there was no man of the men of the house at home.

to do his work - Rav and Shmuel differ on this. One says: "to do his work" — literally; the other: "He went in to do his 'needs' [i.e., to live with her]" (*Sotah* 36b).[8]

and there was no man - Is it possible that in a house as large as that of the wicked Potiphar there was no man? It was taught in the forum of R. Yishmael: "That day was a holiday, and they had all gone to visit their idols. She feigned sickness, saying to herself: 'There is no day more propitious than today for Joseph to live with me' " (*Ibid.*).[9]

40:10   And in the vine, three branches, the buds sprouting blossoms, the clusters ripening into grapes.

And in the vine, etc. - It was taught: "R. Eliezer the Modai said: 'The vine is Jerusalem; the three branches are, respectively, the Temple, the king, and the high priest; the buds sprouting blossoms are the young priests; the clusters ripening into grapes are the libations' " (*Chullin* 92a).[1]

three branches [serigim] - R. Chiyya b. Abba said in the name of Rav: "These are the three high potentates [*sarei geim*] that arise from Israel in every generation." Rava said: "These are the three archangels of the gentiles [*sarei goyim*] that plead Israel's cause in every generation" (*Ibid.*).[2,3]

40:11　And the cup of Pharaoh in my hand; and I took the grapes, and I pressed them into Pharaoh's cup, and I gave the cup into Pharaoh's hand.

And the cup of Pharaoh in my hand - Rava said: "These three 'cups' mentioned in respect to Egypt in the cup-bearer's dream — what do they signify? One [cup of destruction] that Egypt drank in the days of Moses, another that it drank in the days of Pharaoh Neho, and yet another, that it is destined to drink together with all of the idol worshippers" (*Ibid.*).[4,5]

And the cup of Pharaoh in my hand - What do these four cups of Pesach correspond to? R. Yehoshua b. Levi said: "To the four cups of Pharaoh: 'And the *cup* of Pharaoh in my hand'; 'And I pressed them into Pharaoh's *cup*'; 'And I gave the *cup* into Pharaoh's hand'; 'And you will give Pharaoh's *cup* into his hand' " (*Yerushalmi, Pesachim* 1:1).[6]

40:16　And the chief baker saw that he had interpreted correctly, and he said to Joseph: "I, too, in my dream, and, behold, three wicker baskets on my head."

that he had interpreted correctly - How did he know? R. Elazar said: "We may deduce from this that He showed each one his own dream and the interpretation of his neighbor's dream" (*Berachoth* 55b).[7]

wicker baskets [salei chori] - There is an allusion here that *chori* are *large* cakes [*salei chori* being *large* baskets (This has certain halachic implications)] (*Yerushalmi, Betzah* 2:6).[8]

40:20   And it was on the third day, the birthday of Pharaoh, that he made a feast for all of his servants, and he remembered the chief butler and the chief baker among his servants.

the birthday, etc. - From here it is to be derived that the king's own birthday is the "birthday festival" of kings (*Yerushalmi, Avodah Zarah* 1:2).[9]

Miketz

41:10 Pharaoh grew wroth with his servants, and he put me in custody of the chief steward: me and the chief baker.

Pharaoh grew wroth with his servants - R. Chiyya b. Abba said in the name of R.Yochanan: "The Holy One Blessed be He caused the master to grow wroth with his servants to do the will of the righteous one. Who? Joseph — as it is written: 'Pharaoh grew wroth with his servants ... and there was with us a Hebrew youth' " (*Megillah* 13b).[1]

41:13 And it was, as he had interpreted for us, so it came to pass, each man, according to his dream, he interpreted.

as he had interpreted - R. Elazar said: "Whence is it derived that all dreams materialize according to their interpretation? From the verse: 'And it was, as he had interpreted for us, so it came to pass.' Rava said: 'This holds true only on condition that the interpretation corresponds to the dream, as it is written (*Ibid.* 12): 'Each man, according to his dream, he interpreted' " (*Berachoth* 55b).[2]

41:14 And Pharaoh sent, and he called for Joseph, and they hastened him from the pit. And he shaved himself, and he changed his garments, and came into Pharaoh.

And he shaved himself - One who sees shaving in a dream should arise and say: "And he shaved himself and he changed his clothes" — before a different verse presents itself, viz. (*Judges* 16:17): "If I am shaved, my strength will depart from me" (*Ibid.* 56b).[3]

41:32 And as to the dream's repeating itself to Pharaoh twice, it is because the thing is established from G-d, and G-d is hastening to do it.

And as to the dream's repeating itself twice - Some say that a dream which repeats itself will materialize, as it is written: "And as to the dream's repeating itself twice, it is because the thing is established" (*Ibid.* 55b).[4]

41:43   And he caused him to ride in the second chariot which he had, and they called before him "Avrech," and he was appointed over the land of Egypt.

and they called before him "Avrech" - [What is "*Avrech*"? Av (a father) and "*rech*"]. From here it is to be derived that "*recha*" refers to kingship (*Bava Bathra* 4a).[5]

41:44   And Pharaoh said to Joseph: "I am Pharaoh, and without you no man will lift up his hand or his foot in the whole land of Egypt."

and without you, etc. - R. Chiyya b. Abba said in the name of R. Yochanan: "When Pharaoh said to Joseph: 'And without you no man will lift up his hand or his foot,' Pharaoh's astrologers said: 'You place above us a slave, whose master bought him for twenty pieces of silver!' At this, Pharaoh said to them: 'I see kingly qualities in him.' They responded: 'If so, he should know the seventy languages.' Thereupon, Gabriel came and instructed him in them — but he could not learn them. Gabriel then added to his name a letter [*h*] from the name of the Holy One Blessed be He, and he mastered them, as it is written (*Psalms* 81:6): 'He placed testimony in Ye*h*osef when he went out over the land of Egypt' " (*Sotah* 36b).[6,7]

41:50   And to Joseph there were born two sons before the advent of the famine year, which were borne to him by Asnat, the daughter of Poti-fera, the priest of On.

And to Joseph there were born, etc. - Resh Lakish said: "It is forbidden to cohabit in the year of a famine, as it is written: 'And to Joseph there were born two sons *before* the advent of the famine year' " (*Ta'anith* 11a).[8]

41:57   And all the earth came to Egypt to buy food from Joseph, for the famine was severe in all the earth.

And all the earth, etc. - R. Yehudah said in the name of Shmuel: "Joseph collected all of the silver and gold in the world and brought it to Egypt, as it is written (47:14): 'And Joseph collected all of the silver.' From here I know only about the silver in Egypt and in Canaan. How do I know that the other lands are included? For it is written: 'And *all* the earth came to Egypt' " (*Pesachim* 119a).⁹

42:1   And Jacob saw that there was food in Egypt; and Jacob said to his sons: "Why should you show yourselves?"

Why should you show yourselves - Jacob said to his sons: "Do not show yourselves to be sated, neither to Esau nor to Ishmael, so as not to excite their envy" (*Ta'anith* 10b).¹

42:5   And the children of Israel came to buy food among those who came, for the famine was in the land of Canaan.

And the children of Israel came - And it is written elsewhere (*Leviticus* 22:32): "And I will be sanctified in the midst of the children of Israel" — Just as the "children of Israel" mentioned here were ten, so the "children of Israel" mentioned there are ten. From here it is to be derived that every prayer service requires at least ten Jews [a *minyan*] (*Yerushalmi, Berachoth* 7:3).²

42:6   And Joseph was the governor of the land; he was the provider for all the people of the land. And Joseph's brothers came, and they bowed down to him with their faces to the ground.

he was the provider - Rava said in the name of R. Shesheth: "One who does not withhold a *halachah* from a disciple's mouth merits blessings, as Joseph, as it is written (*Proverbs* 11:26): 'A blessing upon the head of the provider,' and 'the provider' is none other than Joseph, as it is written: 'And Joseph was the provider for all the people of the land' " (*Sanhedrin* 92a).³

42:8   And Joseph recognized his brothers, but they did not recognize him.

but they did not recognize him - R. Chisda said: "This teaches us that he left without a beard, and came before them with a beard" (*Yevamoth* 88a).⁴

42:28   And he said to his brothers: "My money has been returned, and here it is in my sack." And their hearts went out, and they trembled before each other, saying: "What is this that G-d has done to us?"

And their hearts went out - When R. Simon b. Zvid died, R. Levi said: "Now if the hearts of Joseph's brothers, who had *found* [Joseph], went out, we, who have *lost* R. Simon, how much more so should our hearts go out!" (*Yerushalmi, Berachoth* 2:8).⁵

What is this that G-d has done - R. Yochanan found Resh Lakish's child sitting and reciting (*Proverbs* 19:3): "A man's foolishness peverts his way, and his heart fumes against the L-rd." Thereupon, he sat down and wondered: "Is there anything written in *Hagiographa* which is not alluded to in the Torah?" To this, the child replied: "Is this *not* alluded to? Is it not written: 'And they trembled ... saying: "What is this that G—d has done to us?" ' " [when they had brought it upon themselves!] (*Ta'anith* 9a).⁶

42:30   The man who is the lord of the land spoke harshly to us, and he accused us of spying out the land.

spoke [dibber] harshly - From here it is to be derived that wherever "*dibber*" is used, harsh speech is connoted (*Makkoth* 11a).⁷

42:36   And Jacob their father said to them: "You have made me destitute. Joseph is not here, and Shimon is not here, and if you take Benjamin, then all of them will come upon me."

Joseph is not here - It was taught: "R. Shimon b. Elazar said: 'One's success or lack of success in his first business dealing after building a house or begetting a child or marrying a woman, though possessing no magical significance, can be indicative of what he might expect in the future.' " R. Elazar said: "This is only on condition that the success or lack of success in question occurs on three consecutive occasions, as it is written: 'Joseph is not here [one], and Shimon is not here [two], and if you take Benjamin [three], then *all* of them will come upon me' " (*Chullin* 95b).[8,9]

42:37   And Reuven said to his father saying: "You may kill my two sons if I do not bring him back to you. Leave him in my care, and I shall return him to you."

You may kill my two sons - Who exemplifies "one who does not ask rightly"? — Reuven, who said: "You may kill my two sons" (*Avoth d'R. Nathan*).[10]

42:38   And he said: "My son shall not go down with you, for his brother has died, and he alone has remained, and if harm befall him on the way, even you will have brought down my old age with sorrow to Sheol."

and if harm befall him on the way - On the way, yes; at home, no? From here it is to be dervied that Satan attacks only in time of danger (*Yerushalmi, Shabbath* 2:6).[11]

43:9   I will be surety for him; you may require him from my hand. If I do not return him to you and present him before you, then I will have sinned against you all of my days.

I will be surety for him - Whence is it derived that a guarantor binds himself? From the verse: "I will be surety for him; you may require him from my hand" (*Bava Bathra* 173b).[1]

I will be surety for him - Who exemplifies "one who asks rightly"? — Judah, who said: "*I* will be surety for him [See (10)above]" (*Avoth d'R. Nathan* 37).[2]

then I will have sinned against you - R. Yehudah said in the name of Rav: "Excommunication on condition [even though the condition for the excommunication is not fulfilled] requires absolution. Whence is this derived? From Judah, who said: '*If* I do not return him to you ... *then* I will have sinned against you' — and R. Shmuel b. Nachmani said in the name of R. Jonathan: 'All of the forty years that Israel was in the desert, Judah's bones rolled around in his casket [though he *had* returned him]; until Moses asked mercy for him' " (*Makkoth* 11b).[3]

43:16 And when Joseph saw Benjamin with them, he said to the doyen of his household: "Bring these men home, and slaughter an animal and prepare it, for the men will eat with me at noon."

and slaughter an animal and prepare it [for eating] - If one slaughters an animal that is subsequently found to be *trefah* [ritually unfit], or if one slaughters for the sake of idol worship, or if one slaughters a non-dedicated animal in the Temple, or a dedicated one outside of it, or if one slaughters a beast or bird that must be stoned — he is not obligated to cover the blood. Why so? Slaughtering that does not result in fitness for eating is not called slaughtering. This is derived from: "And slaughter an animal and prepare it [for eating]." Just as there, slaughtering creates fitness for eating, so, in all cases, slaughtering must create fitness for eating (*Chullin* 85a).[4]

and slaughter an animal and prepare it [for eating] - R. Yossi b. R. Chanina said: " 'And slaughter an animal' — he bared the *shechitah* zone for them; 'And prepare it for eating' — he extracted the thigh-sinew before them" (*Chullin* 91a).[5,6]

43:28 And they said: "Your servant, our father, is in good health; he is still alive. And they bowed down their heads and made obeisance."

Your servant, our father - R. Yehudah said in the name of Rav: "Why was Joseph referred to as 'bones' in his lifetime [50:25]? Because he did not protest on behalf of his father's honor. For his brothers said: 'Your servant, our father,' and he said nothing to them" (*Sotah* 13a).[7,8]

43:34 And he took and sent portions to them from before him,
and Benjamin's portion was five times as much as any of
theirs. And they drank and became inebriated with him.

And they drank and became inebriated with him - R. Yossi b. R.
Chanina said: "From the day that Joseph had left his brothers, they had
not tasted the taste of wine, as it is written: 'And they drank and became
inebriated *with him*,' the implication being that until then they had not
drunk" (*Shabbath* 139a).[9]

44:3 The morning dawned, and the men were sent away, they
and their asses.

The morning "ohr" - We do not have: "*Ohr* is morning," but "The
morning *ohr*," as one would say: "The morning dawned." [This has
certain halachic implications] (*Pesachim* 2a).[1]

The morning dawned - R. Yehudah said in the name of Rav: "One
should always enter his lodgings when it is still light and leave on his
journey when it is light, as it is written: 'When the morning dawned, the
men were sent on their way' " (*Ibid.*).[2]

The morning dawned [haboker ohr] - It is written (19:23): "The sun
rose upon the earth," and (*Leviticus* 22:7): "And the sun set and
disappeared." Rising is compared to setting. If setting means
*dis*appearance of the sun *from* people, then rising means appearance of
the sun *to* people. [Why, then, does the rising of the morning star mark
the beginning of the day, if the sun has not yet appeared at that time?]
R. Ba answered: "It is written: 'haboker *ohr*' [lit., "the morning light"]
— the Torah called 'light' morning" (*Yerushalmi, Berachoth* 1:1).[3]

44:16 And Judah said: "What shall we say to my lord?" What
shall we speak, and how shall we vindicate ourselves? G-d
has found out the iniquity of your servants. Behold, we
are servants to my lord, both we and him with whom the
cup is found."

and how shall we vindicate ourselves [nitztadak] - R. Nachman b. Yitzchak said: "Where is *notarikon* [acronymics] evidenced in the Torah? It is written: 'And how shall we vindicate ourselves [*nitztadak*]?' *N* i *tz t* a *d* a *k* - Notarikon: *N*echonim anachnu [We are right]; *Tz*addikim anachnu [We are righteous]; *T*ehorim anachnu [We are pure]; *D*akkim anachnu [We are clean]; *K*edoshim anachnu [We are holy]" (*Shabbath* 105a).[4]

Vayigash

45:3 And Joseph said to his brothers: "I am Joseph; is my father still living?" And his brothers could not answer him because they were confounded before him.

And his brothers could not, etc. - R. Elazar, when he came to this verse, would cry, saying: "Now, if under the rebuke of flesh and blood it is written: 'And his brothers could not answer him because they were confounded before him,' how much more so under the rebuke of the Holy One Blessed be He!" (*Chagigah* 4b).[1]

45:12 Behold, your eyes and the eyes of my brother Benjamin see, just as my mouth that speaks.

your eyes, etc. - What is the intent of "Your eyes and the eyes of my brother Benjamin"? R. Elazar said: "He said to them: 'Just as I harbor no ill feeling against Benjamin, who was not a party to my being sold, in the same way, I harbor no ill feeling against you' " (*Megillah* 16b).[2]

just as my mouth that speaks - What is the intent of "Just as my mouth"? R. Elazar said: "He said to them: 'Just as my mouth, so is my heart' " (*Ibid.*).[3]

45:14 And he fell on the throats of Benjamin, his brother, and Benjamin cried on his throat.

on the throats of Benjamin - How many throats did Benjamin have? R. Elazar said: "The meaning is that he cried over the two Temples that were destined to be in the territory of the tribe of Benjamin, and which were destined to be destroyed" (*Ibid.*).[4]

and Benjamin cried, etc. - R. Elazar said: "He cried over the sanctuary of Shiloh, which was destined to be in the portion of Joseph and to be destroyed" (*Ibid.*).[5]

45:22   To all of them he gave to each man changes of clothing, and to Benjamin he gave three hundred pieces of silver and five changes of clothing.

and five changes of clothing - Is it possible that this righteous one [Joseph] should go astray with respect to the self-same object [clothes (the coat of many colors)] that brought so much suffering to him! R. Binyamin b. Yefet said: "Joseph was thereby intimating to Benjamin that a descendant [Mordecai] would issue from him, who would emerge from the king's presence wearing five royal vestments, as it is written (*Esther* 8:15): 'And Mordecai emerged from the king's presence in royal apparel: blue, and white, and a great crown of gold, and a wrap of fine linen and of gold' " (*Ibid.*) [6,7]

45:23   And to his father he sent as follows: ten asses laden with the good of Egypt, and ten she-asses laden with corn, bread, and food, for his father, for the journey.

with the good of Egypt - what is the intent of "with the good of Egypt"? R. Binyamin b. Yefet said in the name of R. Elazar: "He sent him old wine, that is especially gratifying to old men" (*Ibid.*).[8]

corn, bread, and food - If "corn" and "bread" are stated, why is "food" mentioned in addition? This is to teach us that all edibles are called "food." We may derive from this that if one takes a vow against "food," all edibles are forbidden to him except water and salt (*Yerushalmi, Nedarim* 1:1).[9]

45:24   And he sent his brothers and they went; and he said to them: "Do not dispute along the way."

Do not dispute along the way - R. Elazar said: "He said to them: 'Do not engage in a halachic discussion, lest you go astray.' " In a *Mishnah* it was taught: "He said to them: 'Do not take overly large strides, and be sure to enter the city when it is still light' " (*Ta'anith* 10b).[10,11]

45:26   And they told him, saying: "Joseph is still alive, and he is
        governor over all the land of Egypt." And his heart
        fainted, for he did not believe them.

for he did not believe them - R. Shimon said: "Such is the punishment
of the liar: even when he tells the truth, he is not believed. For so we find
with respect to Jacob's sons. It is written (37:33): 'And he recognized it
and said: "It is the coat of my son."' Therefore, in the end, even though
they spoke the truth, he did not believe them, as it is written: 'And his
heart fainted, for he did not believe them' " (*Avoth d'R. Nathan*).[12]

45:27   And they told him the words of Joseph, which he had said
        to them, and he saw the wagons that Joseph had sent to
        carry him, and the spirit of Jacob their father revived.

and the spirit of Jacob their father revived - Some say: "What is the
intent of: 'And the spirit of Jacob their father revived'?" The Holy
Spirit, which had departed from him, returned to him at that moment"
(*Ibid.*).[13]

46:1   And Israel journeyed, and all that was his, and he came to
        Beer-Sheva, and he slaughtered offerings to the G-d of his
        father, Isaac.

to the G-d of his father, Isaac - It is not written: "to the G-d of his
father, Abraham." R. Yochanan said: "This teaches us that one must
give more honor to his father than to his father's father." [*Medrash
Rabbah*] We may derive from this that one is, indeed, duty-bound to
honor his father's father, but that his father's honor takes precedence
(*Rama* to *Yoreh Deah* 240:24).[1]

46:2   And G-d said to Israel in the visions of the night, saying:
        "Jacob, Jacob"; and he said: "Here I am."

Jacob, Jacob - The connotation is one of endearment and of impelling
(*Torath Cohanim*, beginning of *Vayikra*).[2]

46:4   I will go down with you to Egypt, and I will bring you up, also up, and Joseph will put his hand on your eyes.

I will go down with you - This teaches us that when Israel went down to Egypt, the *Shechinah* [the Divine Presence] went down with them (*Mechilta, Beshalach*).[3]

and I will bring you up - This teaches us that when Israel went up from Egypt, the *Shechinah* [the Divine Presence] went up with them (*Ibid.*).[4]

also up [gam aloh] - The Rabbis taught: "If one sees a camel [*gamal*] in a dream, it is a sign that Heaven had decreed death upon him and he had been rescued from it." R. Chama b. R. Chanina said: "Whence is this derived? From the verse: 'And I will bring you up [deliver you] also up [*gam aloh* - similar to *gamal*]' " (*Berachoth* 56b).[5]

also up - What is the intent of "also up"? "I will bring you up, and I will also bring up the remnants of the tribes." This teaches us that each tribe brought up with it the bones of its chieftain (*Yerushalmi, Sotah* 1:10).[6]

46:7   His sons, and the sons of his sons with him; his daughters, and the daughters of his sons, and all his seed he brought with him to Egypt.

His sons, and the sons of his sons - This teaches us that the sons of the sons of sons are included in the category of the sons of sons; for included in the seventy souls that came to Egypt with Jacob were Chetzron and Chamol, the sons of Peretz, the son of Judah, and the Torah includes them in the designation "sons of sons" (*Mabit, Responsa, Choshen Mishpat* 20).[7]

46:15   These are the sons of Leah, whom she bore to Jacob in Padan Aram, with Dinah, his daughter; all the souls of his sons and daughters were thirty-three.

These are the sons of Leah, etc. - "These are the sons of Leah, whom she bore to Jacob ... and Dinah, *his* daughter" ... the males are attributed to the female and the female to the male. From here the statement: "If the husband 'sows' first, the child is a girl; if the wife, a boy" (*Niddah* 31a).[8]

46:21   And the sons of Benjamin: Bela and Becher and Ashbel, Gera and Naaman, Aichi and Rosh, Mupim and Chupim and Ard.

And the sons of Benjamin, etc. - It was taught: "They were all called by Joseph's name: *Bela* - he was swallowed up [*nivla*] among the nations; *Becher* - he was the first-born [*bechor*] to his mother; *Ashbel* - the L-rd [*El*] sent him into captivity [*shevi*]; *Gera* - he lived [*gar*] in inns; *Naaman* - he was exceedingly pleasant [*naim*]; *Aichi Varosh* - he is my brother [*ach*] and my head [*rosh*]; *Mupim Vechupim* - he did not see my marriage canopy [*chupah*] and I did not see his; *Ard* - he went down [*yarad*] among the nations; others say: his face was like a rose [vered]" (*Sotah* 36b) (See 37:2).[9-11]

46:23   And the sons of Dan, Chushim.

And the sons of Dan, Chushim - It was taught in the forum of Chezkiah: " 'And the sons of Dan, Chushim' — they were as numerous as the leaves [*chushim*] of reeds" (*Bava Bathra* 143b).[12]

46:26   All the souls who came to Jacob to Egypt, who came out of his loins, besides the wives of Jacob's sons, all the souls were sixty-six.

who came out of his loins [yerecho] - It is to be dervied from here that if one wills his belongings to those "who come out of my loins" [*yerechai*] or to those "who come out of *chalatzai*" [similar to *yerechai*], his daughters, too, are included; for Dinah was one of the seventy souls and the Torah includes her in those "who came out of his loins" (*Decisions* of the *Mahariv*).[13]

46:27   And the sons of Joseph, who were born to him in Egypt, were two souls; all of the souls of the house of Jacob who came into Egypt were seventy.

all of the souls ... seventy - Abba Chalifa asked R. Chiyya b. Abba: "They are summed up as seventy, but counted individually they number only sixty-nine!" R. Chiyya answered: "So said R. Chama b. R. Chanina: 'This [the seventieth] is Yocheved, who was conceived upon the way and born between the city walls, as it is written (26:59): "whom she *bore* to Levi in Egypt" — her birth was in Egypt, but not her conception' " (*Bava Bathra* 123a,b).[14,15]

47:2   And from the end of his brothers he took five men, and he presented them to Pharaoh.

he took five men - Ravah asked Rabbah b. Mari: "Who are these five men?" Rabbah answered: "Those whose names appear twice in immediate succession [Dan, Zevulun, Gad, Asher, Naftali]" [in Moses' blessing (*Deuteronomy* 33)] (*Bava Kamma* 91a).[1]

47:6   The land of Egypt is before you. In the best of the land, place your father and your brothers; let them dwell in the land of Goshen. Now if you know that there are among them any able men, then make them rulers over my cattle.

In the best of the land place your father - R. Chiyya taught in the name of R. Hoshia: "Why do we eat *chazeret* [a kind of lettuce] on Pesach? To impress upon ourselves that just as *chazeret* is sweet in the beginning but bitter afterwards, so were the Egyptians to our forefathers in Egypt. In the beginning they said: 'In the best of the land place your father and your brothers,' and in the end (*Exodus* 1:14): 'And they made their lives bitter with hard bondage, in mortar and in brick' " (*Yerushalmi, Pesachim* 2:5).[2,3]

then make them rulers over my cattle - R. Yossi opened with remarks in honor of the host, expounding: "Now if Egypt drew Israel close only for its own benefit, as it is written: 'Now if you know that there are among them any able men, then make them rulers over my cattle' — the Torah still commanded (*Deuteronomy* 23:8): 'Do not hate an Egyptian, because you were a stranger in his land' — then one who hosts a Torah scholar, and feeds him, and gives him to drink, and benefits him with his possessions — how much more so is he to be commended!" (*Berachoth* 63b).[4]

47:9 And Jacob said to Pharaoh: "The days of the years of my sojournings are one hundred and thirty years. Few and sore have been the years of my life, and they have not attained to the years of the life of my fathers in the days of their sojournings."

one hundred and thirty years - It was taught: "When our father Jacob was blessed by his father, he was sixty-three years old. From then, it was fourteen years until Joseph was born, giving us seventy-seven. It is written: (21:46): 'And Jacob was thirty years old when he stood before Pharaoh' — making it 107. Seven years of plenty and two of famine give us 116. It is written: 'And Jacob said to Pharaoh: "The days of the years of my sojournings are one hundred and thirty years."' But they were 116! — This teaches us that the fourteen years that he spent in the yeshiva of Ever are not reckoned" (*Megillah* 16a).[5,6]

47:14 And Joseph collected all of the silver which was found in the land of Egypt and in the land of Canaan for the food which they bought, and Joseph brought the silver to Pharaoh's house.

And Joseph collected, etc. - R. Yehudah said in the name of Shmuel: "Joseph collected all of the silver and gold in the world and brought it to Egypt, as it is written: 'And Joseph collected all of the silver ...' and when the Jews left Egypt, they brought it up with them, as it is written (*Exodus* 12:36): 'And they emptied out Egypt' " (*Pesachim* 119a; see 41:57).[7]

47:21 And as for the people, he removed them into cities from one end of the borders of Egypt to the other.

he removed them into cities - Why so? So that they should not call his brothers "exiles" (*Chullin* 60b).[8]

47:22 Only the land of the priests he did not buy, for the priests had a portion assigned to them by Pharaoh. And they ate

48:4   And He said to me: "Behold, I will make you fruitful and multiply you, and I will make you a congregation of nations, and I will give the land to your children after you for an everlasting possession."

and I will make you a congregation of nations - Who was born to him at that time? Benjamin. It is to be understood, then, that this is what G—d was telling him: "There will be born to you now another congregation" — whence it is derived that even one tribe is called a congregation (*Horiyoth* 5b).[2]

and I will make you a congregation of nations - R. Acha b. Yaakov said: "The tribe of Levi is not called a congregation, for it is written: 'For I will make you fruitful and multiply you, and I will make you a congregation of nations' followed by 'and I will give the land to your children after you for an everlasting possession' — all who possess land are called a congregation, and all [as Levi] who do not possess land are not called a congregation" (*Ibid.* 6b).[3]

48:5   And now, your two sons who were born to you in the land of Egypt, before I came to you into Egypt — Ephraim and Menashe will be to me as Reuven and Shimon.

Ephraim and Menashe, etc. - It was taught: "If a woman curses her husband's father in his [her husband's] presence, she is divorced without receiving the amount stipulated in her *kethubah* [marriage contract.] R. Yehudah said in the name of Shmuel: "This need not be specifically in his presence, but applies even if she curses his father in the presence of his children [for 'grand-children are considered, as children.'] A device for remembering this is: 'Ephraim and Menashe will be to me as Reuven and Shimon' " (*Kethuvoth* 72b).[4,5]

48:6   And the children that you beget after them will be yours; in the name of their brothers they shall be called in their inheritance.

they shall be called in their inheritance - They shall be like Ephraim and Menashe in their inheritance, and not in other respects [i.e., to be considered distinct tribes] (*Horiyoth* 6b).[6]

48:7   And when I came from Padan, Rachel died unto me, in the land of Canaan, on the way, when there was but a little way to come to Ephrat, and I buried her there on the way of Ephrat, which is Bethlehem.

And when I came from Padan - It was taught: "R. Elazar b. Yaakov said: (*Leviticus* 19:26): 'You shall not resort to enchantment nor augury' — though there is no license for enchantment, there is for signs — with the provision that there be three such signs, as in: 'And when I came from Padan, Rachel died unto me'; (42:36): 'Joseph is not here and Shimon is not here' " (*Yerushalmi, Shabbath* 6:9; see 42:36).[7,8]

Rachel died unto me - It was taught: "A woman dies unto her husband alone, as it is written: 'Rachel died unto me' " (*Sanhedrin* 22b).[9]

48:10   And the eyes of Jacob grew heavy with age; he could not see. And he brought them near to him, and he kissed them, and he embraced them.

grew heavy with age [zoken] - R. Chama b. R. Chanina said: "All the days of our forefathers there was never a hiatus in their learning. When Jacob was old, he was still engaged in learning, as it is written: 'And the eyes of Jacob grew heavy with *zoken*' " [*zoken* connotes learning] (*Yoma* 28b).[10]

48:15   And he blessed Joseph, and he said: "The G-d before whom my fathers, Abraham and Isaac, walked; the G-d who sustained me all my life long until this day."

the G-d who sustained me - R. Yochanan said: "A man's being sustained is more imposing than his being redeemed; for in connection with redemption it is written (16): 'The *angel* who redeems me,' whereas with respect to sustenance it is written: 'The *G-d* who sustained me' " (*Pesachim* 118a).[11]

48:16   The angel who redeemed me from all evil, bless the youths
        and let there be called upon them my name and the name
        of my fathers, and let them grow into a multitude in the
        midst of the land.

my name and the name of my fathers - See 28:13.[12]

and let them grow into a multitude [Veyidgu larov] - The children of
Joseph are not vulnerable to the evil eye, as it is written: 'Veyi*dg*u
larov" [*dag* = fish]. Just as the fish of the sea are concealed by the water
and are not vulnerable to the evil eye, so the children of Joseph are
invulnerable to the evil eye (*Berachoth* 20a).[13]

48:19   And his father refused, and he said: "I know, my son, I
        know. He, too, will be a people, and he, too, will be great;
        but his younger brother will be greater than he, and his
        seed will be filled among the nations."

filled among the nations - When will he be "filled among the nations"?
When the sun will stand still for Joshua [(a descendant of Ephraim) and
the nations will be 'filled' with his glory.] [Here it is intimated that the
sun was destined to stand still in the time of Joshua the son of Nun]
(*Avodah Zarah* 25a).[14]

48:22   And I have given you one portion above your brothers,
        which I took from the hand of the Emori with my sword
        and with my bow.

one portion, etc. - From here it is derived that the share of Joseph was
twice the amount of one share, and not twice the amount of all the other
shares put together. R. Pappa said to Abbaye: "How do we know that
the extra portion was not simply a palm tree?" Abbaye answered: "For
it is written (*Ibid.* 5): 'Ephraim and Menashe will be to me as Reuven
and Shimon' " [implying that their shares are equal in size] (*Bava
Bathra* 123a).[15-17]

with my sword and with my bow - Did he acquire it with his sword and
bow? Is it not written (*Psalms* 44:7): "For I trust not in my bow, and my

sword will not save me"? — "My sword" is prayer; "My bow" is imploration (*Ibid.*).[18]

49:1   And Jacob called his sons, and he said: "Gather together and I will reveal to you what will happen to you in the end of days."

Gather together and I will reveal - R. Shimon b. Lakish said: "Jacob desired to reveal to his children the 'end of days' [the time of the Messiah], and the *Shechinah* [the Divine Presence] departed from him" (*Pesachim* 56a).[1]

49:3   Reuven, you are my first-born, my might, and the first of my strength, an access of dignity and an access of power.

my might and the first of my strength - He had never emitted semen until then [the conception of Reuven] (*Yevamoth* 76a).[2]

49:4   Swift as water, you shall not be exalted. For you went up on your father's bed. Then you defiled my bed on which he went up.

Swift [pachaz] - R. Eliezer Hamodai said: "Turn the word around and expound it [acronymically]; zeazatah [you shook (when tempted by Potiphar's wife)]; *h*irtatah [you recoiled]; *p*archah chet mimechah [the sin flew away from you (i.e., you were rescued from it)]" (*Shabbath* 55b).[3]

Then you defiled my bed, he went up - It was taught: "Others say: 'Reuven defiled two beds: one, the *Shechinah*'s; the other, his father's, as it is written: "Then you defiled my bed, He went up" — read it not 'my *bed*' [*yetzui*], but 'my *beds*' [*yetzuai*]' " (*Ibid.*).[4]

49:6   In their counsel let not my soul come, and in their assembly let not my soul be united. For in their wrath they killed a man, and in their wilfullness they razed an ox.

In their counsel let not my soul come - "In their counsel" — this refers to those who spied out Eretz Yisroel: "And in their congregation" — this refers to the congregation of Korach (*Sanhedrin* 109b).[5]

And in their wilfullness, etc. - Once King Ptolemy assembled seventy-two elders in seventy-two different houses and told each of them: "Transcribe for me [into Greek] the Torah of Moses your teacher." The Holy One Blessed be He placed goodly counsel into the heart of each of them, and they all wrote as one: "For in their wrath they killed an ox [instead of "a man" (so as not to give Ptolemy a pretext to call Jews murderers)], and in their wilfullness they razed a manger" (*Megillah* 9a).[6]

49:7   Cursed is their wrath, for it is fierce. I will divide them in
          Jacob and scatter them in Israel.

Cursed is their wrath, for it is fierce - It was taught: "Issi b. Yehudah said: 'This is one of the ambiguous verses.' " [i.e., Does "cursed" [*arur*] refer to the last word of the preceding verse ("the accursed ox" [Shechem]), or to their wrath?] (*Yoma* 52b).[7]

49:8   Judah, *you*, shall your brothers praise. Your hand is on
          the nape of your foes. Your father's children will bow
          down before you.

Your hand is on the nape of your foes - R. Yochanan said: "What is the meaning of (*Esther* 6:13): 'and his wise men and Zeresh his wife said to him: "If Mordecai is of the seed of the Yehudim, you will not prevail against him" ' "? They said to him: 'If he comes from the other tribes, you will prevail against him; but if he comes from the tribe of Yehudah, Binyamin, Ephraim or Menashe, you will not prevail against him.' Yehudah - as it is written: 'Your hand is on the nape of your foes'; the others- as it is written (*Psalms* 80:3): 'Before Ephraim, and Binyamin, and Menashe, stir up Your might' " (*Megillah* 16a).[8]

Your hand is on the nape of your foes - It is written (II *Samuel* 1:18): "To teach the children of Judah the use of the bow. Is it not written in the book of the just?" What is "the book of the just"? This is the book of Abraham, Isaac, and Jacob, who were called "just," as it is written (*Numbers* 23:10): 'Let me die the death of the just.' And where is it intimated [that the men of Judah are archers]? "Judah, your brothers will praise you; your hand is on the nape of your foes." Which weapon requires that the hand be opposite the nape? The bow (*Avodah Zarah* 25a).[9-11]

Your hand is on the nape of your foes - In the beginning the gentiles decreed *shmad* [enforced conversion] upon the tribe of Judah, it being a tradition handed down by their forefathers that it was Judah who had killed Esau, as it is written: "Your hand is on the nape of your foes" (*Yerushalmi, Kethuvoth* 1:5).[12]

49:10 The sceptre shall not depart from Judah, nor the ruler's staff from between his feet, until Shiloh comes, and the congregation of the peoples be his.

The sceptre shall not depart form Judah - [Even] priests are not anointed as kings. Why so? R. Yuden said: "In keeping with: 'The sceptre shall not depart from Judah' " (*Yerushalmi, Sotah* 88:3).[13]

The sceptre ... nor the ruler's staff - "The sceptre" — this alludes to the Babylonian exilarchs, who ruled Israel with the rod; "nor the ruler's staff from between his feet" — this alludes to the descendants of Hillel, who teach Torah to the masses (*Sanhedrin* 5a).[14]

nor the ruler's staff from between his feet - From this it is derived that the Sanhedrin sat in the portion of Judah (*Zevachim* 54b, see Rashi).[15]

until Shiloh comes - It was said in the forum of R. Dimmi: "The name of the Messiah is 'Shiloh,' as it is written: 'Until Shiloh comes.' " (*Sanhedrin* 98b).[16]

49:11 He binds his foal to the vine, and, to his choice vine, the colt of his ass. He washes his garments in wine, and his clothes in the blood of grapes.

He binds his foal to the vine, etc. - When R. Dimmi came, he said: "What is the intent of: 'He binds his foal to the vine'? — There is no vine in Eretz Yisroel whose harvesting does not require the services of a foal" (*Kethuvoth* 111b).[17]

and to his choice vine, the colt of his ass - It was taught: "One who sees a choice vine in a dream may expect the coming of the Messiah, as it is written: 'And to his choice vine [the Messiah] the colt of his ass [that he will ride upon]' " (*Berachoth* 57a).[18]

and to his choice vine, the colt of his ass - When R. Dimmi came, he said: "What is the intent of: 'And to his choice vine, the colt of his ass'? There is no choice vine, in Eretz Yisrael that does not produce the burden of two asses. Now, lest you say that it contains no wine, it is written: 'He washes in wine his garments.' And, lest you say it is not red, it is written: 'And in the blood of grapes.' And, lest you say that it does not make one heady, it is written: 'He becomes heady.' And, lest you say that it is tasteless, it is written: 'His eyes will be red [*chachlili*] with wine' — every palate [*chaich*] that tastes it will say: '*li, li*' ['It is mine! It is mine!'] And, lest you say that it is satisfying to the young, but not to the old, it is written: 'And his teeth will be white with milk.' Read it not 'And his teeth [*shinayim*] will be white,' but 'his years [*shanim* (i.e., his hair)] will be white'" (*Kethuvoth* 111b).[19-21]

49:12   His eyes will be red with wine, and his teeth will be white with milk.

His eyes will be red with wine - What is the plain meaning of this verse? When R. Dimmi came, he said: "The Congregation of Israel says before the Holy One Blessed be He: 'L-rd of the Universe, look upon me with Your eyes, that are more 'fragrant' than wine, and show me Your teeth, that are more 'refreshing' than milk' " (*Ibid.*).[22]

and his teeth will be white with milk - R. Yochanan said: "It is better to 'whiten' [expose in a smile] one's teeth to one's friend than to give him milk to drink, as it is written: '*ULVN shinayim mechalav*' — do not read it '*Uleven shinayim*' ['and his teeth will be white'], but '*Ulevon shinayim*' ['and he shall whiten his teeth']" (*Ibid.*).[23]

49:13   Zevulun shall dwell at the sea-shore, and he shall be a haven for ships; and his flank shall be upon Siddon.

Zevulun shall dwell at the sea-shore - A certain man was in the habit of saying: "What is a bush on the sea-shore is a cypress on the mainland." When they looked into his genealogy, they found that he came from the tribe of Zevulun — as it is written: "Zevulun shall dwell at the sea-shore" (*Pesachim* 4a).[24,25]

and his flank [lit., "thigh"] shall be upon Siddon - R. Levi said: "It is here intimated that the mother of Jonah the prophet came from the tribe of Asher, for it is written: 'And his thigh shall be upon Siddon' — the thigh from which he emerged was from Siddon [the territory of Asher] (*Yerushalmi, Succah* 1:1).[26]

49:14 Issachar is rich in possessions, couching down between the sheep folds.

Issachar is rich in possessions [chamor garem] - R. Yochanan said in the name of R. Shimon b. Yochai (*Isaiah* 32:20): "'Blessed are you that sow beside all waters, that let the feet of the ox [*shor*] and ass [*chamor*] range freely' — "Sowing" connotes charity, as it is written (*Hosea* 10:12): 'Sow to yourselves through charity,' and "waters" connotes Torah, as it is written (*Isaiah* 55:1): 'Ho! everyone that thirsts, come to the waters.' All who engage in Torah and lovingkindness merit the inheritance of two tribes. They merit the canopy [inheritance] of Joseph [who is referred to as "*shor*" (6)], as it is written: (22): 'Whose branches run over the wall' the ['canopy'], and they merit the inheritance of Issachar [who is referred to as "*chamor*"], as it is written: 'Issachar is rich in possessions' [*chamor garem*]" (*Bava Kamma* 17a).[27,28]

Issachar is rich in possessions - See 30:16.

49:16 Dan will judge his people, as one of the tribes of Israel.

Dan will judge - They said about one who was in the habit of saying: "Judge my judgment" — "He must come from Dan, as it is written: 'Dan will judge his people' " (*Pesachim* 4a).[29,30]

will judge his people as one - R. Yochanan said: "Samson [who came from the tribe of Dan] judged Israel as their Father in heaven, as it is written: 'Dan will judge his people as One' " (*Sotah* 10a).[31]

49:17   Dan shall be a serpent upon the way, an adder upon the path, biting the horse's heels, so that its rider falls backwards.

Dan shall be a serpent - R. Chama b. R. Chanina said (*Judges* 13:25): "'And the spirit of the L-rd began to move him [Samson]' — the prophecy of our father Jacob began to be realized, as it is written: 'Dan shall be a serpent upon the way' " (*Ibid.*).[32]

Shefifon - R. Yochanan said: "Samson was limp in both his legs, as it is written: '*Shefifon* ['double limping'] upon the path' " (*Ibid.* 10a).[33]

49:19   Gad will troop upon a troop, and he will overcome at last.

Gad will troop upon a troop - A troop will come to engulf him, and he will engulf them (*Yerushalmi, Ibid.* 8:10).[34]

49:21   Naftali is a hind let loose; he gives goodly words.

Naftali is a hind let loose - He is light as a hind (*Ibid.* 13a).[35]

Imre SHFR - R. Avahu said: "Read it not: '*Imrei shafer*' [goodly words], but '*Imrei sefer*' [words of the book, i.e., the contract attesting to Jacob's purchase of the Machpelah grave from Esau]" (*Ibid.* 13a).[36]

49:22   Joseph is a fruitful son, a fruitful son above the eye; his issue steps over the wall.

ALI ayin - Read it not "*alei* ayin" [*on* the eye], but "*olei* ayin" [*above* the eye]. From here it is to be derived that the seed of Joseph are invulnerable to the evil eye (*Berachoth* 20a).[37]

above the eye - When Israel came to Shiloh, sacrificial mounds were prohibited, and secondary consecrated offerings and the second tithe could be eaten wherever the eye could see it [Shiloh], as it is written: "Joseph is a fruitful son, a fruitful son above the eye" — that eye which refused to derive enjoyment and sustenance from what did not belong to it [i.e., the wife of Potiphar] — that eye will merit and 'eat' as far as it can see (*Zevachim* 118b).[38,39]

Banot tza'adah - See 14

49:24   And his bow returned to its strength, and the seeds of his
        hands scattered, from the strength of Jacob. From there,
        the shepherd of the stone of Israel.

Vateshev be'etan kashto - R. Yochanan said in the name of R. Meir:
"When Potiphar's wife solicited Joseph and seized his garment, his
father's image appeared to him in the window and said: 'Joseph, your
brothers' names are destined to be inscribed upon the stones of the
Ephod, and yours among them. Do you desire your name to be erased
from among them?' Immediately: '*Vateshev be'etan kashto*' — his 'bow'
[organ] returned to its strength [its normal state], '*vayafozu zroei
yadav*' [lit., "and the seeds of his hands scattered"] — he stuck his
hands into the ground and semen was emitted from beneath his finger-
nails" (*Sotah* 36b).[40]

the strength of Jacob - Who caused him to be inscribed on the stones of
the Ephod? The strength of Jacob. "From there, the shepherd of the
stone of Israel" — From that experience he merited becoming a leader,
as it is written (*Psalms* 80:2): "O shepherd of Israel, give ear; the leader
of the sheep — Joseph" (*Ibid.*).[41]

the stone of Israel - R. Avin said [When the image of Joseph's father
appeared to him,] "there also appeared to him the image of his mother,
Rachel, as it is written: 'From there, the shepherd of the stone of
Israel'" [there being a Biblical allusion to "woman" in the word "*even*"
(stone)] (*Yerushalmi, Horiyoth* 2:5).[42]

49:26   The blessings of your father are potent above the blessings
        of my parents to the utmost bounds of the everlasting
        hills. They shall be on the head of Joseph, and on the head
        of the Nazirite among his brethren.

the Nazirite among his brethren - R. Melai said in the name of R.
Yitzchak Magdelah: "From the day Joseph was separated from his
brothers he did not taste wine, as it is written: 'And on the head of the
Nazirite among his brethren'" (*Shabbath* 139a. See 43:44).[43]

49:27   Benjamin is a wolf that tears. In the morning he shall
        devour the prey, and at night he shall divide the spoil.

Benjamin is a wolf that tears - Rava expounded (*Psalms* 132:1):
"'Remember L-rd, to David, all of his afflictions [over the building of
the Temple], how he swore to the L-rd ... And if I give sleep to my eyes
until I find out a place for the L-rd ... Lo, we heard of it at Efrat; we
found it in the forest field' — "We heard of it at *Efrat*" — this refers to
Joshua, who comes from the tribe of *Ephraim*; "We found it in the
forest field" — this refers to Benjamin, as it is written: 'Benjamin is a
wolf that tears.' " [i.e., In the Book of Joshua it was found that the
Temple was to be situated in the territory of Benjamin] (*Zevachim*
54b).[44]

49:28   All these are the tribes of Israel — twelve. And this is what
        their father spoke to them. And he blessed them; each
        according to his blessing, he blessed them.

the tribes of Israel - What was written on the breast-plate? On the
stones were inscribed the names of the tribes, and on the bottom was
written: "The tribes of Israel" (*Yerushalmi, Yoma* 7:3).[45]

49:33   And Jacob made an end of commanding his sons, and he
        gathered his legs into the bed, and he expired and he was
        gathered to his people.

and he expired and he was gathered - R. Yochanan said: "Our father
Jacob did not die." R. Nachman asked R. Yitzchak: "Was it in vain,
then, that the mourners mourned him and the embalmers embalmed
him!" He answered: "I derive this from the exegesis of the verse
(*Jeremiah* 30:10): 'Therefore, fear not, my servant, Jacob ... for I will
save you from afar, and your children from the land of their captivity'
— he is compared to his children: just as his children are alive, so he is
alive" (*Ta'anith* 5b).[46]

and he expired and he was gathered - R. Tarfon said: "Man dies from
inactivity, as it is written: 'And he expired [ceased from activity] and he
was gathered [died]' " (*Avoth d'R. Nathan* 11).[47]

50:3   And forty days were fulfilled for him, for so are fulfilled
        the days of those who are embalmed. And Egypt wept for
        him seventy days.

seventy days - R. Avahu said: [Why did the gentiles merit (the pleasure
of thinking the Jews would be destroyed) between the letters of Haman
(ordering their destruction) and those of Mordecai (rescinding
Haman's edict)?] "For the seventy days that the Egyptians showed
lovingkindness to our father Jacob" (*Yerushalmi, Sotah* 1:10).[1]

50:5   My father made me swear, saying: "Behold, I am going to
        die. In my grave that I dug for myself in the land of
        Canaan, there shall you bury me." And now, let me go up
        and bury my father, and I will return.

My father made me swear - It was taught: "When Joseph said to
Pharaoh: 'My father made me swear,' the latter said: 'Have your oath
rescinded,' whereupon Joseph answered: 'Well, then, I shall also have
my oath to you rescinded, wherein I swore to you not to reveal that you
do not understand the holy tongue [Hebrew].' At this, Pharaoh said to
him: 'Go up and bury your father, as you swore' " (*Sotah* 36b).[2]

that I dug for myself - R. Yochanan said in the name of R. Shimon b.
Yehotzadak: "'In my grave that *kariti* for myself' — '*kariti*' connotes
'buying'; for in the sea-towns 'buying' is referred to as '*kirah*' " (*Ibid.*
13a).[3]

50:7   And Joseph went up to bury his father, and with him went
        up all the servants of Pharaoh, the elders of his house, and
        all the elders of the land of Egypt.

And Joseph went up - "As one measures, so is it measured unto him."
Joseph had the merit of burying his father, and there were none among
his brothers greater than he. He, therefore, merited being attended to by
Moses, than whom there was no one greater in Israel, as it is written
(*Exodus* 13:19): "And Moses took the bones of Joseph with him" (*Ibid.*
9b).[4]

And Joseph went up, etc. - Why in the beginning do we have: "And Joseph went up to bury his father; and there went with him all the servants of Pharaoh" and [afterwards] "all of the household of Joseph, and his brothers, and his father's household" — whereas at the end we have (14): "And Joseph returned to Egypt — he, his brothers, and [deferentially, *after* his brothers,] all who went up with him"? R. Yochanan answered: "In the beginning, before the Egyptians had seen the honor accorded the Jews [by their countrymen], they did not accord them honor, and afterwards, when they had seen the respect in which they were held, they deferred to them, too" (*Ibid.* 13a).[5]

50:10 And they came to the threshing-floor of the thorn-fence, which is beyond the Jordan, and there they mourned him with very great and sore mourning. And he made for his father seven days of mourning.

to the threshing-floor of the thorn-fence [atad] - Now does a fence have a threshing-floor! R. Avahu said: "The intent is that they encircled Jacob's casket with crowns, as a threshing-floor is encircled with a thorn-fence. The children of Esau, and Ishmael, and Keturah came, and hung their crowns on Jacob's casket" (*Ibid.* 13a).[6,7]

to the threshing-floor of Atad - R. Shmuel b. Nachmani said in the name of R. Jonathan: "We searched through all of Scripture and did not find one place called 'Atad." What, then, is signified by 'Atad.' The intent is that the Canaanites were deserving to be threshed with thorns [*atad*], but were saved in the merit of: 'And the Canaanites, the dwellers of the land, saw [participated in] the mourning in the threshing-floor of Atad'" (*Yerushalmi, Sotah* 1:10).[8,9]

great and sore mourning - It was taught: "Even the horses, and even the asses" (*Sotah* 13a).[10]

seven days of mourning - R. Chisda said: "A man's soul mourns over him all seven days, as it is written (*Job* 14:22): 'And his soul mourns over him,' and 'And he made for his father seven days of mourning' " (*Shabbath* 152a).[11]

seven days of mourning - It was taught: "From where in Scripture is it derived that the mourning period is seven days? From the verse: 'And he made for his father seven days of mourning' " (*Yerushalmi, Moed Katan* 3:5).[12]

50:11   And the Canaanites, the dwellers of the land, saw the mourning in the threshing-floor of the thorn-fence, and they said: "This is a sore mourning for Egypt." Therefore, its name was called "Mourning for Egypt beyond the Jordan."

And the Canaanites, the dwellers of the land, saw - [It was taught that the Canaanites, too, particpated in the mourning over Jacob. How so?] "They loosened their shoulder straps." The Rabbis said: "They stood at attention" (*Yerushalmi, Sotah* 1:10).[13,14]

This is a sore mourning - R. Yuden said in the name of R. Shalom: "We are hereby taught that they pointed with their fingers and said: 'This is a sore mourning for Egypt' " (*Ibid.*).[15]

50:14   And Joseph returned to Egypt — he, his brothers, and all who went up with him to bury his father after he had buried his father.

after he had buried - Now did Joseph himself bury him? Is it not written: "And his sons carried him, and *they* buried him"? [The meaning, then, must be that they all occupied themselves with his interment, but, as far as the actual burial is concerned,] they said: "Let Joseph himself bury him, for our father is honored more in being buried by a king than by commoners" (*Sotah* 13a).[16]

50:16   And they commanded [word] unto Joseph, saying: "Your father comanded before his death, saying:"

Your father commanded - R. Ila said in the name of R. Elazar b. R. Shimon: "One may alter the truth for the sake of peace, as it is written: 'And they commanded Joseph saying: "Your father commanded before his death [saying ... 'Forgive your brothers' sin' " (and we do not find that he had done so!)]' " (*Yevamoth* 65b).[17]

50:17   So shall you say to Joseph: "Please, I beg you: forgive, I
        beg you, the iniquity of your brothers and their sin, for
        they did evil to you. And now, forgive, I beg you, the
        iniquity of the servants of the G-d of your father." And
        Joseph wept when they spoke to him.

Please, I beg you; forgive, I beg you - R. Yossi b. R. Chanina said: "One
who begs a favor of his friend should not solicit it more than three
times, as it is written: 'Please, *I beg you*; forgive, *I beg you* ... and now,
forgive, *I beg you*' " (*Yoma* 87a).[18]

50:21   And now, do not fear. I will feed you and your little ones.
        And he comforted them, and he spoke to their hearts.

and he spoke to their hearts - R. Binyamin b. Yefet said in the name of
R. Elazar: "We are hereby taught that he told them things which are
accepted by the heart, viz.: 'If ten candles [the brothers] cannot
extinguish one candle [Joseph], how can one candle extinguish ten
candles?' " (*Megillah* 16b).[19]

50:25   And Joseph took an oath of the children of Israel, saying:
        "G-d will surely remember you, and you shall bring up my
        bones from here."

and you shall bring up my bones - R. Chanina said: "There was a deep
motive here. Joseph knew himself to be completely righteous, and if the
righteous dead who are buried outside of Eretz Yisroel came to life at
the resurrection, why did he tax his brothers with carrying him four
hundred parasangs? It was because he did not accept upon himself the
suffering of rolling through tunnels to Eretz Yisroel at the time of the
resurrection" (*Kethuvoth* 111a) (See 47:30).[20]

my bones - R. Yehudah said in the name of Rav: "Why was Joseph
referred to as 'bones' in his lifetime? Because he did not protest on
behalf of his father's honor. For his brothers said (43:28): 'Your
servant, our Father,' and he said nothing to them" (*Sotah* 13a).[21,22]